IN THE BALANCE

ALL ROYALTIES FROM THE SALE OF THIS VOLUME WILL BE DONATED TO THE CANADIAN CENTRE OF INTELLIGENCE AND SECURITY STUDIES TO PROMOTE STUDY OF ISSUES CONCERNING THE ADMINISTRATION OF JUSTICE AND NATIONAL SECURITY IN DEMOCRACIES.

In the Balance

THE ADMINISTRATION OF JUSTICE AND NATIONAL SECURITY IN DEMOCRACIES

Christopher K. Penny, editor

NORMAN PATERSON SCHOOL OF INTERNATIONAL AFFAIRS
CARLETON UNIVERSITY

IRWIN LAW

In the Balance: The Administration of Justice and National Security in Democracies

Published in 2011 by

Irwin Law Inc.
14 Duncan Street
Suite 206
Toronto, ON
M5H 3G8

www.irwinlaw.com

ISBN: 978-1-55221-194-6
e-book isbn: 978-1-55221-220-2

Cataloguing in Publication available from Library and Archives Canada

The publisher acknowledges the financial support of the Government of Canada through the Canada Book Fund for its publishing activities.

We acknowledge the assistance of the OMDC Book Fund, an initiative of Ontario Media Development Corporation.

Printed and bound in Canada.

1 2 3 4 5 15 14 13 12 11

Table of Contents

Acknowledgements

This volume resulted from the International Conference on the Administration of Justice and National Security in Democracies, held in Ottawa in June 2007 and organized jointly by the Courts Administration Service and the Canadian Centre of Intelligence and Security Studies at Carleton University. The Conference brought together members of the judiciary, government officials, and academics from democracies around the world to share their views on the continuing importance and ongoing challenges of the administration of justice and the rule of law in the context of modern threats to national security, in particular those posed by transnational Islamist terrorism.

The key proponents of the Conference were the Honourable Allan Lutfy, Chief Justice of the Federal Court of Canada, and Professor Martin Rudner, then-Director of the Canadian Centre of Intelligence and Security Studies. Each recognized the pressing need to bring together individuals directly involved with the administration of justice and the democratic response to terrorism to share their expertise, in order to "promote and pursue innovative ideas aimed at upholding respect for the rule of law, and sustain mutual understanding in respective democratic countries and around the world." Without their advocacy and support, this extraordinary international event would not have taken place.

In addition to Chief Justice Lutfy and Professor Rudner, the members of the Conference Steering Committee were: the Honourable Simon Noël (Justice, Federal Court, and Committee Chair); the Honourable Richard Mosley (Justice, Federal Court); Raymond Guenette (then-Chief Administrator, Courts

Administration Service); Maurice Archdeacon (National Security Educational Advisor to the Federal Court); Gerry Montpetit (then-Director General, Courts Administration Service); David Power (Senior Counsel, Courts Administration Service); Paul Waksberg (Director General, Finance, Courts Administration Service); and, Sylvia MacKenzie (Legal Officer, designated proceedings of the Federal Court). Their efforts resulted in a remarkable Conference program and highlighted the considerable benefits to be gained from partnerships among various supporters of the rule of law, both within and between democracies worldwide.

As well as thanking the various authors whose work is presented in this volume, I would like to acknowledge the significant contributions of the other participants at the Conference: Sami Aoun (Université de Sherbrooke); Stewart Bell (*National Post*); Yves Boisvert (*La Presse*); the Honourable Leonie M. Brinkema (United States District Judge, Eastern District of Virginia); the Right Honourable Lord Carlile of Berriew (Independent Parliamentary Reviewer of Terrorism Legislation, United Kingdom); Jean Chichizola (*Le Figaro*); the Honourable R. Elkerbout (Judge, Netherlands Court of Justice); the Honourable Baltasar Garzon (Judge, National Court, Spain); Gerard Hervuoet (Université Laval); Fred Hitz (University of Virginia Law School); the Honourable Royce Lamberth (Judge, United States District Court for the District of Columbia); Ian Leigh (Faculty of Law, University of Durham); the Right Honourable Beverley McLachlin, P.C. (Chief Justice, Supreme Court of Canada); the Honourable Richard Mosley (Justice, Federal Court of Canada); the Honourable Dennis O'Connor (Associate Chief Justice, Court of Appeal for Ontario); Charlie Savage (*Boston Globe*); the Honourable Antonin Scalia (Justice, United States Supreme Court); and Ruth Wedgwood (Paul H. Nitze School of Advanced International Studies, The Johns Hopkins University).

The Conference—and this resulting volume—would not have occurred without the generous financial support of the Courts Administration Service.

I would like to thank all of those involved with this volume for their patience and commitment. This has been a long process, but I hope you agree that the final product was worth the wait.

On a personal note, I would like to recognize the substantial contribution of my wife, Karima Karmali, who has been a constant source of inspiration and support in this and all things.

CKP

NOTE

The following chapters developed from papers presented at the International Conference on the Administration of Justice and National Security in Democracies in June 2007. Authors were provided a subsequent opportunity to revise their conference paper prior to publication in this volume. Unless otherwise apparent, the opinions and statements of law contained in the following chapters should be considered current as of February 2008.

CHAPTER 1

Introduction: The Administration of Justice and National Security in Democracies

CHRISTOPHER K. PENNY
NORMAN PATERSON SCHOOL OF INTERNATIONAL AFFAIRS

> Whatever the shape of our respective systems of government, respect for the rule of law and for the authority of strong and independent judges is a necessary feature of legitimate governance. It cannot be compromised, and must be continually sustained. In countries where it is under threat, the rule of law must be pursued. In countries where it is established, it must be fiercely guarded. Whatever the situation, judges are the principal defenders of the rule of law, and judicial education is the best resource we have to sustain each other in this role.[1] (The Right Honourable Beverley McLachlin, P.C., Chief Justice of Canada)

Rule of law is the essential foundation of all democratic societies. At the same time, one of the principal roles of any democratic state—if not its paramount obligation—is to provide for the security of its citizens. Faced with the continuing threat of domestic and transnational terrorism, how can democracies achieve the related goals of public safety and national security while at the same time maintaining and promoting the rule of law and protecting (other) individual rights and freedoms?

There is no single answer to this modern existential question. Instead, democracies worldwide continue to struggle to balance these often (albeit not necessarily) competing values. As members of the broader international

1 "Remarks of the Right Honourable Beverley McLachlin, P.C." (Address to the 2d International Conference on the Training of the Judiciary, 1 November 2004) online: The Supreme Court of Canada www.scc-csc.gc.ca/court-cour/ju/spe-dis/bm04-11-01-eng.asp.

community, democratic states are certainly not alone in facing the threat of terrorism. However, their inherent respect for individual liberty and the rule of law poses particular challenges and presents unique opportunities for counteracting its ongoing dangers.

Fundamental to any democratic response to the complex security threat posed by terrorism is the effective domestic administration of justice. National judiciaries around the world are increasingly being called upon to address legal issues arising from the fight against it. But what exactly is the proper role for the administration of justice in the defence of democracy against this threat? When should judges balance national security considerations with the protection of individual human rights? How should they go about doing so?

The following chapters present various perspectives on these and other issues of significance to democracies engaged in the struggle against terrorism, authored by members of the judiciary, government officials, and academics drawn from Australia, Canada, France, Israel, the Netherlands, the United Kingdom, and the United States of America.

The resulting volume is divided into five parts. Part I establishes overall context, illustrating the specific contemporary threat posed to democracies by Islamist terrorism. Part II develops overarching themes, examining various national perspectives on balancing human rights and national security concerns in the fight against it. Part III follows with an overview of the challenges posed by the actual conduct and reporting of national security proceedings. Part IV addresses the moral and legal implications of the use of torture for the administration of justice and the rule of law in democracies. Formal mechanisms for the oversight and review of national security measures are discussed in Part V.

In Chapter 2, Lorenzo Vidino delineates the threat posed to Western democracies by Islamist *jihadist* terrorism, situating this phenomenon in its evolving historical and contemporary context. In doing so, he distinguishes the extremist political ideology of Islamism from more general religious adherence to the teachings of Islam, and argues that modern Islamist terrorism poses a unique and particularly violent threat to democracies. His introductory chapter traces the evolution of *jihadist* terrorist movements in democracies from isolated groups targeting their countries of origin to their later coordination and greater targeting of American interests (and influence in the Islamic world) beginning in the mid-1990s, often under the aegis of al-Qa'ida. He observes that 9/11—and the resulting weakening of central al-Qa'ida direction—has led to more fragmented *jihadist* networks targeting the United States and other Western states, not only due to the Afghanistan and Iraq invasions but also as a result of their perceived discrimination against domestic Muslim communities. While recognizing the positive place of law in the fight against *jihadist* terrorism, Vidino concludes that its role is limited. First and foremost, he argues that the struggle against terrorism is ideological, not legal, and that the underlying appeal of Islamism must instead be eliminated.

In Chapter 3, the Honourable Aharon Barak draws upon his extensive judicial experience in Israel—and his own landmark decisions—to argue that "judges in modern democracies have a major role to play in protecting democracy," not only against the threats posed by terrorism but also against state excesses in the fight against it. Countering Cicero's famous maxim, "silent enim leges inter arma," he instead asserts that "[w]e need laws most in times of war." His chapter highlights the overall importance of judicial review (and its prerequisite, judicial independence), recognizing that its long-term benefits outweigh any short-term restrictions it may place on the war against terrorism. At the same time, he underscores the difficult balance often required between considerations of human rights and national security in this context. Barak recognizes that courts will not solve the problem of terrorism. Instead, he argues that their role is "to ensure the constitutionality and legality of the fight against [it]." In doing so, judges will make a substantial contribution to democracy, whether the state wins or loses in specific cases. As Barak argues, "[o]nly a strong, safe and stable democracy may afford and protect human rights, and only a democracy built on the foundations of human rights can exist with security."

In Chapter 4, the Honourable Richard Posner critiques the domestic response of the United States to the threat posed by Islamist terrorism, arguing that its sui generis nature "challenges conventional legalistic thinking." In doing so, he highlights serious problems resulting from the law enforcement focus favoured by the Federal Bureau of Investigation (and, more broadly, the Department of Justice) in its lead role in domestic counter-terrorist activities, noting that evidence gathering, arrest, and prosecution differ substantially from the preventive intelligence efforts necessary to effectively combat this threat. Posner maintains that the United States is "overinvested in criminal law as a response to terrorism," and that it should instead "tailor a legal regime to the distinctive character of the current terrorist threat" that would allow greater flexibility than (now) permitted by criminal courts; a criminal conviction should not be the principal goal of domestic counter-terrorism measures. In many cases, including terrorist surveillance, he submits that executive and legislative oversight of counter-terrorism efforts may be more appropriate than judicial review. While recognizing that the current struggle against terrorism requires balancing competing interests, Posner highlights serious problems resulting from "overemphasizing legally enforceable rights at the expense of recognition of values of equal importance embodied in governmental powers," in particular the protection of public safety.

In Chapter 5, Jean-Claude Marin argues that terrorism achieves its most significant victory when democracies sacrifice their underlying values in the interests of efficiency in the fight against it. Reviewing the French experience with terrorism—and, in particular, its use of legal and judicial mechanisms to combat it—he questions whether there is really a choice to be made between the protection of national security and justice. Marin outlines French legislative and judicial responses to terrorism, including provisions restricting terrorist support. He draws on two recent cases to illustrate various factors that indicate culpable support of terrorism, which does not necessarily require knowledge of specific terrorist acts so long as there is knowledge of the terrorist objectives of the group in question. He notes that general legal principles remain applicable to combating terrorism, with certain modifications (for example, increased provisional detention), and that issues arising in this context also occur in the context of fighting organized crime and illegal immigration. Addressing the need to protect civil liberties while safeguarding public order, he argues that "[t]out est question de proportion et d'équilibre" ("everything is a question of proportionality and balance"). For each democracy, the specific balance will reflect its culture, history, and experience with terrorism; however, such balancing is assisted with dialogue between various democracies, particularly in light of the international threat posed by Islamist terrorism. As Marin argues, this balance is fragile, requiring constant vigilance and adaptation.

In Chapter 6, Stanley Cohen examines the judicial treatment of Canada's response to terrorism in the wake of 9/11, noting that "national security law and policy cannot and should not be regarded as static or frozen." Instead, he traces the ongoing "dialogue" between various systemic actors, recognizing that Canada "has a refined and sophisticated system of checks and balances that encourages the kind of democratic discourse involving the public, the press, and our elected representatives that is the lifeblood of a truly free society." Cohen reviews key recent jurisprudence addressing various aspects of Canada's counter-terrorism laws in light of the Canadian Charter of Rights and Freedoms, highlighting ongoing tensions (and the difficult balance) between state secrecy and the presumption of an open court. While recognizing the ideal role of the judiciary as a "check on governmental or police abuse or excess," Cohen argues that these recent cases "reveal a judicial reluctance to accept the balance struck in our national security laws between openness and secrecy." Nonetheless, he submits that they should be read for more than "what they have struck down or qualified," maintaining that "[t]oo little attention is paid to what the courts have sustained and to our independent judiciary's reasons for why they have upheld so much of what has been enacted."

In Chapter 7, the Honourable Sir Andrew Collins observes that historically in the United Kingdom, "the common law—or perhaps I should say the judges—has not sought to intervene when national security has been said to be the justification for particular actions by the executive." However, he submits that "recently there have been indications that national security will not always provide a complete answer for the executive," and that this has resulted primarily from the domestic implementation of the European Convention on Human Rights. His chapter traces the handling of national security claims in United Kingdom courts, highlighting decreasing judicial deference to such arguments, with particular reference to its implications for disclosure of evidence to terrorist suspects and the establishment of the special advocate system. While recognizing the "shortcomings" of the use of special advocates, Collins argues that "the system is the best that can be devised to balance the need to protect individuals from being subjected to restrictions on or deprivation of their liberty and the need to protect citizens from the risk of terrorism"; however, he maintains that recent judicial decisions may not be helpful for maintaining this delicate and important balance.

In Chapter 8, the Honourable Ian Bruce Josephson discusses the practical challenges posed by the actual conduct of terrorism trials, drawing on his personal experience adjudicating the recent Air India trial in Vancouver (relating to the 1985 bombing of Air India flight 182, which killed 329 people). In particular, Josephson highlights the substantial positive impact of various modern courtroom technologies for the effective and efficient administration of justice, noting that one must first overcome the "great inertia in the judicial system" that often militates against its use. He describes, among other things, the significant benefits arising from electronic evidence management systems in the Air India trial, which allowed the orderly presentation and recall of roughly fourteen hundred exhibits, with tens of thousands of pages of related documents, as well as their dissemination throughout the courtroom (not only to the judge, but also to various counsel, witnesses, media, and others in attendance). Although recognizing that such technology does have some downsides, and that it isn't the "end all, be all," Josephson observes that it can nonetheless substantially ease the overall burdens placed on judges when adjudicating terrorism trials of such magnitude and complexity.

In Chapter 9, the Right Honourable Lord Hutton addresses a range of legal issues concerning media reporting of national security proceedings, informed by recent judicial decisions from the United Kingdom and the European Court of Human Rights. These cases demonstrate the importance (and difficulty) of judicial balancing of various competing democratic values: provision of intelligence to defendants viewed in light of national security claims to non-disclosure; reporting on issues of public interest in relation to secretive intelligence operations; effective political reporting by the media weighted against the protection of individual reputations from unfounded allegations; and freedom of expression contrasted with the right to a fair trial free from outside influence. In each instance, Hutton discusses the rationale for judicial establishment of reasonable but limited restrictions on media reporting and disclosure of information founded on protection of national security and the maintenance of other related democratic interests.

In Chapter 10, Angela Gendron considers the ethics of counter-terrorism, arguing that "[r]ather than weighing public safety against individual rights, we might do better to see them both as interdependent parts of the critical political-cultural infrastructure on which democracies depend." Beginning with an assessment of the "conflict between personal liberties and community safety," she observes that law often serves as the "intermediary" in the "discourse between politics and morality." Gendron recognizes that moral dangers may result both from overreacting to terrorism and from underestimating its threat, and that the resulting challenge "is to find ways within the rule of law which will enable us to be both more effective against those who threaten us and preserve the civil values that define us." The moral dilemma this poses—where each available alternative gives rise to "harmful consequences"—is illustrated by the contentious issue of whether there is ever a moral justification for the use of torture (as distinct from the current absolute legal prohibition). Here, Gendron examines in detail the arguments of (and between) moral idealists and realists, identifying an "element of pious pragmatism" in current democratic responses supporting a legal prohibition while accepting that, in some circumstances, individuals may feel compelled to act outside the law. In the struggle against terrorism, she concludes that, "in the final analysis, it behooves society to decide where the moral line should be drawn before an emergency threatens."

In Chapter 11, the Honourable Yorick Aler addresses questions relating to the use in criminal proceedings of evidence derived from the practice of torture in third countries, drawing in part on his own experience adjudicating the "Eik" trial in Rotterdam (which raised but did not hinge on related issues). While Aler identifies an absolute legal prohibition on torture and on the direct use of resulting incriminatory statements against torture victims, he notes that substantial legal challenges remain concerning associated issues such as the use of new evidence deriving from such statements. He submits that an "appealing" test in such circumstances is whether the evidence carries "enough of the smell of the torture chamber" (citing the views of Lord Hoffman). Though admitting that "my nose becomes rather sensitive in such cases," Aler recognizes the need to balance law enforcement counter-terrorism interests against the prohibition on torture and corresponding state obligations to suppress and discourage this practice. Nonetheless, he supports restricting use of the "fruit of the poisonous tree" on the basis that, in addition to the interests of the accused, "the role of the judiciary in guaranteeing human rights is also at stake, just as the need to preserve the integrity of the judicial process."

In Chapter 12, the Honourable Sir Duncan Ouseley examines issues related to the removal to their countries of nationality of foreign nationals posing a security threat, referring to the practice of the United Kingdom and his own experience chairing its Special Immigration Appeals Commission. Such return is prohibited where there exist "substantial grounds for believing that there is a real risk that the individual would face torture or cruel, inhuman, or degrading treatment" (a prohibition arising from recent decisions of the European Court of Human Rights, criticized by Ouseley as "the judicial arrogation of a power truly belonging to the legislature or to the treaty-making powers of the executive"). Recognizing that returned Islamist terrorists would likely face such threats, the United Kingdom has sought assurances from foreign countries that they would not resort to torture in such cases. Ouseley addresses the subsequent treatment of these assurances, noting that "the judicial role in deciding whether the degree of risk would breach international obligations was vital" and highlighting various specific issues considered important to such determinations (such as the parties to and scope of the assurances). He argues that states have a right to protect themselves and their citizens by removing foreign nationals posing a threat, and "if the exercise of that right is inhibited in order to protect the deportees' human rights, taking further measures which then enable the lawful deportation of such individuals is likewise legitimate. It is for the courts to judge whether the measures proposed are effective enough to that end."

In Chapter 13, Ian Carnell provides a "satellite view" of Australia's counter-terrorism experience since 9/11, highlighting areas of continuing controversy including: the need to balance individual rights with the essential authority of security agencies; the introduction and application of preventive measures, including criminal offences; and, the nature of media responsibilities (contrasted with media rights). While recognizing the "absolutely vital role" of the judiciary, Carnell argues that "non-judicial mechanisms are also important in safeguarding the rule of law." He observes that the counter-terrorism powers that were most controversial when introduced (such as control orders and preventive detention) "have not provided the dire consequences which some commentators warned would eventuate," in part due to "the close attention these measures received in development, and the inclusion of non-judicial forms of monitoring and review in the schemes implemented." Though understanding the pressure for governments to act quickly, Carnell questions Australia's self-reflection to date, maintaining that "a key test for liberal democracies in the area of counter-terrorism is willingness to revisit what was done, and if necessary modify the measures introduced, to ensure balance and proportionality. This is particularly so if some elements may be counterproductive—such as adding to the sense of alienation and discrimination which members of Muslim communities can suffer."

In Chapter 14, the Right Honourable Sir Peter Gibson reviews security oversight mechanisms in the United Kingdom, with particular emphasis on the role of the Intelligence Services Commissioner (drawing on his own experience in this position). Gibson observes that while intelligence services are provided "extensive and intrusive powers" to fight terrorism, the governments that rely on them "also recognise the need to reassure the public that those services are properly accountable and subject to the rule of law." He notes that the United Kingdom only recently acknowledged the existence of its intelligence services (MI5, MI6, and the Government Communications Headquarters) and subsequently accepted "the need for their accountability." In addition to political and parliamentary oversight, formal review mechanisms now include the Intelligence Services Commissioner (one of two independent judicial reviewers). Gibson outlines the key statutory review functions of the commissioner, and using review of executive surveillance warrant authority as an example, he notes the balance required between a measure's necessity (for example, "in the interests of national security") and the proportionality of its impact. Although required to report annually, the exercise of the commissioner's authority is not itself subject to comprehensive review, leading Gibson (citing Juvenal) to wonder in conclusion, "[w]ho will keep watch on those who keep watch?"

In Chapter 15, The Honourable Gary Filmon draws on his experience as chair of Canada's Security and Intelligence Review Committee to assess its role "safeguarding human rights while promoting national security." Filmon describes the establishment of the Canadian Security Intelligence Service and the review mechanisms designed to keep its "powers in check," with particular emphasis on the independent external review provided by SIRC. He notes that SIRC has two primary roles: "to conduct retrospective reviews into CSIS operations; and, . . . to investigate complaints against CSIS." While these functions are often treated separately, Filmon argues that "Canada's experience suggests that there are real benefits in having them under one roof." While SIRC authority is not binding, he notes that CSIS has implemented the majority of its recommendations. Filmon argues that "democracies must use every resource at their disposal to counter threats to national security, but in doing so must uphold the principles of accountability, respect for individual rights and absolute adherence to the rule of law." In conclusion, he maintains that, in the view of SIRC, "the demands of public safety and democratic values are not in conflict with each other; rather, they are complementary."

Taken together, these contributions illustrate the enormous challenge as well as the critical importance of balancing individual rights and national security in the administration of justice. Whether viewed as competing or complementary, upholding each of these interests is essential to protecting democracies worldwide in their fight against terrorism.

While each democracy must confront terrorism in its own way, they are nonetheless bound together in a common struggle and further united by their inherent respect for individual rights and the rule of law. Faced with similar issues, democracies (and their various members) have much to learn from one another. Realizing the mutual benefits of interaction between proponents of the rule of law was the primary purpose of the International Conference on the Administration of Justice and National Security in Democracies. It remains the principal goal of this volume.

Obviously, maintaining the rule of law is necessary but not in itself sufficient as a democratic response to terrorism. In examining its requirements, one must not lose sight of its larger context, including the need for democracies to maintain the political will to combat violent extremism and, perhaps most importantly, to reduce its initial attraction. Judges alone will not end the threat of terrorism. Nor will they eliminate its appeal. However, as the following chapters illustrate, the balanced administration of justice is indispensable to preventing democratic societies from undermining their own fundamental values—and their own long-term interests—in the struggle against it.

PART ONE

CONTEXT

CHAPTER 2

Islamist Terrorism: Assessing Threats to Democracy

LORENZO VIDINO
BELFER CENTER, KENNEDY SCHOOL OF GOVERNMENT, HARVARD UNIVERSITY

The focus of this chapter is Islamist terrorism, its presence in the West, and the challenges it poses. Before delving into such analysis, it is necessary to clarify the terminology I will use. Since 9/11, policymakers, academics, and journalists have been endlessly debating how to define the violence perpetrated by individuals and groups that openly claim to act in defence of Islam. A clear-cut differentiation between the religion of Islam and a politicized interpretation of it must be made. While the term "Islamic terrorism" would not serve such purpose, "Islamist terrorism" does, as it identifies the roots of today's violence not in Islam, but, rather, in the political ideology commonly referred to as Islamism.

Throughout history acts of terror have been inspired by all sorts of ideologies and extreme interpretations of many religions, and Islamism hardly has the monopoly over the use of violence. Still today, radical forms of Christianity, Judaism, Hinduism, and other religions are used as a motivation for acts of violence. Nevertheless, at this point in time, Islamism unquestionably surpasses all other ideologies in inspiring violence. Islamist terrorism's global reach, combined with the frequency and lethality of the attacks perpetrated by individuals claiming to be inspired by some form of it, constitute an unparalleled source of concern for policymakers worldwide.

What is then Islamism, the ideology that feeds most of today's terrorism? Although politicized and radical interpretations of Islam have occurred throughout history, Islamism established a new life over the past three hundred years as the Muslim world attempted to respond to the state of crisis in which it found itself. Starting with the *Treaty of Karlowitz* (1699), which sanctioned the beginning of the decline of Ottoman power in Eastern Europe, the Muslim world began a rapid decline that led it to succumb to European powers. For centuries the world of Islam had prospered while Europe was entangled in the darkness of the Middle Ages. Yet, by the eighteenth century, it was lagging behind Europe in military, scientific, and economic achievements. This state of inferiority, which became painfully evident with the conquest and colonization of large segments of Islamic lands, led to various forms of intellectual responses.

Some Muslim intellectuals and leaders argued that the Muslim world's state of military and economic inferiority was due to its failure to fully embrace modernity. The West, argued such voices, was ahead because it had freed itself from the chains of religion and had placed faith only in the private sphere, enforcing a strict separation of church and state. Muslims could emulate the West's military and economic achievements only if they fully embraced modernity and realized that religion had no place in public life. Such secularist thinking is epitomized by the radical reforms implemented by Mustafa Kemal to shape modern Turkey after the fall of the Ottoman Empire.

A different response to the state of crisis of the Muslim world came from a group of intellectuals that, like the secularists, believed that Muslims should embrace modernity, but claimed that Islam was compatible with modernity. Rather than completely doing away with their religion, argued such voices, Muslims should find ways to blend the positive influences of Western culture (such as technology and rational thought) with their own cultural, moral, and religious customs.

Finally, a third ideological response to the crisis of the Muslim world came from those who believed that such a state of weakness was a direct byproduct of the lack of piety of most Muslims. The only way to revive Islam's glory, argued such voices, was to refer to the past. Muslims should act and structure their societies exactly like the prophet Mohammed and his early followers had. Only by returning to such a pure form of Islam and eliminating all external influences that had corrupted Islam over the centuries could Muslims regain their God-mandated status of primacy in the world.

Islamism springs from this third ideological response to the state of crisis of the Muslim world. Its core belief is that Islam has been corrupted by outside influences and that most Muslims are only nominally so, while not living their lives according to the norms set out by the prophet Mohammed. This state of ignorance of Islam (which Egyptian Islamist thinker Sayyid Qutb termed "*jahiliya*") is the reason for the weakness of the Muslim world and only by returning to a pure form of Islam can Muslims regain their due place in the world.

As with most large social movements, Islamism comprises different factions and currents that differ from one another on the interpretation of various concepts and on how they propose to implement their vision. Some Islamists use violence to achieve their goals, claiming that God allows them to do so. Others adopt only peaceful methods, working within the political framework and disseminating their worldview at the grassroots level. Hardly a monolithic bloc, the Islamist movement is ridden with internal divisions that, in some cases, even develop into violent confrontations. Despite these differences, all Islamist groups agree on the final goal: the creation of an Islamic state in which a pure Islamic system of life can thrive.

A key element in the Islamic state envisioned by Islamists is the law. Most Islamists believe that the sole source of legislation should be God. All man-made laws are, therefore, illegitimate, as they represent an attempt of man to substitute himself to God. Any system of government that is not based on Islamic law (*sharia*) is equally illegitimate. This vision of God's primacy on all aspects of life, including the law, has been perfectly described in the writings of Abul A'la Maududi, one of the foremost Islamist ideologues of the twentieth century. "Human beings must, individually or collectively, surrender all rights of overlordship, legislation and exercising of authority over others," wrote the Pakistani intellectual in 1976. "No one should be allowed to pass orders or make commands on his own right and no one ought to accept the obligation to carry out such commands and obey such orders."

Only a minority of Muslims subscribe to this view. Yet militant Islamists have been extremely cunning at exploiting grievances (some of them quite legitimate) that are widespread throughout the Muslim world. Conflicts in Iraq, the Palestinian territories, Chechnya, the Philippines, and even events such as the Danish Mohammed cartoon controversy have all been framed by Islamists as part of a large Western conspiracy to subjugate and humiliate Muslims. Only a strictly Islamic society, argue Islamists, can have the strength to prevent such injustices and avenge the sense of humiliation and powerlessness that many Muslims feel worldwide. Today, political Islam has managed to portray itself in the eyes of many Muslims as the only valid alternative to all the ideologies that have failed in the Muslim world, from nationalism to socialism and even democracy, which is often seen as a Western tool to dominate the Muslim world.

While originating in the Muslim world, Islamism has found fertile ground among the masses of Muslim immigrants that have settled in Western countries over the past fifty years. Although only a minority of "Western Muslims" embrace some form of political Islam, its presence in the West is quite significant and diverse. Terrorist attacks in New York and Washington (September 2001),

Madrid (March 2004), and London (July 2005), and the myriad of terrorist plots thwarted over the past few years, have clearly shown that the West faces an enormous challenge from terrorism of Islamist inspiration. Yet terrorism is only the tip of the iceberg, the most visible manifestation of a larger problem. The West, and Europe in particular, today faces a tripartite threat from radical Islam, of which the terrorist is only the most immediate and evident, but not necessarily the most dangerous one. At the risk of incurring the unavoidable trap of oversimplification, today we can identify three different kinds of Islamist organizations operating in the West and visualize them as a pyramid:

1. At the top are groups that openly advocate an extremist Islamist agenda and resort to violence to further it. Violent *jihadists* are a few thousand individuals who openly challenge the societies they live in and are willing to spill blood to achieve their goals.
2. Below them are groups that openly support an Islamist agenda but, at least publicly, oppose violence. Transnational groups such as Hizb ut Tahrir, which advocates the establishment of a global caliphate through peaceful means, belong to this category.
3. Finally, the base, the largest section of the pyramid, is occupied by groups that publicly purport to support democracy and the integration of Muslim communities within the Western mainstream, but quietly work to radicalize the West's Muslim population. The Muslim Brotherhood and its various offshoots belong to this category.

Each of these aspects of radical Islam has a different presence, structure, and *modus operandi*. Each, consequently, presents a different kind of challenge to Western policymakers and intelligence agencies. Moreover, the differences between the three categories are not always clear-cut. It is not uncommon for individuals linked to organizations at the bottom of the pyramid to climb up and become further radicalized. The first two levels often work as conveyor belts to the third level, providing the ideological background to the use of violence. They tell young Muslims that the West is at war with Islam and that they should aim at establishing an Islamic state, while stopping short of advocating violence to achieve such goal. It is not difficult to understand that some young, disenfranchised Muslims might decide to take it upon themselves to take the next step and use violence in the belief that it will further the goals of the *ummah*.

Nevertheless, although the legal system can combat terrorist activities, there is very little that Western authorities can do to confront the actions of groups that belong to the lower levels of the pyramid. Unless they cross a certain line (which, according to the laws of each country, can include incitement of violence or racial and religious hatred), such groups generally act within their rights of free expression and cannot be prosecuted for their words. As troubling as the rhetoric might be, Western countries must respect their freedom to advocate the destruction of democracy and its replacement with a strict Islamic order. Not allowing them to do so would go against the very principles that shape the West. The response to their rhetoric, therefore, must not be at the judicial level, but, rather, at the ideological.

A. THE THREAT OF *JIHADIST* TERRORISM

Although all three levels of the pyramid constitute a danger, albeit of different kinds, the most imminent threat to the West comes from terrorism. Even though they have increased their presence and propensity to attack the West over the past few years, *jihadist* networks have been operating in Western countries since the 1980s. The number of *jihadis* living in the West received a significant boost between the end of the 1980s and the beginning of the 1990s when hundreds of veterans of the Afghan war against the Soviet Union settled in Europe. Attempting to avoid incarceration and other forms of repression in their native countries, where local governments perceived them to be a threat to stability, veterans of the Afghan war sought, and in most cases received, political asylum in various European countries. This phenomenon occurred in the United States and Canada only to a lesser degree. Most of the Afghan Arabs, in fact, chose to relocate to Europe because of the presence of large Arab and Muslim diaspora communities on the continent; they recognized the ample fundraising and recruiting opportunities these communities could provide. The liberal asylum and immigration policies adopted by most European countries also made many Afghan Arabs prefer Europe to the United States.

Once they relocated in Europe, most of the Afghan Arabs—committed *jihadis* who had dedicated their life to the establishment of Islamic regimes—continued their subversive activities. Taking advantage of Europe's freedoms and wealth, the Afghan Arabs used their new host countries as bases of operations to spread their propaganda, recruit militants, and raise funds for their struggle against secular regimes in their countries of origin. Organizations such as the Egyptian Gamaa Islamiya or the Algerian Armed Islamic Group (GIA) created sophisticated networks throughout Europe that provided crucial support to the organizations' efforts in North Africa.

The Afghan Arabs' assiduous propaganda efforts began to attract a small but increasing number of Muslims residing in the West. Some European-born, second- and third-generation Muslims, as well as recent immigrants to the continent with no prior involvement with radical Islam, found the message of the Afghan Arabs appealing. Facing socioeconomic and identity issues, some European Muslims attempted to find an answer to their problems in the most militant interpretation of Islam, becoming the ideal recruits for committed radicals who were just establishing their presence in Europe.

During this first phase of the presence of Islamic fundamentalism in Europe, most radical organizations showed no violent intent toward their new host countries, which they viewed only as temporary and extremely convenient bases of operations. Even though it was apparent from the sermons and propaganda of the "European Afghan Arabs" that they strongly disapproved of Europe's liberal moral standards, secularized society, and perceived anti-Muslim biases, the radicals targeted only the regimes of their countries of origin. European countries were spared the militants' furor, provided they did not interfere with the *jihadis'* struggles in North Africa and the Middle East. In fact, the only attack against a European country carried out during the first half of the 1990s was the series of bombings that bloodied France in the summer of 1995, a campaign orchestrated by Algerian militants to punish the French government for its support of the Algerian regime.

This first phase is also characterized by the operational separation of the various *jihadi* groups operating in the West. Even though they all shared the same ideological bases, radical outfits from different nationalities tended to maintain a certain degree of autonomy from one another. Aside from isolated episodes, the coordination among them tended to be limited to statements of support of their brethrens' cause. While all groups aimed at the establishment of an Islamic state, each focused on doing so in its own country.

Yet, by the mid-1990s, this localized approach to *jihad* was progressively being supplanted by a new stance, which was being shaped by forces in Europe and Afghanistan. Militants of different nationalities began to meet inside the most radical mosques of Europe, establishing and quickly strengthening links among various organizations. Whereas in the past each Islamist group had fought alone against its own enemy, their interaction within the Islamist networks fashioned in cities such as London, Milan, and Brussels, made the *jihadis* realize that they were all bound by a common ideology and that it would be in their best interest to cooperate among themselves. Also, by 1998 Osama Bin Laden and Ayman al Zawahiri had perfected al-Qa'ida's reorganization in Afghanistan, creating a global platform that was formalized with the launch of the World Islamic Front against Jews and Crusaders.

Bin Laden's project was the zenith of a phenomenon that was already under way in the Afghan training camps, on the battlefields of Bosnia, Chechnya, and Kashmir, and in the most radical mosques of large European cities. Moreover, Bin Laden and other al-Qa'ida leaders expressed the idea that the best strategy to topple secular regimes in the Muslim world was to block the economic and military support they received from the United States and other Western countries. Therefore, the *jihadist* movement had to switch its emphasis to one of attacking America and making a continued American presence in the Middle East too painful to bear. Al-Qa'ida, in Bin Laden's mind, was to become the umbrella organization for *jihadi* groups throughout the Muslim world; united under its banner, all would fight together against both secular regimes in the Muslim world and their "protectors" in the West.

By the end of the 1990s most of the networks that had been formed throughout Europe had fallen into the orbit of Bin Laden's project. Al-Qa'ida established only a small direct presence on the Continent, but for the most part co-opted already existing networks, particularly the Algerian ones, and treated them as franchises. Because of their familiarity with the West, "European" militants were used for various operations planned by al-Qa'ida against the United States, including the failed Millennium bombing of the Los Angeles International Airport in 2000 and the attacks of 11 September 2001. In the first case, al-Qa'ida dispatched London- and Montreal-based militants affiliated with the Algerian Salafist Group for Preaching and Combat (GSPC) to the United States. In the case of 9/11, al-Qa'ida trained a group of previously unaffiliated, Germany-based *jihadi* enthusiasts and dispatched them to America to carry out its deadliest operation.

The two attacks are indicative of important developments that characterize this second phase of *jihadism* in the West. The Millennium bombing shows how a group that was still fighting a bloody civil war in its country of origin was willing to put its forces at the service of al-Qa'ida's global project, signalling a clear break with the national focus that *jihadi* groups had in the past. European Islamist networks had become "delocalized," focusing less on their initial regional targets and more on the global *jihad*. The 9/11 hijackers, on the other hand, represent a clear indication that the West is home to small clusters of radicals who, while unaffiliated with any organization at their outset, can be easily co-opted and used by the global *jihadi* movement.

B. POST-9/11 DEVELOPMENTS

The aftermath of the attacks of 9/11 brought significant changes to the relationship between European networks and al-Qa'ida, triggering the development of a third phase. The resulting US invasion of Afghanistan and the global crackdown on al-Qa'ida–linked networks limited the ability of al-Qa'ida's core to control its cells and affiliated groups worldwide. On the run and in hiding, al-Qa'ida's leadership became unable to function as it previously had and was forced to relinquish much of its control on its global network. While a certain level of coordination still existed, European networks began to operate more autonomously, loyal to al-Qa'ida's ideology but virtually independent in their day-to-day operations.

As they became more independent, European cells progressively began to change their focus. Global conflicts such as Afghanistan, Palestine, and, even more importantly, Iraq continued to attract the attention of European *jihadi*s, many of whom travelled to regions where al-Qa'ida was battling American forces. Nevertheless, since 9/11, a new phenomenon has increasingly emerged that might be called the "re-localization" of *jihad*. While still perceiving themselves as part of the global *jihadi* movement, networks operating on the ground in Europe, as in other areas of the world, started to pay more attention to their immediate environment. Viewing all Western countries, both those that joined American efforts in Afghanistan and Iraq and those that did not, as hostile to Islam, they began to focus their wrath on all of them, often placing equal emphasis on global political affairs and domestic issues involving tensions between the local Muslim communities and the native population. Therefore, in the eyes of *jihadis* operating in Europe, countries such as Spain, the United Kingdom, and Italy bear equal guilt for discriminating against their Muslim population as for having sent troops to Iraq. And even countries that have distanced themselves from American efforts in the Middle East are considered enemies, because their media criticize Islam and, more generally, because their societies are not Islamic.

The "re-localization" of *jihad* has led to the growth of homegrown *jihadist* networks. Over the past few years, homegrown clusters of European-born, self-radicalized, violence-prone Islamists have sprung up in most European countries. Yet, the panorama of *jihadi* networks in Europe is quite complex and, for a more accurate analysis, could be described on a continuum. At one extreme, one can identify quintessential homegrown groups such as the Hofstad Group in the Netherlands: small domestic clusters of radicals that have developed no ties to external groups and act in complete operational independence. At the opposite side of the spectrum are cells that respond to the traditional model used by al-Qa'ida–affiliated groups in the 1990s: compartmentalized cells inserted in a well-structured network and subjected to a hierarchy whose heads are often outside Europe.

In between these two extremes, there is a whole spectrum of realities, positioned according to the level of autonomy of the group. The most recurring model seems to be that of the cell that carried out suicide attacks in London on 7 July 2005: a small group of young men, most of them born and/or raised in Europe who knew each other either from the neighbourhood or from the mosque. Their radicalization took place in Europe and only one or two members of the group travelled out of the country (Pakistan, in this case) to link up with foreign-based, well-structured groups ideologically or operationally affiliated with al-Qa'ida.

C. WHAT CAN THE LAW DO?

Since 9/11 most Western countries have significantly improved their counter-terrorism efforts in order to better face the new threat of Islamist terrorism. Law enforcement and intelligence agencies have been given more powers to investigate and dismantle terrorist networks. New laws that better define and broaden the crimes related to terrorism have been passed. Harsher penalties have been inflicted on individuals convicted of terrorism-related charges. Most of such measures were badly needed. Nevertheless, it is necessary to ask certain questions not only at the International Conference on the Administration of Justice and National Security in Democracies, but also, more generally, in public debates. Do such measures strike the right balance between security concerns and civil rights guarantees? Are individuals accused of terrorism given a fair trial? When does free speech become incitement to commit acts of terror?

All these questions need to be asked in order to assess what the law can and cannot do in fighting today's terrorism. But, in doing so, we must keep in mind that the law can only play a limited role. As we saw, the West is not fighting against an organization, but rather against an ideology. The law can provide short-term solutions. Arresting or deporting terrorists, outlawing organizations or shutting down extremist websites are necessary measures that, nevertheless, do not tackle the ideology that motivates young Muslims to use violence. The long-term solution to the problem is neither legal nor military, but rather strictly ideological. Only when the appeal of radical Islam is eliminated will the violence cease.

PART TWO

LAW AND THE CHALLENGE OF TERRORISM

CHAPTER 3

Human Rights in Times of Terror: A Judicial Point of View

THE HONOURABLE AHARON BARAK[1]
PRESIDENT EMERITUS, SUPREME COURT OF ISRAEL

A. THE ROLE OF THE JUDGE: TO PROTECT DEMOCRACY

I see the role as a judge on the Supreme Court or on a Constitutional Court of a democracy as the protection of the constitution and of democracy.[2] We cannot take the continued existence of a democracy for granted. This is certainly the case for new democracies, but it is also true for the old and well-established ones. The approach that "it cannot happen to us" can no longer be accepted. Anything can happen. If democracy was perverted and destroyed in the Germany of Kant, Beethoven, and Goethe, it can happen anywhere. If we do not protect democracy, democracy will not protect us. I do not know if the Supreme Court judges in Germany could have prevented Hitler from coming to power in the 1930s. But I do know that one of the lessons of the Holocaust and of the Second World War is the need to have democratic constitutions and ensure that they are put into effect by Supreme Court judges whose main task is to protect democracy. It was this awareness in the post–World War II

1 This article is based on selections from Aharon Barak, "Foreword: A Judge on Judging: The Role of a Supreme Court in a Democracy" (2002) 116 Harv. L. Rev. 16 and Aharon Barak, "The Role of a Supreme Court in a Democracy, and the Fight against Terrorism" (2004) 58 U. Miami L. Rev. 125; Aharon Barak, "Human Rights in Times of Terror—A Judicial Point of View" (2008) 28 L.S. 493.

2 For a comprehensive analysis of my thesis, see Aharon Barak, *The Judge in a Democracy* (Princeton, NJ: Princeton University Press, 2006) [Barak].

era that helped disseminate the idea of judicial review of legislative action and make human rights central.[3] And it shaped my perspective that the main role of the Supreme Court judge in a democracy is to maintain and protect the constitution and democracy. As I noted in one of my opinions:

> The struggle for the law is unceasing. The need to watch over the rule of law exists at all times. Trees that we have nurtured for many years may be uprooted with one stroke of the axe. We must never relax the protection of the rule of law. All of us—all branches of government, all parties and factions, all institutions—must protect our young democracy. This protective role is conferred on the judiciary as a whole, and on the Supreme Court in particular. Once again we, the judges of this generation, are charged with watching over our basic values and protecting them against those who challenge them.[4]

According to my approach, judges in modern democracies have a major role to play in protecting democracy. We should protect it both from terrorism and from the means the state wishes to use to fight terrorism. Judges are, of course, tested daily in their protection of democracy, but judges meet their supreme test when they face situations of war and terrorism. The protection of the human rights of every individual is a duty much more formidable in situations of war or terrorism than in times of peace and security. If we fail in our role in times of war and terrorism, we will be unable to fulfill our role in times of peace and tranquillity. It is a myth to think that it is possible to maintain a sharp distinction between the status of human rights during a period of war and the status of human rights during a period of peace. It is self-deception to believe that we can limit judicial rulings so that they will be valid only during wartime, and that we can decide that things will change in peacetime. The line between war and peace is thin; what one person calls peace, another calls war. In any case, it is impossible to maintain this distinction in the long term. We should assume that whatever we decide when terrorism is threatening our security will linger many years after the terrorism is over. Indeed, we judges must act with coherence and consistency. A wrong decision in a time of war

---

3 See generally Mauro Cappelletti, *Judicial Review in the Contemporary World* (Indianapolis: Bobbs-Merrill, 1971); Douglas Greenberg *et al.*, eds., *Constitutionalism and Democracy: Transitions in the Contemporary World* (Oxford: Oxford University Press, 1993); C. Neal Tate & Torbjorn Vallinder, eds., *The Global Expansion of Judicial Power* (New York: New York University Press, 1995); Marina Angel, "Constitutional Judicial Review of Legislation: A Comparative Law Symposium" (1983) 56 Temp. L.Q. 287.

4 H.C. 5364/94, *Velner v. Chairman of the Israeli Labor Party*, 49(1) P.D. 758 at 808 [citations omitted].

and terrorism plots a point that will cause the judicial curve to deviate after the crisis passes.[5] In one of my judgments I wrote:

> [I]f we fail in our task in times of war and terror, we will not be able to carry out our task properly in times of peace and calm. From this viewpoint, a mistake by the judiciary in a time of emergency is more serious than a mistake of the legislature and the executive in a time of emergency. The reason for this is that the mistake of the judiciary will accompany democracy even when the threat of terror has passed, and it will remain in the case law of the court as a magnet for the development of new and problematic rulings. This is not the case with mistakes by the other powers. These will be cancelled and usually no-one will remember them. This was well expressed by Justice Jackson in *Korematsu v. United States*, where he said:
>
>> A judicial construction of the due process clause that will sustain this order is a far more subtle blow to liberty .... A military order, however unconstitutional, is not apt to last longer than the military emergency .... But once a judicial opinion rationalizes such an order to show that it conforms to the Constitution, or rather rationalizes the Constitution to show that the Constitution sanctions such an order, the Court for all time has validated the principle of racial discrimination in criminal procedure and of transplanting American citizens. The principle then lies about like a loaded weapon ready for the hand of any authority that can bring forward a plausible claim of an urgent need .... A military commander may overstep the bounds of constitutionality, and it is an incident. But if we review and approve, that passing incident becomes the doctrine of the Constitution. There it has a generative power of its own, and all that it creates will be in its own image.[6]

Moreover, democracy ensures us, as judges, independence. It strengthens us, because of our political non-accountability against the fluctuations of public opinion. The real test of this independence comes in situations of war and terrorism. The significance of our non-accountability becomes clear

---

5 See *Korematsu v. United States*, 323 U.S. 214 at 245–46 (1944) (Jackson J., dissenting). See also Patricia Hughes, "Judicial Independence: Contemporary Pressures and Appropriate Responses" (2001) 80 Can. Bar Rev. 181 at 186 (noting the general agreement that "judicial independence is both an individual and a systemic, institutional or 'collective' quality").

6 H.C. 7052/03, *Adalah v. The Minister of Interior* (14 May 2006, forthcoming in Isr. L.R.) at 34–35 [*Adalah*].

in these situations, when public opinion is more likely to be near-unanimous. Precisely in these times of war and terrorism, we must embrace our supreme responsibility to protect democracy and the constitution. We should always reflect history—not hysteria. Admittedly, the struggle against terrorism turns our democracy into a "defensive democracy" or even a "fighting or militant democracy."[7] Nonetheless, this defence and this militant fight must not deprive our regime of its democratic character. Judges in the highest court of the modern democracy should act in the spirit of defensive fighting or militant democracy, as opposed to uncontrolled democracy.

B. THE BATTLE AGAINST TERROR: WITHIN THE LAW

There is a well-known saying that when the cannons speak, the Muses are silent. A similar idea was expressed by Cicero in his maxim "*Silent enim leges inter arma*" ("In battle, indeed, the laws are silent").[8] These statements are regrettable; I hope they do not reflect the way things are.[9] I am convinced they do not reflect the way things should be. Every battle a country wages—against terrorism or against any other enemy—must be waged in accordance with rules and laws. There is always law according to which the state must act. There are no black holes in which there is no law.[10] And the law needs Muses. We need the Muses most when the cannons speak. We need laws most in times of war.[11] In one of my judgments I wrote:

7 In contemporary Germany, the militant democracy (*streitbare Demokratie*) is one of the foundations of the constitutional structure. See David P. Currie, *The Constitution of the Federal Republic of Germany* (Chicago: University of Chicago Press, 1994) at 213; Donald P. Kommers, *The Constitutional Jurisprudence of the Federal Republic of Germany*, 2d ed. (Durham, NC: Duke University Press, 1997) at 37. See also András Sajó, ed., *Militant Democracy* (Utrecht: Eleven International Publishing, 2004).

8 Cicero, *Pro Milone*, trans. by N.H. Watts, 5th ed. (Cambridge, MA: Harvard University Press, 1972) at 16.

9 See *Re Application under s. 83.28 of the Criminal Code*, 2004 SCC 42, [2004] 2 S.C.R. 248 at 260: "So, while Cicero long ago wrote '*inter arma silent legas*' (the laws are silent in battle) we, like others, must strongly disagree . . ." [citations omitted] (Iacobucci and Arbour JJ.). *Compare* William H. Rehnquist, *All the Laws But One: Civil Liberties in Wartime* (New York: Alfred A. Knopf, 1998) at 224.

10 Johan Steyn, "Guantanamo Bay: The Legal Black Hole" (2004) 53 I.C.L.Q. 1.

11 See Harold Hongju Koh, "The Spirit of the Laws" (2002) 43 Harv. Int'l L.J. 23 at 23:

> In the days since, I have been struck by how many Americans — and how many lawyers — seem to have concluded that, somehow, the destruction of four planes and three buildings has taken us back to a state of nature in which there are no laws or rules. In fact, over the years, we have developed an elaborate system of domestic and

> The decision has been laid before us, and we must stand by it. We are obligated to preserve the legality of the regime even in difficult decisions. Even when the artillery booms and the Muses are silent, law exists and acts and decides what is permitted and what is forbidden, what is legal and what is illegal. And when law exists, courts also exist to adjudicate what is permitted and what is forbidden, what is legal and what is illegal. Some of the public will applaud our decision; others will oppose it. Perhaps neither side will have read our reasoning. We have done our part, however. That is our role and our obligations as judges.[12]

The struggle against terrorism is not conducted outside the law, but within the law, using tools that the law makes available to a democratic state. Terrorism does not justify the neglect of accepted legal norms. This is how we distinguish ourselves from the terrorists themselves. They act against the law, by violating and trampling it. In its war against terrorism, a democracy acts within the framework of the law and according to the law. Indeed, the war against terrorism is a war of a law-abiding nation and law-abiding citizens against lawbreakers. It is, therefore, not merely a war of the state against its enemies; it is also a war of the law against its enemies.

C. THE NEED FOR A BALANCED APPROACH

Democracies should conduct the struggle against terrorism with a proper balance between two conflicting values and principles. On the one hand, we must consider the values and principles relating to the security of the state and its citizens. Human rights cannot justify undermining national security in every case and in all circumstances. Human rights are not a stage for national destruction.[13] The Constitution is not a suicide pact. As I stated in one case:

> A constitution is not a prescription for suicide, and civil rights are not an altar for national destruction (*cf.* the remarks of Justice Jackson in *Terminiello v. Chicago*). The laws of a people should be interpreted on the basis of the assumption that it wants to continue to exist. Civil rights depend upon the

---

international laws, institutions, regimes, and decision-making procedures precisely so that they will be consulted and obeyed, not ignored, at a time like this.

12 H.C. 2161/96, *Rabbi Said Sharif v. Military Commander*, 50 (4) P.D. 485 at 491.

13 See E.A. 2/84, *Neiman v. Chairman of Central Elections Committee for Eleventh Knesset*, 39(2) P.D. 225 at 310 [*Neiman*]. Compare *Terminiello v. Chicago*, 337 U.S. 1 at 37 (1949) (Jackson J., dissenting) [*Terminiello*].

> existence of the State, and they should not be made into a spade with which to bury it.[14]

On the other hand, we must consider the values and principles relating to human dignity and freedom. National security cannot justify undermining human rights in every case and under all circumstances. National security does not grant an unlimited licence to harm the individual.

Every balance that is made between security and freedom will impose certain limitations on both security and freedom. A proper balance will not be achieved when human rights are fully protected, as if there were no terrorism. Similarly, a proper balance will not be achieved when national security is afforded full protection, as if there were no human rights. The balance and compromise are the price of democracy. Only a strong, safe, and stable democracy may afford and protect human rights, and only a democracy built on the foundations of human rights can exist with security. It follows that the balance between security and freedom does not reflect the lack of a clear position. On the contrary, the proper balance between security and freedom is the result of a clear position that recognizes the need for security and the need for human rights.

When I speak about the balance, I don't mean an external normative process that changes the scope of rights and the protection accorded them because of terror. I mean the ordinary process and the ordinary balancing rules we have that take place when we address the relationship between individual rights and the needs of society. In this latter process, rights are not absolute. They may be limited to serve the needs of society. In a judgment that dealt with the battle on terror, I wrote:

> Israeli constitutional law has a consistent approach to human rights in periods of relative calm and in periods of increased fighting. We do not recognize a clear distinction between the two. We do not have balancing laws that are unique to times of war. Naturally, human rights are not absolute. They can be restricted in times of calm and in times of war. I do not have a right to shout "fire" in a theatre full of spectators (see the analogy of Justice Holmes in *Schenck v. United States*). War is like a barrel full of explosives next to a source of fire. In times of war the likelihood that damage will occur to the public interest increases and the strength of the harm to the public interest increases, and so the restriction of the right becomes possible within the framework of existing criteria. Indeed, we do not have two sets of laws or balances, one for times of calm and the other for times of terror. This idea was well expressed by

14 *Neiman, ibid.* The judgment cited is *Terminiello, ibid.*

Lord Atkin more than sixty-five years ago, during the Second World War, in a minority opinion where he said:

> In England amidst the clash of arms the laws are not silent. They may be changed, but they speak the same language in war as in peace. It has always been one of the pillars of freedom, one of the principles of liberty for which ... we are now fighting, that the judges ... stand between the subject and any attempted encroachments on his liberty by the executive, alert to see that any coercive action is justified in law (*Liversidge v. Anderson*).[15]

When the court rules on the balance between security and freedom during times of terrorist threats, it often encounters complaints from both sides. The supporters of human rights argue that the court gives too much protection to security and too little to human rights. The supporters of security argue that the court gives too much protection to human rights and too little to security. Frequently, the persons making these arguments read only the judicial conclusion without considering the judicial reasoning that seeks to make a proper balance between the conflicting values and principles. None of this intimidates the judge. He must and does rule according to his best understanding and conscience.[16]

This balance is based upon the view that in democracy, not all means are acceptable. The ends do not justify the means. Thus, we ruled that parts of the separation fence in the West Bank, which is intended to prevent terrorists from the West Bank from entering Israel, are not legal. We determined that the additional security attained by the location chosen for the security fence by the army is not proportional to the harm which that fence location causes to the fabric of the lives of the local inhabitants. In one case I wrote:

> Ends do not justify the means. It is a manifestation of the idea that there is a barrier of values which democracy cannot surpass, even if the purpose whose attainment is being attempted is worthy.[17]

In one case we decided that the executive branch has no authority to authorize (*ante*) torture, though the interrogators may act out of necessity and have a (*post*) defence in criminal law. This (*ante*) prohibition is comprehensive, and applies even in a "ticking bomb" situation. In my judgment I wrote:

---

15 *Adalah*, above note 6 at 33–34.

16 See H.C. 428/86, *Barzilai v. Government of Israel*, 40(3) P.D. 505 at 585 (Barak J., dissenting).

17 H.C. 8276/05, *Adalah—The Legal Center for Arab Minority Rights in Israel v. The Minister of Defense* (unpublished, para. 30 of my judgment).

> We are aware that this judgment of ours does not make confronting that reality any easier. That is the fate of democracy, in whose eyes not all means are permitted, and to whom not all the methods used by her enemies are open. At times democracy fights with one hand tied behind her back. Despite that, democracy has the upper hand, since preserving the rule of law and recognition of individual liberties constitute an important component of her security stance. At the end of the day, they strengthen her and her spirit, and allow her to overcome her difficulties.[18]

In one of my last judgments, I had to deal with the constitutionality of a statute that imposed a temporary flat ban of family unification between an Israeli and his West-Bank or Gaza spouse. The reason for the ban was that in twenty-six cases the non-Israeli spouse, who came to Israel by the program of family unification, was directly involved in terrorist activities. I decided that the statute is unconstitutional as it affects in a non-proportional way the right to family unification, which is a constitutional right derived from the right to dignity. In my judgment I wrote:

> Examination of the test of proportionality (in the narrow sense) returns us to first principles that are the foundation of our constitutional democracy and the human rights that are enjoyed by Israelis. These principles are that the ends do not justify the means; that security is not above all else; that the proper purpose of increasing security does not justify serious harm to the lives of many thousands of Israeli citizens. Our democracy is characterized by the fact that it imposes limits on the ability to violate human rights; that it is based on the recognition that surrounding the individual there is a wall protecting his rights, which cannot be breached even by the majority. This is how the court acted in many different cases. Thus, for example, adopting physical measures ("torture") would without doubt increase security. But we held that our democracy was not prepared to adopt them, even at the price of a certain harm to security. Similarly, determining the route of the separation fence in the place decided by the military commander in Beit Sourik Village Council would have increased security. But we held that the additional security was not commensurate with the serious harm to the lives of the Palestinians. Removing the family members of suicide bombers from their place of residence and moving them to other places ("assigned residence") would increase security in the territories, but it is inconsistent with the character of Israel as a "democratic freedom-seeking and liberty-seeking state." We must adopt this path

18 H.C. 5100/94, *Public Committee against Torture in Israel v. The State of Israel*, 53(4) P.D. 817 at 845 [*PCAT v. Israel*].

> also in the case before us. The additional security achieved by abandoning the individual check and changing over to a blanket prohibition involves such a serious violation of the family life and equality of many thousands of Israeli citizens that it is a disproportionate change. Democracy does not act in this way. Democracy does not impose a blanket prohibition and thereby separate its citizens from their spouses; democracy does not prevent them from having a family life; democracy does not impose a blanket prohibition and thereby give its citizens the option of living in it without their spouse or leaving the state in order to live a proper family life; democracy does not impose a blanket prohibition and thereby separate parents from their children; democracy does not impose a blanket prohibition and thereby discriminate between its citizens with regard to the realization of their family life. Indeed, democracy concedes a certain amount of additional security in order to achieve an incomparably larger addition to family life and equality. This is how democracy acts in times of peace and calm. This is how democracy acts in times of war and terror. It is precisely in these difficult times that the power of democracy is revealed. Precisely in the difficult situations in which Israel finds itself today, Israeli democracy is put to the test.[19]

D. THE ISRAELI CASE

I will describe now the way we approach the battle on terror in Israel.[20] Please recall, that in Israel we had not only September 11, but also September 10 and September 12. By describing our way of dealing with terror, I do not make a general claim that ours is the best way, and every judge in a democracy should do the same. I am not so naïve. Of course, every country should reflect, in its war of terror, its history, its constitutional structure and aspirations, the way it solves non-terrorist cases, and the role of courts in its legal tradition. My claim is much more restricted. I do claim that the way our Supreme Court is doing it is the proper way for Israel, for whom security threats are part of ordinary life. Other legal systems will have to make their own reflections. As in any other area of comparative law the foreign law is only a source of inspiration—a mirror through which we see ourselves—like a good book or article that gives us confidence in the path we take. In my description, I am concentrating on

19 *Adalah*, above note 6 at 93–94.

20 See Israel Supreme Court, *Judgments of the Israel Supreme Court: Fighting Terrorism within the Law*, vol. 1 (Jerusalem: Israel Supreme Court, 2004) and Israel Supreme Court, *Judgments of the Israel Supreme Court: Fighting Terrorism within the Law*, vol. 2 (Jerusalem: Israel Supreme Court, 2006).

the role of the judge. Judges are not conducting the battle on terror. Judges will not solve the problem of terror. That is the duty of the other branches of government. Judges are adjudicators. Their duty within the constitutional scene is to say what the law is, and to what extent are the means used by the state according to law.

Our starting point in Israel has been that the doors of the Supreme Court—which in Israel serves as a court of first instance for complaints against the executive branch—are open to anyone wishing to complain about the activities of a public authority. There are no areas without judicial review.[21] The open door approach is expressed in a number of ways. First, it is very rare that the court would close its doors on grounds of non-justiciability.[22] At times the state may argue that most of its counterterrorism activities are beyond the reach of the judiciary because they take place outside the country, because they constitute an act of state, or because they are political in nature. All these arguments were made before us in the Israeli Supreme Court, and they were rejected when human rights were directly affected. Thus, we have ruled in petitions concerning the power of the state to arrest suspected terrorists[23] and the conditions of their confinement in Israel or outside it.[24] We have decided petitions concerning the rights of suspected terrorists to legal representation and the means by which they may be interrogated.[25] We have ruled about the legality of the fence Israel is building to provide security from terrorists crossing its borders. Recently, we ruled regarding the legality of targeted killings. The rule that guided us in all of those judgments was that there is no place for an argument of non-justiciability when the petition regards human rights. When a claim of violation of a human right is raised, the suit is always justiciable.

Second, the court opens its doors to anyone claiming that civil rights have been violated. Everyone has standing. This is the general approach of the court in time of peace.[26] We apply it also in times of terror. It is used mainly by civil

---

21 See H.C. 910/86, *Ressler v. Minister of Defence* 42(2) P.D. 441 at 458.

22 *Ibid.*

23 See H.C. 3239/02, *Maraab v. Commander in Judea and Samaria*, 57(2) P.D. 349 [*Maraab*].

24 See H.C. 3278/02, *The Center for Defense of the Individual Founded by Dr. Lotta Salzberger v. IDF Commander in the West Bank*, 57(1) P.D. 385; H.C. 5591/02, *Yassin v. Commander of Kziot Military Camp*, 57(1) P.D. 403; H.C. 253/88, *Sajadia v. Minister of Def.*, 42(3) P.D. 801.

25 *Maarab*, above note 23 at 377 (the right to legal representation). See *PCAT v. Israel*, above note 18 (means of interrogation).

26 The Israeli Supreme Court's general approach is that in cases of serious violation of the rule of law, everyone in Israel has standing. For an analysis of this approach, see Barak, above note 2 at 190.

rights associations that come to us in defence of human rights of those sectors of society that most people do not wish to protect—including, of course, suspected terrorists.

Third, our judgments regarding many of the terrorist cases committed outside Israel are based on international law dealing with humanitarian law or human rights law applicable to international armed conflicts. Thus, terrorists in many cases are not viewed as regular criminals. To the extent that they take part in hostilities, they are not protected against attack. This international law is part of our common law.

In applying customary international law, national judges should take the judgment of the International Court of Justice (ICJ) very seriously. Even if the judgment of the ICJ in The Hague is only advisory, it is of great weight.[27] The ICJ is the highest judicial body in international law. Its interpretation of international law should be given its full appropriate weight. We should also look to decisions of other international courts like the European Court of Human Rights in Strasbourg. We cite their judgment regularly, though we are not party to the *European Convention on Human Rights*. Judgments of national courts applying international law should be consulted. Of course, academic writings on international law are of great importance. I myself felt quite restrained in my freedom to interpret international law, as I am not the only judicial player in the field, especially when I have to interpret an international treaty or customary international law.

In all these decisions—and there have been thousands of them—we recognized, on the one hand, the power of the state to protect its security and the security of its citizens. On the other hand, we emphasized that the rights of every individual must be preserved, including those of the individual suspected of being a terrorist. The balancing point between the conflicting values and principles is not fixed. It differs from case to case and from issue to issue. The damage to national security caused by a given terrorist act and the nation's response to the act affects the way in which the freedom and dignity of the individual are protected. To the extent that the terrorist activity takes place in Israel, we apply the regular criminal law. Our Parliament has generally not created a special criminal law of the enemy.

The fight against terrorism requires the interrogation of terrorists. Such interrogations must be conducted according to the ordinary rules of interrogation. Physical force must not be used. We decided specifically that the persons

---

27 H.C. 7957/04, *Mara'abe v. The Prime Minister of Israel* (15 September 2005), para. 56 of my judgment.

being interrogated must not be tortured.[28] A democracy—even a defensive or militant democracy—should not (*ante*) bureaucratize the use of torture, though it may view such acts (*post*) as triggering the defence of necessity in criminal law.

E. JUDICIAL REVIEW OF THE BATTLE ON TERROR

Judicial review of the battle against terrorism, by its very nature, raises the question of the timing and scope of judicial review. There should not be a theoretical difference between applying review at a time that the state is under threats of terrorism and doing so at a time after the terrorism is gone. We should never postpone our judgment until terror is over, because the fate of a democracy and of human beings may hang in the balance. Protection of human rights would be bankrupt if, during combat, courts—consciously or unconsciously—decided to review the behaviour of the executive branch only after the period of emergency ended.

What is the scope of judicial review in time of terror? The answer to this question should vary according to the essence of the concrete question raised. On the one end of the spectrum stands the question "What is the law on the battle against terror?" That question is within the realm of the judicial branch. The court is not permitted to liberate itself from the burden of that authority. The question which the court should ask itself is not whether the executive branch's understanding of the law is a reasonable understanding. The question should be is it the correct understanding. We have not accepted the *Chevron* doctrine.[29] On the other end of the spectrum is the decision, made on the basis of the knowledge of the military professionals, to execute a military operation. That decision is the responsibility of the executive branch. It has the professional-security expertise to make that decision. The Court will ask itself only if a reasonable military commander could have made the decision that was made. If the answer is yes, the Court will not exchange the military commander's security discretion within the security discretion of the Court. Judicial review regarding the military means to be taken is the regular review of reasonableness. True, "military discretion" and "state security" are not magic words that prevent judicial review. However, the question is not what I would decide in the given circumstances, rather whether the decision that the military com-

---

28 *PCAT v. Israel*, above note 18 at 835.

29 *Chevron U.S.A., Inc. v. Natural Resources Defense Council, Inc.*, 467 U.S. 837 (1984).

mander made is a decision that a reasonable military commander was permitted to make. On that subject, special weight is to be granted to the military opinion of the official who bears the responsibility for security.

Between these two ends of the spectrum, there are intermediate situations. Each of them requires a meticulous examination of the character of the decision. One of those legal aspects is the decision about proportionality. By proportionality I mean the legal concepts that require that any limitation of human rights—whether by statute or by an administrative regulation—should fulfill the following requirements: (a) there should be a rational connection between the goal to be achieved and the means used; (b) there are no less restrictive means to achieve that goal; and, (c) the benefit to the public interest achieved by the means is proportional to the harm caused to the human rights. Many judgments I gave dealing with the battle on terror were dealing with proportionality. Thus, in occupied territories, the military cannot take possession of land, if the harm to the local population does not fulfill the requirements of proportionality. Similarly, under customary international law the state cannot harm civilians while fighting terror if such harm does not fulfill the proportionality requirement. In a recent case, I dealt with targeted killings. It was decided that the state cannot target a terrorist that takes direct part in terrorist activities if the collateral damage to civilians will be non-proportional.

Who decides about proportionality? Is it a military decision to be left to the reasonable application of the military, or a legal decision within the discretion of the judges? Our answer is that the proportionality of military means used in the fight against terror is a legal question, left to the judges. In the case, regarding the proportionality of the harm which the separation fence causes to the fabric of life of the local inhabitants, I wrote:

> The military commander is the expert regarding the military quality of the separation fence route. We are experts regarding its humanitarian aspects. The military commander determines where, on hill and plain, the separation fence will be erected. That is his expertise. We examine whether this route's harm to the local residents is proportionate. That is our expertise.[30]

Proportionality is not a standard of precision. At times there are a number of ways to fulfill its conditions. A zone of proportionality is created. It is the borders of that zone that the Court guards. The decision within the borders is the executive branch's decision. That is its margin of appreciation.

The decision should not rest on issuing general declarations about the balance of human rights and the need for security. Rather, the judicial ruling must

---

30 H.C. 2056/04, *Beit Sourik Village Council v. The Government of Israel*, 58(5) P.D. 845.

impart guidance and direction in the specific case before the court. Justice Brennan correctly noted, "[A]bstract principles announcing the applicability of civil liberties during times of war and crises are ineffectual when a war or crisis comes along unless the principles are fleshed out by a detailed jurisprudence explaining how those civil liberties will be sustained against particularized national security concerns."[31]

From a judicial review point of view, the situation in Israel is unique. Petitions from suspected terrorists reach the Supreme Court—which has exclusive jurisdiction on the matter—in real time. The judicial adjudication takes place not only during combat, but also while the events being reviewed are taking place. For example, the question of whether the General Security Service may use extraordinary methods of interrogation (including what has been classified as torture) did not come before us in the context of a criminal case in which we had to rule, ex post, on the admissibility of a suspected terrorist's confession.[32] Rather, the question arose at the beginning of his interrogation. At the start of the interrogation, the suspect's lawyer came before us and claimed, on the basis of his past experience, that the General Security Service would use force against his client. We summoned the state's representative—the same day or the next day—and we heard arguments, and made a decision in real time.

Often the court will encounter the argument from the executive that security considerations led to an action of the government, followed by a request that the court be satisfied with this statement. Such a request should not be granted. "Security considerations" are not magic words. The court must insist on hearing the specific security considerations that prompted the government's actions. The court must be persuaded that the security considerations actively motivated the government's action and were not merely a pretext. The court must be convinced that the security measures adopted were proportional. Indeed, in several of the many security cases that the Supreme Court heard, senior army commanders and heads of the security services testified before us. Only if we were convinced that the security consideration was the dominant one and that the security measure was proportionate, did we dismiss the challenge against the security action.[33] In dismissing challenges to security actions,

31 William J. Brennan, Jr., "The Quest to Develop a Jurisprudence of Civil Liberties in Time of Security Crises" (1988) 18 Isr. Y.B. Hum. Rts. 11 at 19.

32 See H.C. 4054/95, *Public Committee against Torture in Israel v. Government of Israel*, 43(4) P.D. 817 [*PCAT v. Israel* (H.C. 4054/95)].

33 In *Secretary of State for the Home Department v. Rehman*, [2001] UKHL 47 at para. 62, Lord Hoffman noted that "the judicial arm of government [needs] to respect the decisions of ministers of the Crown on the question of whether support for terrorist activities in a foreign country constitutes a threat to national security." I hope the meaning of

we should not be naïve or cynical. We should analyze the evidence before us objectively. In the case dealing with review under the *Geneva Conventions*, of the state's decision to assign Arab residents from the West Bank to the Gaza Strip, I noted that:

> In exercising judicial review ... we do not make ourselves into security experts. We do not replace the military commander's security considerations with those of our own. We take no position on the way security issues are handled. Our job is to maintain boundaries, and to guarantee the existence of conditions that restrict the military commander's discretion.... We do not, however, replace the commander's discretion with our own. We insist upon the legality of the military commander's exercise of discretion and that it fall into the range of reasonableness, determined by the relevant legal norms applicable to the issue.[34]

Is it proper for judges to review the legality of the fight on terrorism? Many argue that the court should not become involved in these matters. These arguments are heard from both ends of the political spectrum. On one side, critics argue that judicial review undermines security. On the other side, critics argue that judicial review gives legitimacy to actions of the government authorities in their battle against terrorism. Both arguments are unacceptable. As to the argument that judicial review undermines security: judicial review of the legality of the battle on terrorism may make the war against terrorism harder in the short term. Judicial review, however, fortifies and strengthens the people in the long term. The rule of law is a central element in national security. As I wrote in a case of pre-trial pardon given to the heads of the General Security Service who committed crimes against terrorists:

> There is no security without law. The rule of law is an element of national security. Security requires us to find proper tools for interrogation. Otherwise, the General Security Service will be unable to fulfill its purpose. The strength of the Service lies in the public's confidence in it. Its strength lies in the court's confidence in it. If security considerations are decisive, the public will have no confidence, and the court will have no confidence in the security service and the lawfulness of its interrogations. Without this confidence, the branches of the state cannot function. This is the case with regard to public confidence

---

these comments is limited to the general principle that a court determines not the means of fighting terrorism but rather the lawfulness of the means employed.

34 H.C. 7015/02, *Ajuri v. IDF Commander in the West Bank*, 56(6) P.D. 352 at 375–76.

> in the courts, and it is the case with regard to public confidence in the other branches of state.[35]

With regard to considerations of legitimacy: to the extent that legitimacy by the court means that the acts of the state are lawful, the court fulfills its traditional role. Both when the state wins and when the state loses, the rule of law and democracy benefit. It should be remembered that the effect of the judicial decision does not occur only in the individual instance that comes before it. Rather, the main effect occurs in determining the general norms according to which the government authorities act, and in establishing the deterrent effect this norm will have. The test of the rule of law arises not merely in the few cases brought before it, since government authorities are aware of the ruling of the court and act accordingly. The argument that judicial review somehow validates the governmental action does not take into account the nature of judicial review. In hearing a case, the court does not examine the wisdom of the battle against terrorism, but only the legality of the acts taken in furtherance of the war. The court does not ask itself if it would have adopted the security measures that were adopted, if it were responsible for security. Instead, the court asks if a reasonable person responsible for security would be within the bounds of the law to adopt the security measures that were adopted. Thus, the court does not express agreement with the means adopted but rather fulfills its role by reviewing the constitutionality and legality of the executive acts.

Naturally, one must not go from one extreme to the other. One must recognize that the court will not solve the problem of terrorism. It is a problem to be addressed by the other branches of government. The role of the court is to ensure the constitutionality and legality of the fight against terrorism. It must ensure that the battle against terrorism is conducted within the framework of the law and not outside it. This is the court's contribution to the struggle of democracy to survive. In my opinion, it is an important contribution, one that aptly reflects the judicial role in a democracy. Realizing this role during the battle against terrorism is difficult. Judges cannot and would not want to escape from this difficulty.

I regard myself as a judge who is sensitive to his role in a democracy. I take the tasks imposed on me—protecting the constitution and democracy—seriously. Despite criticism often heard, I have continued on this path for twenty-eight years. I hope that by doing so, I am serving my legal system properly. Indeed, as judges in the highest court, we must continue on our path according to our consciences.

---

35 H.C. 428/86, *Barzilai v. Government of Israel*, 40(3) P.D. 505 at 622 [citation omitted].

Judges have a North Star that guides them: the fundamental values and principles of constitutional democracy. A heavy responsibility rests on our shoulders. Even in hard times, we must remain true to ourselves. I discussed this in the opinion considering whether extraordinary methods of interrogation—torture or inhuman treatment—may be used against a terrorist in a "ticking bomb" situation:

> Deciding these petitions weighed heavily on this Court. True, from the legal perspective, the road before us is smooth. We are, however, part of Israeli society. We know its problems, and we live its history. We are not isolated in an ivory tower. We live the life of this country. We are aware of the harsh reality of terrorism in which we are, at times, immersed. Our concern that this decision will hamper the ability to properly deal with terrorists and terrorism disturbs us. We are, however, judges. Our fellow-citizens demand that we act according to the law. This is also the same standard that we set for ourselves. When we sit at trial, we too stand trial.[36]

36 *PCAT v. Israel* (H.C. 4054/95), above note 32 at 845.

CHAPTER 4

On Being Overinvested in Law as a Weapon Against Terrorism

THE HONOURABLE RICHARD A. POSNER[1]

JUDGE, UNITED STATES COURT OF APPEALS FOR THE SEVENTH CIRCUIT

It is no secret that the United States is a highly legalistic country. Law pervades the political culture, as well as popular culture. And so it is not surprising that law has been ubiquitous in the nation's response to the menace of global Islamist terrorism revealed by the terrorist assault on the United States on 11 September 2001. Despite the Federal Bureau of Investigation's negligent failure to have detected and prevented the impending assault and the demonstrable incompatibility between intelligence and criminal investigation, the Bureau, and its parent, the Department of Justice, remain entrusted with the lead role in domestic intelligence, a key counter-terrorism tool. The result has been an overemphasis on criminal law enforcement as a method of countering terrorism. Legalistic excess is further exemplified by the attempt to force international terrorism into legal categories—namely, crime and war—that it does not fit, rather than trying to tailor a legal regime to the distinctive character of the current terrorist threat; by the attempt to govern national security surveillance by warrant requirements enforced by a secret court rather than by administrative methods for assuring accountability; and, by overemphasizing legally enforceable rights at the expense of recognition of values of equal importance embodied in governmental powers. These and related points are the focus of this paper.

---

1 This is the revised text of the keynote address given at the International Conference on the Administration of Justice and National Security in Democracies, in Ottawa on 12 June 2007. I have drawn heavily on my book (published after the conference), *Countering Terrorism: Blurred Focus, Halting Steps* (Lanham, MD: Rowman and Littlefield, 2007).

A. DOMESTIC INTELLIGENCE

The Bureau's traditional and still dominant conception of intelligence is of information that can be used to obtain a criminal conviction. A crime is committed having a definite time and place and usually witnesses and often physical evidence and even suspects, and the crime can usually be placed in a pigeonhole familiar to criminal investigators. These circumstances enable a criminal investigation to be tightly focused and create a high probability that the information gathered in the investigation will lead to an arrest and a successful prosecution. They thus give the FBI a well-defined, readily achievable mission.

National security intelligence, especially counter-terrorist intelligence, is different. The aim is to *prevent* the crime, not wait for it to occur and use it as the jumping-off point for an investigation. The key to prevention is detection in advance. That requires casting a very wide investigative net, chasing down ambiguous clues, assembling tiny bits of information—and often failing to detect the impending attack because there is as yet no crime, no definite time and place from which to start the investigation, no witnesses, no physical evidence.[2]

And when a terrorist plot *is* discovered, prosecution is not necessarily the best response. "In intelligence work, a trial is often a symptom of failure—

---

2 The contrast between criminal law enforcement and national security intelligence has been well explained by a former director of Canada's domestic intelligence service, the Canadian Security Intelligence Service:

> Law enforcement is generally reactive; it essentially takes place after the commission of a distinct criminal offence. Police officers are results-oriented, in the sense that they seek prosecution of wrongdoers. They work on a "closed" system of limits defined by the *Criminal Code*, other statutes and the courts. Within that framework, they often tend to operate in a highly decentralized mode. Police construct a chain of evidence that is gathered and used to support criminal convictions in trials where witnesses are legally obligated to testify. Trials are public events that receive considerable publicity. Security intelligence work is, by contrast, preventive and information-oriented. At its best, it occurs before violent events occur, in order to equip police and other authorities to deal with them. Information is gathered from people who are not compelled by law to divulge it. Intelligence officers have a much less clearly defined role, which works best in a highly centralized management structure. They are interested in the linkages and associations of people who may never commit a criminal act—people who consort with others who may be a direct threat to the interests of the state.

Ward Elcock, John Tait Memorial Lecture (delivered at the Canadian Association for Security and Intelligence Studies Conference, Vancouver, 16–18 October 2003), online: Canadian Security Intelligence Service www.csis-scrs.gc.ca/nwsrm/spchs/spch17102003-eng.asp.

failure to turn the uncovering of an agent against the enemy or to manipulate the information going to a hostile group."[3] From an intelligence standpoint, arrest and prosecution should be postponed until the terrorist network has been fully traced and its methods, affiliates, financiers, suppliers, and camp followers identified. Even then, a more effective tactic, because more discreet, may be to disable the network by sowing suspicion among its members, as by revealing to them who has been talking to the government, rather than to risk revealing in a public trial the intelligence techniques used to detect the terrorist ring and the knowledge gained through their use.

When a preventive strategy is employed, moreover, much of what is prevented is possible or incipient or intended criminal activity, rather than a prosecutable crime. This deprives the FBI agent, oriented toward arresting and prosecuting criminals, of a satisfactory sense of closure to an investigation:

> The FBI is a law enforcement organization, the critics said: cops who are good at capturing suspects *after* a crime has been committed, but with little aptitude for the tedious work of intelligence gathering and *preventing* a crime by a highly sophisticated foreign terrorist group. Agents were in love with their guns and badges and racking up arrests—which, since the FBI's beginning in 1908, was the way they got ahead in the organization. "Door kickers," as one 40-year CIA officer put it when asked what major attribute FBI agents brought to the job.[4]

Because it engages in disruption as well as detection, a domestic intelligence agency such as the Canadian Security Intelligence Service or Britain's MI5 is better called a security service—in fact, MI5's official title is the "Security Service"—than just an intelligence agency. It not only collects and analyzes intelligence data, but it also attempts to eliminate, though by methods other than those of criminal investigation and prosecution (intelligence officers have, for example, no power of arrest)—instead, by methods traditionally associated with intelligence agencies—the terrorist dangers it uncovers. That is not

3 K.G. Robertson, "Intelligence, Terrorism and Civil Liberties" in Paul Wilkinson & Alasdair M. Stewart, eds., *Contemporary Research on Terrorism* (Aberdeen: Aberdeen University Press, 1987) at 557.

4 Jeff Stein, "FBI under the Gun" *CQ Weekly* (1 May 2006) at 1153 [emphasis in original]. For a case study of the FBI's ineptitude in recruiting agents in the US Muslim community, see Peter Waldman, "Hard Sell — A Muslim's Choice: Turn U.S. Informant or Risk Losing Visa" *Wall Street Journal* (11 July 2006) A1. The FBI agent seems not to have realized that recruiting an undercover agent from the ethnic community in which the undercover agent will be working is a delicate courtship rather than a one-night stand.

congenial work for most FBI special agents, even, or perhaps especially, when it takes rather gentle forms, suggestive of "community policing."

The highly publicized arrests and indictments in June 2006 of seven Muslims (most of them Americans) in Miami on suspicion of plotting to blow up buildings there along with the Sears Tower in Chicago illustrate the tenacity of the FBI's culture of criminal investigation.[5] The Bureau was able to plant an informant in the group, and the members asked him to supply them with money, uniforms, machine guns, explosives, and other materials. He gave them a video camera to case possible targets, and some boots; but "by May [2006], the indictment suggests, the plan had largely petered out because of organizational problems."[6] Because the group had no money or backers (except the FBI's informant!), no skills or experience, had organizational problems, and had been penetrated, it was not an imminent threat;[7] there was no urgency about arresting its members. The group had wanted to get in touch with foreign terrorists but had been unable to do so. The informant might have helped them do so—might even have helped them become part of a serious terrorist network, enabling the Bureau to ascertain the network's scope and membership, methods and tradecraft, even goals and specific plans. The opportunity to exploit the penetration in this fashion was lost by the arrests—about which the Attorney General boasted to an extent that, given the ineptness of the defendants, evoked ridicule.[8]

---

5 Peter Whoriskey & Dan Eggen, "Terror Suspects Had No Explosives and Few Contacts: Sears Tower Plan Never Finished, Authorities Say" *Washington Post* (24 June 2006) A3.

6 *Ibid.*

7 Yet the FBI's public affairs officer describes the plot of the Miami Seven as one of five principal terrorist plots thwarted by the bureau in the year ending in September 2006. John Miller, "Law Enforcement, American Style" *The New York Times* (14 September 2006) A27. Although Miller says that the FBI is "transforming itself into an intelligence-driven organization," the title of his piece conveys a more accurate sense of the bureau's approach to counter-terrorism.

8 Richard Cohen, "Terror Alert: Severe Risk of Hype" *Washington Post* (27 June 2006) A21. An earlier example of premature arrest and prosecution was that of the "Lackawanna Six," who had attended al-Qa'ida training camps in Afghanistan before 9/11 (thus providing material support for terrorism) but apparently had decided not to join the jihad. Marc Sageman, *Understanding Terror Networks* (Philadelphia: University of Pennsylvania Press, 2004) at 68, 152. See also Richard A. Posner, *Uncertain Shield: The U.S. Intelligence System in the Throes of Reform* (Lanham, MD: Rowman and Littlefield, 2006) at 97. But it seems the Justice Department and FBI were not responsible for the decision to arrest the suspects so soon. Responsibility rested rather with the CIA, which hyped the threat posed by the suspects, and with the Bush Administration's "one percent doctrine." See Matthew Purdy and Lowell Bergman, "Where the Trial Led: Between Evidence and Suspicion; Unclear Danger: Inside the Lackawanna Terror Case" *The New York Times* (12 October 2003) A1; and text at note 27 in chapter 1 of Posner, *ibid.* What

A senior Justice Department official said: "We can't afford to wait.... [The suspects in Miami] were of significant concern, and we're not going to allow them to run into somebody who has the means to carry out what they were talking about."[9] That is the wrong attitude. Finding a "somebody who has the means" to carry out a terrorist attack, as the "Miami Seven" did not, is more important than prosecuting, as soon as enough evidence to sustain a prosecution has been obtained, plotters who pose no immediate threat to the nation's security. The undiscovered "somebody" is the real threat. Having penetrated the group, the FBI was in a position to manipulate it to the end of discovering, or even creating, links to persons capable of mounting terrorist attacks without the Bureau's assistance. Conceivably, the group may have been in such disarray that it was not worth cultivation, but if so, what did the Justice Department mean by saying that its members were of "significant concern"?

The Miami Seven were eventually tried. One was acquitted; the jury was hung on the rest, and at this writing the case is about to be retried.[10]

Risk aversion, an abiding characteristic of bureaucracy,[11] plays a big role in the FBI's early-arrest policy. Early arrests assure that members of the group won't escape the Bureau's grasp and commit terrorist attacks. Minuscule as that risk may be in a case such as that of the Miami Seven, should it materialize—delay in making arrests enabling an attack to succeed—the Bureau would find itself unable as a practical matter to defend itself in the court of public opinion. Yet a refusal to take a small risk may create a much greater one—the proper approach is to compare the expected benefits of pouncing with the expected benefits of waiting.

When the Bureau penetrates a drug gang, it has no compunctions about allowing the gang members to continue selling drugs while agents gather

---

was particularly unfortunate about the premature arrest of the Lackawanna Six was that because "recruitment of agents in place is a difficult task because of the strong emotional bonds among members of the jihad, making them reluctant to betray their friends and their faith . . . the best avenue for penetration lies in recruitment from the pool of those who went through the training but decided not to join the jihad." Sageman, *ibid.* at 180. "The aggressive policy of prosecuting [the Lackawanna Six] without exploring ways to use them to penetrate the jihad was a mishandled opportunity." *Ibid.* at 181.

9 Christopher Drew & Eric Lichtblau, "Two Views of Terror Suspects: Die-Hards or Dupes" *The New York Times* (1 July 2006) A1 and A10.

10 Kirk Semple, "National Briefing: South; Florida: Delay in Retrial of Six in Terror Plot" *The New York Times* (8 January 2008) 20. See also Kirk Semple, "National Briefing: South; Florida: Terror Conspiracy Retrial Begins" *The New York Times* (2 February 2008) 16.

11 See, for example, Murray J. Horn, *The Political Economy of Public Administration: Institutional Choice in the Public Sector* (Cambridge: Cambridge University Press, 1995) at 122.

evidence against as many members as possible. No one seems to worry that by doing this the Bureau is allowing illegal activity to continue during a protracted investigation. But if a terrorist act, however minor, were committed because the FBI had failed to pounce at the first opportunity—it had a suspect on a long tether, and the tether broke—there would be an avalanche of adverse publicity that the Bureau is not prepared to face.

The FBI's primary focus is and will remain the investigation of non-terrorist federal crimes, a vital national need that has shaped its organization, incentive structure, and culture. It resists blurring that focus by transforming itself into an intelligence agency. Just as crime-fighters do not make the best intelligence officers, intelligence officers don't make the best crime-fighters. The Bureau doesn't want to compromise its main mission by switching emphasis to one that it regards as secondary—understandably, since we know there's a great deal of ordinary federal crime but do not know the magnitude of the terrorist threat inside the United States—and to a degree incompatible with the effective performance of the main mission. Already there is concern that the reallocation of resources from conventional crime to terrorism is impairing the Bureau's ability to solve bank robberies and other staple offences within its jurisdiction.[12]

B. CRIME VERSUS WAR

The aim of criminal investigation is to develop evidence that will enable a criminal to be convicted. But when the criminal is a terrorist, procuring a conviction—even deciding to prosecute—can become a daunting challenge quite apart from the concerns that I have expressed with the overuse of prosecution as a counter-terrorist tool. The criminal justice system has been designed for dealing with ordinary crimes, not with terrorism, especially terrorism of the magnitude that the nation may be facing. Consider the rules of criminal procedure that entitle a person who is arrested to a prompt hearing before a judge to determine whether there is probable cause to believe he's committed a crime, that entitle the defendant to trial by jury, that require that criminal trials be open to the public, that entitle the defendant to confront the witnesses against him and require the government to disclose at trial all its evidence, that limit the use of hearsay evidence, that exclude evidence seized in violation of the Constitution, and that require proof of guilt beyond a reasonable doubt. The

12 See Dan Eggen, "Violent Crime in U.S. Continues to Surge: Homicide Increase Largest in Big Cities" *Washington Post* (19 December 2006) A1.

requirement of a prompt hearing forces the government to tip its hand and impairs its ability to extract information from a suspect. A public trial gives terrorist defendants a platform for propaganda and recruitment—for broadcasting their grievances and preening themselves as martyrs—and may yield clues to the government's investigative methods, reveal classified information, and make the intelligence services of foreign nations, on which we rely heavily for assistance in the struggle against global terrorism, reluctant to share intelligence information with our intelligence agencies, fearing that it will become public in our court proceedings.[13] Public trials also create a risk of witness intimidation, and public jury trials invite intimidation of jurors as well.

Requiring proof beyond a reasonable doubt—rather than just requiring, as in civil cases, that the plaintiff show that the defendant is more likely than not to have committed the wrong of which the plaintiff is complaining—weights false positives (convicting innocent persons) much more heavily than false negatives (acquitting guilty persons). So do other rules of the criminal process, such as the rule excluding evidence designed to establish the defendant's propensity to engage in the conduct of which he has been accused and the rule forbidding the trier of fact to infer guilt from the defendant's refusal to take the stand. The criminal law's systematic weighting of false positives more heavily than false negatives is questionable when the defendant is a terrorist determined to wreak mayhem on a large scale.

Other countries have greater flexibility to tailor their judicial procedures to the special problems posed by terrorism; we are boxed in to an extent by our eighteenth-century Constitution as it has been interpreted by the Supreme Court. But the qualification "to an extent" is vital, and so is "as it has been interpreted." We are less tightly boxed in by the Constitution, even as "amended" by the Supreme Court's countless constitutional decisions, than many civil libertarians believe.[14] One often hears it said, with relief on the part of civil libertarians and anxiety on the part of national security experts, that the Constitution prevents us from emulating the tough measures that England has taken to fight terrorism. If true, this is unfortunate because England has a much longer history of dealing with serious terrorist threats than the United States does. Queen Elizabeth I faced grave danger from religious fanatics, yearning for martyrdom, dispatched to England by foreign powers with which England was at war in the sixteenth century. Germany peppered England with spies during

---

13 Jennifer E. Sims, "Foreign Intelligence Liaison: Devils, Deals, and Details" (2006) 19 Int'l J. Intel. & Count. Intel. 195 at 211.

14 See Richard A. Posner, *Not a Suicide Pact: The Constitution in a Time of National Emergency* (Oxford: Oxford University Press, 2006) [Posner].

World War II. The provisional wing of the Irish Republican Army waged clandestine war against England for decades. And today England faces a more serious threat of homegrown Islamist terrorism than does the United States. We should learn from the experience that England has accrued over the centuries.

Although our political and legal culture derives from England, our *Bill of Rights* has, it is true, no direct counterpart in English law. But the difference between the two nations' civil liberties cultures is narrowing as a result of England's having signed the *European Convention on Human Rights*. And in considering the effect of our *Bill of Rights* on measures to combat terrorism we must bear in mind the difference between what the *Bill of Right*s actually says and how the Supreme Court has interpreted its words; judicial interpretations of the Constitution are mutable, whereas the words themselves can be changed only by the cumbersome procedures for formally amending the Constitution. A tradition of flexible interpretation permits judicial departures from, as well as judicial elaborations of, the actual language of the Constitution. Terms like "due process of law," "unreasonable searches and seizures," "freedom of speech," and "*habeas corpus*" are not self-defining; nor have judges been willing to confine them to the meaning they had for the framers or to the core meaning that they would have to be given to have any significance at all. Because American judges do not adhere strictly to precedent, the meaning impressed by judicial decisions on constitutional text is tentative, especially when a case arises that is not within the heartland of a previous decision because of the novelty of its facts or a shift in the social or political context of the relevant issues.

The consequence is that novel constitutional cases are essentially addressed to judicial discretion, and cannot be decided by subsumption or other deferential interpretive techniques. Novel constitutional cases in fact invite and receive what is in reality a policy or legislative judgment, and the essence of such a judgment is balancing (often, to be sure, intuitively) the considerations pro and con one outcome versus another. So if in times of perceived national emergency the government claims a right to detain a suspected terrorist incommunicado for a period of time necessary to interrogate him thoroughly or to protect the government's sources from being compromised as a result of knowledge of the suspect's arrest, the courts will decide the validity of the government's claim by balancing the government's interests (just described) against the interest of the suspect, who might turn out to be innocent.

There is nothing novel or illiberal in trading liberty off against safety. We do it all the time, for example, in limiting the ownership of guns or requiring seatbelts and infant seats in automobiles. It is no answer that while there is a right to due process of law, there is not a right to be safe against terrorism. That is true in the sense that one cannot sue the government for failing to protect one from terrorists. But that does not mean that safety is any less a constitutional *value* than due process is. All it means is that for rather obvious reasons of practicality, courts will not tell the government how much, and where, to spend on public safety. So there is no legally enforceable right to a particular level of police protection or national defence, but public safety is as important to any sensible construal of the scope of constitutional rights as the values underlying those rights are.

A complication, however, is that judges in a common law system such as that of the United States, are with rare exceptions generalists rather than specialists. Few know much about the menace of terrorism or the efficacy and limitations of alternative measures for countering it. This should make judges cautious about setting their judgment against that of the officials and staffs (the staffs more than the political-level officials) of the executive and legislative branches, who have the relevant knowledge. Because the Constitution is so difficult to amend, judges should treat it as a loose garment rather than as a straitjacket.[15] An eighteenth-century document should not be interpreted to bar measures essential to the defence against twenty-first century threats. And indeed courts in the United States generally have deferred to executive and legislative judgments concerning national security because they are in so poor a position to question them. That is the sensible response. New national security measures, or the enhancement of old ones, are adopted usually in times of felt emergency, and are relaxed when the emergency passes or its gravity diminishes or is reassessed downward. The curtailment of liberty may be excessive at first ("better safe than sorry"), but the excess is temporary, and so the costs of overreaction to perceived threat are truncated.

England is a liberal democracy, like the United States, and Americans living in or visiting England, and therefore fully subject to English law while they are there, do not walk in fear that they are at the mercy of a secret police. Like all other nations of the European Union, England has abolished capital punishment. It is in most respects more liberal than the United States. Yet both before and especially after 11 September 2001, England has deployed counterterrorism measures that frighten our civil libertarians, such as:[16]

---

15 *Ibid.*; see also Eric A. Posner & Adrian Vermeule, *Terror in the Balance: Security, Liberty, and the Courts* (Oxford: Oxford University Press, 2007).

16 The sources for this list are as follows: Antonio Vercher, *Terrorism in Europe: An International Comparative Legal Analysis* (Oxford: Oxford University Press, 1992) [Vercher]; Dana Keith, "In the Name of National Security or Insecurity?: The Potential Indefinite Detention of Noncitizen Certified Terrorists in the United States and the United Kingdom in the Aftermath of September 11, 2001" (2004) 16 Fla. J. Int'l L. 405; Helen Fenwick and Gavin Phillipson, "Legislative over-breadth, democratic failure and

1. conducting criminal trials without a jury if there is fear of jurors' being intimidated by accomplices of the defendant;
2. placing persons suspected of terrorism under "control orders" that require them to consent to being questioned or monitored electronically or forbidden to associate with certain persons, and that limit their travel;
3. detaining terrorist suspects for up to twenty-eight days (with judicial approval) for questioning, without charges being lodged;
4. conducting deportation proceedings from which the alien and his lawyer may be excluded—the alien is not entitled to be fully informed of the reasons for deporting him; "his" lawyer is appointed by and, more importantly, is responsible to the government rather than to the defendant; and evidence that is classified may be concealed from the defendant;
5. indefinitely detaining aliens who have been ordered deported but cannot actually be removed from the country (there may be no country willing to take them);[17]
6. criminalizing persons who encourage terrorism by "glorifying" it in words that imply that the listener should engage in the glorified activity;
7. authorizing the issuance of search warrants by security officials rather than just by judges;
8. conducting traffic analysis and other data mining of Internet communications without a warrant[18] (Internet service providers are required to install devices to enable Internet communications to be intercepted in transit); a warrant must be obtained to read an intercepted communi-

---

the judicial response: fundamental rights and the UK's anti-terrorist legal policy," in Victor V. Ramraj, Michael Hor, & Kent Roach, eds., *Global Anti-Terrorism Law and Policy* (Cambridge: Cambridge University Press, 2005) at 455; Kent Roach, "Must We Trade Rights for Security?: The Choice between Smart, Harsh, or Proportionate Security Strategies in Canada and Britain" (2006) 27 Cardozo L. Rev. 2157; Laura K. Donohue, "Anglo-American Privacy and Surveillance" (2006) 96 J. Crim. L. & Criminology 1059 [Donohue]. The British post-9/11 terrorism legislation is, however, strongly criticized in Dirk Haubrich, "September 11, Anti-Terror Laws and Civil Liberties: Britain, France and Germany Compared" (2003) 38 Gov't and Opposition 3, as being insufficiently sensitive to civil liberties.

17 The judicial committee of the House of Lords, England's highest court, has invalidated this practice. The situation in England is now similar to that in the United States: a deportee who cannot be removed from the country can be kept in custody indefinitely only if he poses a continuing danger to the country. *Zadvydas v. Davis*, 533 U.S. 678 (2001).

18 A warrant is not required in order "to monitor patterns, such as web sites visited, to and from whom e-mail is sent, which pages are downloaded, of which discussion groups a user is a member, and which chat rooms an individual visits." Donohue, above note 16 at 1179–80.

cation, but it may be granted by an executive official rather than a judge; and

9. authorizing judges to issue "Public Interest Immunity Certificates" to intelligence agencies, allowing them to withhold from public judicial proceedings highly sensitive information concerning informants or techniques.[19]

Contrary to the widespread belief that England has gone much further in curtailing the legal rights of terrorist suspects than our *Bill of Rights* would permit, most of the measures that I have listed would not violate the *Bill of Rights*. The *Bill of Rights* gives illegal aliens many fewer rights in deportation proceedings than enjoyed by defendants in criminal proceedings; allows criminal suspects to negotiate for "control" orders in lieu of incarceration; and does not require that searches be conducted by warrants, whether issued by judges or by other officials, but only that they not be "unreasonable." Nor does the Constitution require a criminal suspect *always* to be brought before a magistrate for a probable-cause hearing within forty-eight hours of his arrest. There is no such requirement in the constitutional text, and although the Supreme Court has imposed such a requirement by way of free interpretation of the Constitution's due process clauses, the Court excepts cases of "bona fide emergency or other extraordinary circumstance."[20]

That exception is important, and codifying it should be a priority in congressional deliberations on strengthening US laws against terrorism. The judicial formulation is too vague to be of much use in terrorist investigations, especially with the FBI gun-shy about testing the outer bounds of its legal authority. Congress needs to decide for how much longer than forty-eight hours it should be permissible to detain a terrorist suspect. The fixing of the outer limit should depend on the likelihood that protracted detention would yield important benefits for national security in additional arrests or a fuller detection, penetration, and disruption of terrorist activities or preparations.

---

19 Britain is not the only country that has a political and legal culture similar to ours and from which we might want to borrow ideas for combating terrorism more effectively. Canada — the foreign nation that is most like the United States — is another. See Kent Roach, "Canada's Response to Terrorism" in Ramraj, Hor, & Roach, eds., *Global Anti-Terrorism Law and Policy*, above note 16 at 511; Richard G. Mosley, "Preventing Terrorism, Bill C-36: The *Anti-Terrorism Act 2001*" (Paper presented at the Canadian Institute for the Administration of Justice conference on Terrorism, Law and Democracy: How Is Canada Changing Following September 11?, 25–26 March 2002), available for purchase online: Canadian Institute for the Administration of Justice www. ciaj-icaj.ca/en/publications/papers-a-articles/criminal-law.

20 *County of Riverside v. McLaughlin*, 500 U.S. 44 at 57 (1991).

Prolonged detention incommunicado increases the likelihood of extracting valuable information concerning the plans and accomplices of the suspect, avoids alerting the accomplices to the fact that their plot has been detected, conceals investigatory tactics, and may also be necessary in order to protect the sources whose information enabled the arrest. Because terrorism inflicts greater costs on society than ordinary crime, the social value of protracted detention of a terrorist suspect is greater than that of protracted detention of an ordinary criminal suspect, and this argues for allowing longer detention in a terrorist case. But there must be limits. The longer the period of detention, the greater the hardship to the person detained (who may, after all, be innocent) and the less likely further detention is to yield significant information or the recruitment of a double agent. The benefits diminish with time, and the costs increase; when the curves cross, the detainee should be brought before a judicial officer to decide whether further detention is necessary. There should be a fixed limit—to start with, perhaps twenty-eight days, with the government required (as under English law) to seek periodic reauthorizations from a judge during the twenty-eight days.

The English measures that would present the most difficult constitutional issues if adopted in this country are forbidding the "glorifying" of terrorism unless the glorification amounts to an incitement to imminent terrorist activity and conducting criminal trials without a jury. Yet the "unless" qualification is critical because glorifying that came within it would be punishable under US law as well, so that the objection to punishing the glorifying of terrorism is less to the principle of the English law than to the vagueness of the word "glorifying." And the *Bill of Rights*' guaranty of the right to a jury in a criminal case can probably be bypassed by trying suspected terrorists (at least if they are foreigners apprehended abroad, or, if American, apprehended in a combat setting) before military commissions, where there is no right to a jury. Just how far such commissions can go to relax the other procedural safeguards that the Constitution imposes on orthodox criminal trials is an unsettled question. It will not be answered until the Supreme Court decides the constitutionality of the *Military Commissions Act* of 2006—the law reauthorizing (in somewhat altered form) the commissions in order to comply with the *Hamdan* decision,[21] which had ruled that the President lacked authority to create the commissions on his own; further congressional action was necessary to authorize their creation.

---

21 *Military Commissions Act of 2006*, codified at 10 U.S.C. §§ 948–49 (2006). Online: US Government Printing Office http://frwebgate.access.gpo.gov/cgi-bin/getdoc.cgi?dbname=109_cong_bills&docid=f:s3930enr.txt.pdf.

And why *military* commissions? Some of the United States' Islamist enemies, such as the Taliban when they ruled Afghanistan, are military, and if they violate the laws of war, trial before a military commission is appropriate. But most terrorists are not soldiers. Homegrown terrorism may become a major threat in the United States, as it has become in England, but it would be odd to describe it as a *military* threat unless it attained a scale that would justify calling it a rebellion. Yet the prosecution of homegrown terrorists might be as problematic for the conventional court system as the prosecution of international terrorists, while a special terrorist court might be as appropriate for the former as for the latter. Many special courts, or courtlike administrative tribunals, have been established under Article I of the Constitution. They do not exercise the "judicial Power of the United States" in the sense that this phrase bears in Article III, and so they are not cabined by conventional features of federal adjudication, such as that criminal cases be tried by life-tenured judges (and often by jurors as well), appointed by the President and confirmed by the Senate. There are abundant foreign precedents for specialized tribunals, and specialized procedures, for terrorist trials. And there is a US precedent in the two foreign intelligence surveillance courts (the Foreign Intelligence Surveillance Court and the Foreign Intelligence Surveillance Review Court), though they are Article III courts rather than Article I courts. A special terrorist court composed of Article III judges, like the two *FISA* courts, would be less likely to roil constitutional waters than an Article I court would be.

The choice of military commissions reflects both America's legalistic tradition and American provincialism. Legalistic thinking tends to be dichotomous, classificatory—a squeezing of novel problems into old categories by main force. We lawyers have a bin called criminal law enforcement and a bin called waging war, and we think that any counter-terrorist measure has to be squeezed into one or the other. We have a history of using military commissions (how lawyers love precedents!); and so to escape some of the constraints of criminal law enforcement we declare "war" on terrorism and convene military commissions to try terrorists. This dichotomizing may even be a factor in the reluctance to consider creating a domestic intelligence agency. The Federal Bureau of Investigation is part of the Justice Department and does criminal investigation. The Defense Department fights terrorism by means that include military commissions and electronic surveillance. A domestic intelligence agency would fit neither box comfortably. So, instead of creating such an agency, we have tried to alter our legal procedures to enable the use in law enforcement of the methods that such an agency would use, such as permitting hearsay and other forms of information that do not fit the rules of evidence, to nail terrorists.

America's cultural provincialism—the instinctive American sense that we have nothing to learn from foreign countries—is reinforced by the inherent provincialism of law. Legal systems differ greatly across countries, even countries that belong to the same legal phylum, as do the English-speaking nations. Much of the difference is superficial, yet nonetheless daunting. Learning a foreign legal system is like learning a foreign language—indeed, it may well require learning the foreign country's language. That is not a problem for US lawyers and judges who want to understand the law of an English-speaking nation. But law is not just a rhetorical artifact. It is also an artifact of a country's political, social, and economic culture and institutions, and they have to be understood too for a legal transplant to avoid being rejected. Yet we should be able to learn, and to benefit from learning, how other democratic countries, especially those with more experience than we have with terrorism, tailor their counter-terrorist measures. The literature is extensive and much of it in English.[22] Without violating the letter or even the spirit of the Constitution, we could experiment with trying terrorists in specialized courts[23] or with using investigatory magistrates empowered to compel testimony from suspected terrorists under pain of holding them in contempt of court if they refused to testify.

So the United States could go quite a distance in the direction of English counter-terrorist law without the necessity of constitutional amendment. One question is why it hasn't, since 9/11; the answer may be that the Bush Administration overestimated what it could do on its own (more precisely, what the courts would permit it to do on its own), without bringing Congress into the picture. But the more interesting question is how far we should want to go in the direction of tougher laws against terrorism. The answer depends in part on how salient a role the formal legal system should play in the struggle against terrorism. As I have already hinted, I believe that we are overinvested in criminal law as a response to terrorism. This is regardless of specific constraints that

---

22 See, besides the references above in note 16, Karin von Hippel, ed., *Europe Confronts Terrorism* (New York: Palgrave MacMillan, 2005); Cyrille Fijnaut, Jan Wouters & Frederik Naert, eds., *Legal Instruments in the Fight against International Terrorism: A Transatlantic Dialogue* (Leiden: Martinus Nijhoff, 2004); Paul Gallis, ed., *European Counterterrorist Efforts: Political Will and Diverse Responses* (Hauppauge, NY: Nova, 2004); Marianne van Leeuwen, ed., *Confronting Terrorism: European Experiences, Threat Perceptions and Policies* (Alphen aan den Rijn, The Netherlands: Kluwer Law International, 2003) [*Confronting Terrorism*]; Human Rights Watch, *Setting an Example? Counter-Terrorism Measures in Spain* (2005) Human Rights Watch Vol. 17, No. 1(D), online: Human Rights Watch www.hrw.org/en/reports/2005/01/26/setting-example-0.

23 See, for example, Vercher, above note 16 at 303–22; Nathalie Cettina, "The French Approach: Vigour and Vigilance," in *Confronting Terrorism*, *ibid.* at 82–83.

the courts and Congress have placed on criminal law enforcement and might be persuaded to relax. The overinvestment is not, at least not primarily, a result of the courts' or Congress's having made investing in criminal law enforcement unprofitable by giving criminal defendants too many rights. Rather it is a symptom of an overlegalized political culture, in which litigation is seen as the answer to every problem. Conservatives rail against trial lawyers, activist judges, vague laws, and the proliferation of tort and other civil suits. What they miss is that our profligate recourse to the criminal process, and our prison population hugely swollen by draconian drug laws, are symptoms of the same underlying problem—an unconscious and often foolish faith in the legal system to alleviate our social and political woes. Democrats and Republicans play leapfrog in advocating new legal remedies for perceived social ills.

Criminal law enforcement is no more likely to win the "war on terrorism" than it is to win the "war on drugs." It is maladapted to both struggles. The United States should be de-emphasizing the effort to prevent terrorism by means of criminal prosecutions, especially but not only in the regular courts, which are not designed for the trial of people who pose a serious threat to national security. Our counter-terrorism efforts could be more effective, and at the same time the dilemma of defeating terrorism while respecting essential civil liberties minimized, if we downplayed the judicial role in counter-terrorism.

This would mean less striving to prevent terrorism by criminal prosecutions, whether in courts or in military tribunals; a diminished use of devices, such as the warrant, that are used mainly in criminal law enforcement; and, an expanded recourse to executive and legislative rather than judicial oversight to curb abuses to which counter-terrorism undoubtedly is prone. It is prone to abuse because of the fear that terrorism engenders and terrorism's political nature, which makes political opinions and advocacy a concern of national security.

It is telling that no one was actually tried by the military commissions established in the wake of 9/11 before they were held unconstitutional by the Supreme Court almost five years later[24] and that criminal prosecutions of terrorists have been few and often trivial.[25] According to one study, "the median sentence for those convicted [since the 9/11 attacks] in what were categorized

---

24 On the difficulties involved in prosecuting cases before a military commission, see Jess Bravin, "At Guantánamo, Even 'Easy' Cases Have Lingered: Balky Intelligence Agencies, War-Torn Crime Scene Hinder Legal Process" *Wall Street Journal* (18 December 2006) A1.

25 New York University Center for Law and Security, *Terrorist Trial Report Card: U.S. Edition: 2001–2006: Executive Summary* (New York: New York University School of Law, 2006).

as 'international terrorism' cases—often involving lesser charges like immigration violations or fraud—was 20 to 28 days, and many received no jail time at all."[26] In fact, terrorist prosecutions seem to be petering out.[27]

The government's failure to have brought anyone to trial before a military commission may have contributed to its losing the *Hamdan* case. Had the Court been reviewing a judgment rendered after a trial conducted by such a commission, it might have been persuaded that the procedures were adequate to prevent miscarriages of justice. The Court can also be criticized, however, for its impatience in refusing to hold its fire until a trial had been held that would have lent concreteness to judicial consideration of the legal issues. It is true that the Court's ruling was based on a lack of legislative authority for the commissions, and such a ruling is, in principle, unrelated to the adequacy of the procedures used by the commissions. But in practice, judges' sense of the "fairness" or "justice" of a proceeding is likely to influence their decision on whether the proceeding is authorized, at least in a close case, which *Hamdan* was.

Criminal law enforcement discourages crime by a combination of deterrence and incapacitation. Contemporary international terrorists are difficult to deter. Not only are many of them suicide attackers, but also as political criminals the others may expect if captured to be released from prison, as part of a swap or a political settlement, before completion of their prison terms. As for incapacitation, locking up terrorists (those who survive the terrorist attack) has only a limited preventive effect because the supply of replacements is so large.[28] Nor is it necessary to put a terrorist on trial in order to be able to imprison him indefinitely. The Constitution does not require a full-scale criminal trial in order to detain a person who is a demonstrable threat to national security.[29]

---

26 Eric Lichtblau, "Study Finds Sharp Drop in the Number of Terrorism Cases Prosecuted" *The New York Times* (4 September 2006) A9.

27 *Ibid.*; Dan Eggen, "Terrorism Prosecutions Drop: Analysis Shows a Spike after 9/11, Then a Steady Decline" *Washington Post* (4 September 2006) A6. Eggen's article summarizes Transactional Records Access Clearinghouse (TRAC), "Criminal Terrorism Enforcement in the United States during the Five Years since the 9/11/01 Attacks" (3 September 2006), online: TRAC Reports http://trac.syr.edu/tracreports/terrorism/169/. For striking examples of hyped FBI terrorist investigations and prosecutions, see Scott Shane and Lowell Bergman, "F.B.I. Struggling to Reinvent Itself to Fight Terror" *The New York Times* (10 October 2006) A23.

28 In economic terms, the supply of terrorists is highly elastic, meaning that if one is killed or captured, creating a demand for a replacement, the demand will be quickly filled by someone from the large reserve army of potential terrorists.

29 Posner, above note 14 at 66–67. But if a terrorist suspect is detained on the ground that he poses a danger to national security, there should be periodic judicial review to determine whether his continued detention is justified.

The Constitution does, of course, require a trial if the government wants to execute a person. But executing terrorists, at least before the political movement to which the terrorists belong has been crushed, is usually a mistake. It creates martyrs, as the English learned to their sorrow when they executed the leaders of the Easter Rebellion in Ireland in 1916. It is one thing to execute an enemy when the alternative is a short prison sentence, or to execute the leaders or for that matter the followers of a defeated movement or regime, as in the case of the Nazi leaders executed after World War II; but Islamist terrorism has not been defeated and it thrives on martyrdom. Obviously, the threat of execution does not deter would-be martyrs, as they do not expect to survive their attacks. But neither, in all likelihood, does it deter the leaders of terrorist movements, even though they do not seek martyrdom. To be a terrorist leader is already to accept a high probability of being killed—the *incremental* probability of death by execution will usually be slight.

Granted, there is more to terrorism than leaders and suicide bombers. Peripheral players are deterrable by threat of criminal punishment.[30] An important example is criminals who sell weapons to terrorists.[31] Nor am I advocating that we turn the other cheek. Just and prudent retribution can be ferocious without being channelled through the legal system. Our military and quasi-military efforts against terrorism have inflicted substantial costs on our terrorist enemies. And however the *Military Commissions Act* of 2006 fares in the courts, the Constitution casts a longer shadow over criminal prosecutions than it does over non-legal (by which I do not mean illegal) methods, even when lethal, of combating terrorism (a longer shadow and also a lengthening one).[32] Most of the rights conferred by the *Bill of Rights*, as expansively interpreted by the Supreme Court, are rights of criminal defendants. Efforts to curtail those rights, whether through judicial interpretation or by shifting prosecution to non-Article III courts, encounter particularly strident opposition from civil libertarians. We shall see that electronic surveillance is less constrained by the Fourth Amendment when it is not used to generate evidence for criminal prosecutions.

Criminal law enforcement may seem the only *domestic* counter-terrorist tool that we have unless martial law is declared and the military turned loose

30 That deterrence retains considerable utility as a method of counter-terrorism is strongly argued in Paul K. Davis & Brian Michael Jenkins, *Deterrence and Influence in Counter-terrorism: A Component in the War on al Qaeda* (Santa Monica, CA: RAND, 2002).

31 See David P. Auerswald, "Deterring Nonstate WMD Attacks" (2006) 121 Poli. Sci. Q. 543.

32 See Jack Goldsmith & Cass R. Sunstein, "Military Tribunals and Legal Culture: What a Difference Sixty Years Makes" (2002) 19 Const. Commentary 261.

on domestic enemies. That is incorrect. Intelligence services, as I pointed out in Part A of this paper, disrupt as well as detect, and not only by engaging in forms of covert action that comply with US law only when they are deployed abroad. The term "covert action" requires careful definition. It is too often equated to efforts to subvert foreign governments. That is indeed the activity in which the Central Intelligence Agency achieved unwanted notoriety. But all the term means or should mean is clandestine activity in support of national security. It covers a wide range of tactics, some clearly inappropriate for domestic intelligence or security operations but others uncontroversially used in combating ordinary crimes and properly usable for domestic counterterrorist work as well. Once detected, a terrorist plot can often be lawfully neutralized without prosecution of the plotters. Some of them can be deported (deportation is civil rather than criminal and administrative rather than judicial, though there is judicial review); some "turned" to work for us by offers of money or other assistance, by threats, or by promises (turning an enemy into a friend is one way of dealing with some enemies); some discredited in the eyes of their accomplices, some paid off, some frightened into sullen quiescence by a "heavy tap on the shoulder" (a warning to the suspect that his activities and inclinations are known to the authorities and that he is being watched); some sent off on wild-goose chases by carefully planted disinformation; some bought off by amnesties; and, some monitored in the hope that they will lead us to their accomplices

And some can be held in administrative detention or otherwise restricted in their movements (if a judge decides they're dangerous) until the terrorist threat abates and then either tried in the regular way or released. For it is not true that preventive detention—detention other than pursuant to a criminal charge or conviction—is alien to the American legal system. An insane person, for example, can be detained indefinitely (though with frequent judicial review) if he is adjudged a serious danger to himself or others. The same thing should be possible if the person is dangerous not because he is insane but because his religion or his politics impels him to mass murder.

The greatest value of allowing detention of terrorist suspects for more than forty-eight hours would lie neither in facilitating prosecution nor in keeping them out of circulation without a prosecution, however, but rather in aiding intelligence by enabling the government to get more complete and timely information about the scope, direction, timing, personnel, and links to other networks of the plot that has been detected.

I am not suggesting that criminal law should be dispensed with in the struggle against modern terrorism, any more than military force should be, though the efficacy of military force as a way of combating terrorism is easily exaggerated as well.[33] If all terrorists were so fanatical as to be undeterrable by threat of criminal punishment, the methods available to intelligence services in the domestic environment would often fall flat. The tap on the shoulder would lack weight if it didn't convey an implicit threat to prosecute a suspect who refused to play ball.[34] And sometimes the heavy tap is inferior to prosecution because it just drives the suspect deeper into a secret terrorist milieu, so that intelligence loses track of him. Moreover, many of the handicaps to using the criminal law against terrorists evaporate when terrorist suspects are prosecuted for violating ordinary crimes—a form of lawful police harassment.[35] That is part of the explanation for those light sentences in the Justice Department's anti-terrorist cases; the defendants were suspected terrorists prosecuted for ordinary crimes. In general, however, when the government is not looking to put a terrorist suspect on trial, it has more constitutional and statutory space in which to seek to neutralize him, using methods that often are more effective than criminal law enforcement.

C. WARRANT FETISHISM

The idea that judicial warrants should be the principal tool for preventing abuses in counter-terrorism surveillance is a particularly perverse example of the United States' overinvestment in legalistic responses to the terrorist threat. It is historically perverse: warrants are actually constrained rather than required or encouraged by the language and historical background of the warrant clause of the Fourth Amendment. The clause *limits* the use of warrants by requiring that they be supported by oath (or affirmation) and probable cause and describe with particularity the person, house, etc., to be searched and the things to be seized. Surveillance, even when it takes the form of wiretapping or other electronic interception and so is deemed a search under the Fourth Amendment, need not—at least if the actual language of the amendment is

33 Our successful campaign against Afghanistan in the wake of the 9/11 attacks was mainly a CIA show, as was the Predator strike that killed terrorist leaders in Yemen, while the invasion and occupation of Iraq by our armed forces have not been anti-terrorist triumphs.

34 Or to detain him indefinitely, without prosecution, on the ground that he is too dangerous to let loose. But if he is that dangerous, the heavy tap on the shoulder would probably not be an effective method of neutralizing him.

35 See, for example, Robert Block, "An L.A. Police Bust Shows New Tactics for Fighting Terror: Officers Use Local Laws to Arrest Small Offenders with High-Risk Potential" *Wall Street Journal* (29 December 2006) A1.

deemed authoritative—be conducted on the authority of a warrant. The Fourth Amendment, interpreted in light of its framers' and ratifiers' understanding as well as its text, permits warrantless surveillance provided that only it is reasonable.

After the Supreme Court ruled in a conventional criminal case that wiretapping and, by implication, other forms of electronic surveillance were to be deemed "searches" within the meaning of the Fourth Amendment, Congress enacted Title III of the *Omnibus Crime Control and Safe Streets Act* of 1968. Title III created procedures for obtaining warrants for electronic surveillance that were modelled on the procedures for conventional search warrants. Ten years later—and thus long before the danger of global terrorism was recognized and the methods of electronic surveillance transformed by the digital revolution—the *Foreign Intelligence Surveillance Act* (*FISA*) was enacted. It is a complicated statute but basically it provides, so far as relates to terrorism, that interceptions in the United States of the international communications of a US citizen, or permanent resident, or of anyone in the United States if the interception is made here, be conducted pursuant to warrants based on probable cause to believe that one of the parties to the communication is a member of a terrorist group.

The statute remains usable for regulating the monitoring of communications of known terrorists, but it is useless for finding out who is a terrorist, even though "the problem of defeating the enemy consists very largely of finding him."[36] Hence the importance of "collateral intercepts"—such as intercepts of communications that seem likely to yield information of intelligence value even if probable cause to believe that a party to the communication is a terrorist is lacking.

It is true that surveillance not cabined by a conventional probable-cause requirement produces many false positives—interceptions that prove upon investigation to have no intelligence value. But that is not a valid criticism. One must not forget the necessity of balancing false positives against false negatives. The failure to detect the 9/11 plot was an exceptionally costly false negative. The intelligence services have no alternative to casting a wide net with a fine mesh if they are to have reasonable prospects of obtaining the clues that will enable the next attack to be prevented. The National Security Agency's electronic surveillance involves an initial sifting, performed by computer search programs, of electronic communications for clues to terrorist activity. The sifting uses both "content filtering" and "traffic analysis" to pick out a tiny percentage of

36 Frank Kitson, cited in Bradley W.C. Bamford, "The Role and Effectiveness of Intelligence in Northern Ireland" (2005) 20 Intelligence and National Security 581 at 586.

communications to be read. Content filtering is Google-like searching for words inside the communication. Traffic analysis is examining message length, frequency and time of communication, and other non-content information that may reveal suspicious patterns; thus traffic analysis can't be foiled by encryption because the information is not content-based. The National Security Agency has obtained call records from telephone companies to aid in its traffic analysis. If the agency has the phone number of a known or suspected terrorist, it can use call records to determine the most frequent numbers called to or from that number and then determine the most frequent numbers called to or from those numbers and in this way piece together a possible terrorist network—all without listening to any conversation. That comes later.

So the search sequence is interception, data mining, and finally a human search of those intercepted messages that data mining or other information sources have flagged as suspicious. Computer searches do not invade privacy because search programs are not sentient beings. Only the human search should raise constitutional or other legal issues.

Communications read by an intelligence officer and thus "searched" in the legal sense could as a technical matter include—what *FISA* forbids unless there is probable cause to believe that a party to the communication is a member of a terrorist group (or an agent of a foreign power)—communications to which a US citizen is a party and communications that are purely domestic rather than international.

Instead of requiring probable cause to believe that the target of an interception is a terrorist, *FISA* could be amended to require merely reasonable suspicion. But even that would be too restrictive; effective surveillance can't be confined to suspected terrorists when the object is to discover who may be engaged in terrorism or ancillary activities. Further attenuation of *FISA*'s standard for obtaining a warrant may be possible. It is possible that the issuance of a warrant could be authorized on the basis of a showing that while probable cause to believe that the target was a terrorist was lacking, national security required making assurance doubly sure by intercepting some of his electronic communications. A model (and an example of how the United States can learn from foreign experience) might be the criterion for issuing a search warrant to the Canadian Security Intelligence Service: it can be issued on the basis of a factually supported "belief, on reasonable grounds, that a warrant . . . is required to enable the Service to investigate a threat to the security of Canada . . . ."[37] Such a criterion might pass muster under the Fourth Amendment, which requires probable cause for the issuance of a warrant but does not state what it is

37 *Canadian Security Intelligence Service Act*, R.S.C. 1985, c. C–23, s. 21(2)(a).

that there must be probable cause to believe. The Supreme Court has said that it must be probable cause to believe that the search will yield contraband or evidence of crime—when the search is part of a criminal investigation.[38] That is an example of my earlier point that the Constitution binds the government more tightly when it is exerting its powers to convict people of crimes. A search intended not to obtain evidence of crime but to obtain information about terrorism might, as under Canadian law, require only probable cause to believe that the search would yield such information.

The lower the standard for getting a warrant, however, the more porous the filter that the requirement of a warrant creates, bearing in mind the *ex parte* character of a warrant proceeding. If all the application need state is that an interception might yield data having value as intelligence, judges would have no basis for refusing to issue the warrant. Alternatively, reliance on warrants could invite legislation to expand the reach of the criminal laws relating to terrorism in order to make it easier to establish probable cause to believe that a search will reveal evidence of crime.

Warrants that satisfy *FISA*'s standard as traditionally understood should continue to be required for all physical searches, because they are far greater intrusions on privacy than an electronic interception is, and for all electronic surveillance for which *FISA*'s existing probable-cause requirement can be satisfied. With these exceptions, civil libertarians' preoccupation with warrants is not only harmful to national security (and possibly to civil liberties, if it induces legislation to expand the reach of the criminal law) but also anachronistic. The government's ready access to the vast databases that private and public entities compile for purposes unrelated to national security has enabled it to circumvent much of the protection of privacy that civil libertarians look to warrant requirements to secure.[39]

It thus is time that we broke our habit of thinking that legal rules are always the best way of preventing abuses. Congress struggled in the *Military Commissions Act* to define the legal limits of coercive interrogation. An alternative would have been to require that the interrogation of terrorist suspects that uses methods forbidden in an ordinary criminal investigation be expressly authorized in writing by the Secretary of Defense, the Attorney General, or the President himself. Accountability would be substituted for deniability and legal hair-splitting. The same substitution is attractive with

38 *Zurcher v. Stanford Daily*, 436 U.S. 547 at 554–55 (1978).

39 See, for example, Arshad Mohammed & Sara Kehaulani Goo, "Government Increasingly Turning to Data Mining: Peek into Private Lives May Help in Hunt for Terrorists" *Washington Post* (15 June 2006) D3; Posner, *Countering Terrorism*, above note 1, c. 6.

regard to the control of electronic surveillance for national security purposes. Congress could, for example, create a steering committee for national security electronic surveillance, composed of the Attorney General, the Director of National Intelligence, the Secretary of Homeland Security, and a retired federal judge or justice appointed by the Chief Justice of the United States. The committee would monitor all such surveillance to assure compliance with the Constitution and laws.

The National Security Agency could be required to submit to the steering committee, to departmental inspectors general, to the Privacy and Civil Liberties Oversight Board (a White House agency created by the *Intelligence Reform Act*), to the congressional intelligence and judiciary committees, and to an independent watchdog agency of Congress modelled on the General Accountability Office, every six months a list of the names and other identifying information of all persons whose communications had been intercepted in the previous six months without a warrant, with a brief statement of why these persons had been targeted.

The responsible officials of the National Security Agency could be required to certify annually to the watchdog groups that there had been no violations of the statute during the preceding year. False certification would be punishable as perjury.

The use of intercepted information for any purpose other than investigating threats to national security could be forbidden. Information would not be usable as evidence or leads in a prosecution for ordinary crime—this to alleviate public concern that wild talk bound to be picked up by electronic surveillance would lead to criminal investigations unrelated to national security. Violations of this provision would be made felonies punishable by substantial prison sentences and heavy fines. But the punishments must not be made too severe lest they cause intelligence officers to steer so far clear of possible illegality that they fail to conduct effective surveillance. The risk of abuses is not great enough to justify savage penalties in order to deter them, because intelligence officers have no interest in assisting in the enforcement of criminal laws unrelated to national security. A neglected point is that violations of privacy and civil liberties tend to emanate from the White House and the top management level of executive branch agencies rather than from the working or middle-management levels.

The utility of electronic surveillance as a counter-terrorist tool would be emasculated by requiring probable cause to believe that an interception would yield evidence of a crime already committed. But the countervailing concern with privacy and related values served by allowing communications to be kept secret from third parties, including government, can be accommodated once it is understood that the objection to surveillance is less to the loss of privacy than to the danger that the persons engaged in the surveillance will use the information they gain from it against persons surveilled who turn out to be innocent of any involvement in terrorist activities. Provided that effective safeguards against such abuses are in place, the cost of infringing privacy can be brought below the benefit to the public safety of widespread surveillance, obviating constitutional objections; for the Fourth Amendment prohibits only "unreasonable" searches and seizures.

Civil libertarians and privacy advocates are also concerned about the privacy of the vast mass of personal data that people turn over to vendors and other service providers with whom they have online transactions. Personal data voluntarily provided to an online bookseller, for example, do not enjoy constitutional protection against being turned over to the government by the bookseller to assist in a terrorist investigation. Similarly, there is no constitutional protection against a city's installing thousands of surveillance cameras on its streets or against the FBI's sending undercover agents into mosques to report on the contents of the sermons delivered by the imams. The value of the data collected by such means to preventing terrorists is potentially very great, but there is an infringement of privacy and a danger that people will be inhibited about expressing unpopular though constitutionally protected ideas and opinions, knowing that their ideas and opinions have become transparent to government security officers. Again there is a need for difficult tradeoffs and again the focus should in my opinion be on assuring, so far as is possible, that personal data are not used by government for any purpose other than the protection of national security.

Finally, to limit the permissible scope of surveillance, "threats to national security" justifying comprehensive electronic surveillance could and should be narrowly defined as threats involving a potential for mass deaths or catastrophic property or other economic damage. That would exclude, for the time being anyway, eco-terrorism, animal-rights terrorism, and other political violence that, though criminal, does not threaten catastrophic harm (yet).

Congressional action is also needed, however, to protect the phone companies that cooperated with the National Security Agency's post-9/11 surveillance programs from potentially immense liability for allegedly having violated federal law protecting the privacy of telephone records; a number of suits are pending. The intelligence system is enormously dependent on informal assistance from private companies in communications, banking, and other industries. At times such assistance is made a legal duty, as in the federal law requiring banks to report cash transactions of ten thousand dollars or more.

Most of the assistance is voluntary. But if voluntary assistance—even when tendered in a national emergency, as in the wake of the 9/11 terrorist attacks—places companies in legal jeopardy, such assistance will dry up.

Why are such ideas (except legal immunities for business) for regularizing domestic surveillance getting little attention from Congress and the administration? One reason is the grip of our legalistic culture, which makes us think that the regulation of national security *must* be modelled on the regulation of criminal law enforcement.

The United States should be playing to its strengths, and one of the greatest of them is technology. We may not be able to prevail against terrorism with one hand tied behind our back. Critics of surveillance argue that since our enemies know that we monitor electronic communications, they will foil us by simply ceasing to use such communications. That is wrong. We know it is wrong because we do intercept terrorist communications.[40] But if it were true that our monitoring caused the terrorists to abandon the telephone and the Internet, that would be an enormous victory for counter-terrorism, as it is extremely difficult to coordinate and execute a major terrorist attack if all communications among the plotters must be face to face to avoid detection. The greater danger is that encryption and other relatively cheap and simple countermeasures will defeat our surveillance.

Opponents of efforts to modify the *FISA* point out that the Foreign Intelligence Surveillance Court has almost never turned down an application for a warrant. In 2005, for example, although more than two thousand applications were filed, not a single one was denied in whole or in part.[41] The inference the critics wish drawn is that the Act is not inhibiting surveillance. The correct inference is that the Justice Department is too conservative in seeking warrants. The analogy is to a person who has never missed a plane in his life because he contrives always to arrive at the airport eight hours before the scheduled departure time. The effect of the legalistic miasma of which I have been complaining in this paper is to cause law enforcement agencies, notably the FBI, to avoid not only violating the law but also steering so close to the wind that they might be accused, albeit groundlessly, of violating the law, or of being "insensitive" to values that inform the law, even when those values have not been enacted into law. So consider, in closing, the "wall" that before 9/11 inhibited communication

40 See, for example, James Bamford, "He's in the Backseat!" *Atlantic Monthly* (April 2006) at 67.

41 Letter from William E. Moschella, Assistant Attorney General, to J. Dennis Hastert, Speaker, U.S. House of Representatives (28 April 2006), online: Federation of American Scientists www.fas.org/irp/agency/doj/fisa/2005rept.html.

between intelligence officers and criminal investigators. Quickly dismantled (or so it is claimed—actually, it was merely lowered) after the 9/11 attacks, the wall was a product of the Justice Department's exaggerated fear of jeopardizing criminal prosecutions by using, as leads or evidence in prosecutions, information obtained by intelligence operations, including *FISA* surveillance:

> The 1995 procedures [that established the wall] dealt only with sharing between agents and criminal prosecutors, not between two kinds of FBI agents, those working on intelligence matters and those working on criminal matters. But pressure from the [Justice Department's] Office of Intelligence Policy Review, FBI leadership, and the *FISA* Court built barriers between agents—even agents serving on the same squads. FBI Deputy Director Bryant reinforced the Office's caution by informing agents that too much information sharing could be a career stopper. Agents in the field began to believe—incorrectly—that no *FISA* information could be shared with agents working on criminal investigations.
>
> This perception evolved into the still more exaggerated belief that the FBI could not share any intelligence information with criminal investigators, even if no *FISA* procedures had been used. Thus, relevant information from the National Security Agency and the CIA often failed to make its way to criminal investigators [emphasis in original].[42]

The legalistic atmosphere that envelops the Justice Department, including the FBI (notice that the Bureau played a role, though not the dominant one, in building the wall), is impeding the nation's response to the terrorist threat without securing civil liberties.

The threat is *sui generis*. It is not a crime problem, primarily, or a war problem, primarily, but its own problem. It requires a tailored solution that, I have tried to show, challenges conventional legalistic thinking.

---

42 National Commission on Terrorist Attacks upon the United States, *The 9/11 Commission Report: Final Report of the National Commission on Terrorist Attacks upon the United States* (Washington, DC: US Government Printing Office, 2004) 79.

CHAPITRE 5

Respect des libertés individuelles et exigences de sécurité nationale : quel point d'équilibre?

LES RÉPONSES JUDICIAIRES FRANÇAISES

JEAN-CLAUDE MARIN

PROCUREUR DE LA RÉPUBLIQUE, TRIBUNAL DE GRANDE INSTANCE DE PARIS, FRANCE

La plus grande victoire du terrorisme international sur les démocraties est de les engager dans une lutte où elles abandonnent toutes leurs valeurs au profit de l'efficacité.

Existe-t-il un choix à faire entre sécurité et justice?

L'État de droit est-il un obstacle (légitime) à la lutte contre le terrorisme dans une optique de sécurité nationale?

Pour tenter de répondre à ces paradoxes apparents, l'expérience française permet peut-être de contribuer à une réflexion qui concerne tous les États démocratiques, lesquels en ont bien à apprendre les uns des autres.

À partir de 1975, et surtout au début des années 1980, la France a eu à faire face à une série d'attentats commis par des groupuscules soutenus, selon la formule consacrée, par des États terroristes, c'est-à-dire des États tels alors que la Libye, l'Iran ou la Syrie, qui fournissaient du soutien financier et logistique, voire de la formation, aux auteurs de ces faits criminels.

Ce furent notamment les actions menées, en France et en Europe, par Illich Ramirez Sanchez, dit « Carlos » ou « Le Chacal », aujourd'hui détenu en France, qui, après l'assassinat, en 1975, de deux policiers de la direction de la Surveillance du territoire (DST) venus l'arrêter, en passant par l'enlèvement à Vienne de 11 ministres de l'OPEP, devait être l'artisan de 3 attentats commis en France en 1982 qui devaient faire 11 morts et 130 blessés.

C'est d'ailleurs à la suite de ces événements, ainsi qu'en considération d'actions terroristes d'extrême gauche menées par le groupe « Action directe » et ayant abouti à l'assassinat de personnalités françaises, dans un contexte où des actions semblables étaient menées en Allemagne et en Italie par des organisations similaires, que la France a choisi, dès cette époque, de faire de la réponse judiciaire l'axe principal de sa politique de lutte contre le terrorisme, contrairement à d'autres États qui, depuis, ont choisi une réponse principalement militaire.

La France s'est ainsi dotée, depuis 1986, d'une législation pénale complète, à la fois spécifique et respectueuse des principes fondamentaux de nos États de droit.

Le terrorisme des années 1980, et nous parlons ici du terrorisme intégriste islamiste, a depuis changé de visage. D'un terrorisme d'État fondé sur des motivations politiques précises, il est devenu un terrorisme beaucoup plus planétaire, global et diffus, pour lequel aucun espace de négociation n'est envisageable puisqu'il s'agit d'un « terrorisme de rejet, essentiellement celui de la démocratie libérale[1] », dont l'objectif est peu ou prou l'instauration d'une sorte de charia mondiale.

Des lois successives sont donc venues depuis 1986, et spécialement après les attentats commis à Paris à l'été 1995, puis à la suite du 11 septembre 2001, compléter et aménager le dispositif initial afin de l'adapter à cette évolution majeure, mais sans jamais en altérer la philosophie d'origine : un système qui comporte certes des accroissements de pouvoirs d'investigation et de contrainte, dérogatoires, afin de lutter efficacement contre le terrorisme, mais un système inscrit dans notre droit commun et qui n'est pourtant pas sans efficacité.

C'est cet équilibre voulu par le législateur que nous exposons maintenant.

A. LE CHOIX D'UNE RÉPONSE JUDICIAIRE INSCRITE DANS LE DROIT COMMUN. . .

Le législateur français a entendu privilégier, dans l'élaboration de l'arsenal de lutte contre le terrorisme, le cadre juridique ordinaire, celui du droit commun, tant sur le plan de l'organisation judiciaire que sur le plan du droit pénal de fond et du droit processuel.

Ce choix repose sur le souci d'assurer le respect des droits fondamentaux de la personne et des exigences du procès équitable telles qu'elles résultent de nos textes constitutionnels et de la *Convention européenne des droits de l'homme.*

1 Philippe Chrestia, maître de conférences en droit public, Université de Corse, « La France et la lutte contre le terrorisme à travers la loi du 23/01/06, relative à la lutte contre le terrorisme », (2006) 6 *Collectivités territoriales—Intercommunalité* 4.

1) C'est ainsi, dans le domaine de l'organisation judiciaire, que la création d'une juridiction d'exception a été exclue.

La solution retenue est celle de la *centralisation*, à Paris, des poursuites, de l'instruction et du jugement des crimes et délits terroristes, jusques et y compris de la procédure d'exécution des peines prononcées.

Le parquet, les juges d'instruction, les juges d'application des peines, le tribunal correctionnel, la Cour d'appel et la Cour d'assises de Paris se sont vu attribuer une compétence nationale dans le domaine terroriste.

Cette compétence est dite « concurrente » de celle des autres juridictions du territoire, ce qui signifie que toute juridiction peut connaître des affaires de terrorisme relevant de sa compétence territoriale jusqu'à ce que le parquet de Paris décide de s'en saisir.

Cette disposition présente l'avantage de ne pas rendre nuls les premiers actes éventuellement accomplis sous l'autorité de l'une de ces juridictions et montre bien à quel point la compétence de droit commun est au cœur du dispositif.

Paris est un parquet et une juridiction de droit commun à compétence nationale et non une juridiction d'exception.

À la centralisation s'est ajoutée au fil du temps la *spécialisation* des magistrats et formations appelés à intervenir dans le domaine du terrorisme : ainsi, au parquet, huit magistrats se consacrent exclusivement à ces dossiers, depuis l'enquête jusqu'au jugement. De même, à l'instruction, huit juges n'instruisent que des affaires de terrorisme.

Il est en effet évident que ces procédures nécessitent une connaissance particulière des réseaux terroristes, de leur histoire, de leur mode de fonctionnement et des corrélations possibles ou probables entre mouvements et entre individus. Cela est si vrai qu'il existe une sorte de « surspécialisation », non rigide, au sein des services du parquet et de l'instruction, entre affaires relatives à l'intégrisme islamiste, affaires basques et affaires corses.

La nécessité d'une spécialisation, initialement cantonnée au service du Procureur de la République et de l'instruction, s'est peu à peu imposée pour les formations de jugement au Tribunal et à la Cour d'appel.

La spécialisation terroriste se double éventuellement de la spécialisation financière en cas d'affaires de financement du terrorisme. Les services de police comme les magistrats du parquet et ceux de l'instruction antiterroristes travaillent alors conjointement avec leurs homologues financiers au sein d'équipes pluridisciplinaires.

La centralisation et la spécialisation ne sont toutefois pas des solutions propres au terrorisme. Le tribunal et le parquet de Paris ont ainsi une compétence nationale en matière de délits boursiers et de lutte contre la corruption de décideurs publics étrangers, de même qu'une compétence sur les deux tiers du territoire national dans le domaine de la santé publique. Ils forment l'un des huit pôles judiciaires spécialisés dans la lutte contre la criminalité organisée et les délits financiers les plus complexes.

Si la lutte contre le terrorisme a pu être un précurseur dans la centralisation et la spécialisation des juridictions et des magistrats, le fait que ce mouvement touche aujourd'hui d'autres domaines du droit pénal montre bien que la lutte contre le terrorisme est partie intégrante de l'organisation pénale française dans son ensemble et ne constitue en rien une « organisation d'exception », mais bien une structure de droit commun spécialisée.

2) Dans le domaine du droit pénal de fond, la loi définit la notion d'acte de terrorisme par référence au droit commun, puisque deux éléments sont nécessaires.

Les crimes ou délits de droit commun, limitativement énumérés dans la liste des articles 421-1 et 421-2 du *Code pénal*, vont des atteintes volontaires à la vie au délit d'initié en passant par l'enlèvement et la séquestration, le détournement d'aéronef, le vol, l'extorsion, l'infraction à la législation sur les armes ou le blanchiment.

Une intention terroriste particulière est définie comme « la relation avec une entreprise individuelle ou collective ayant pour but de troubler gravement l'ordre public, par l'intimidation ou la terreur ».

Dans ce cas, la peine encourue est plus élevée que celle qui l'aurait été pour le délit ou le crime de droit commun fait sans intention terroriste.

Sont également réprimées les infractions terroristes par nature, mais dont les éléments constitutifs ou le mode de preuve ne diffèrent en rien des infractions de droit commun. Il s'agit du financement d'une entreprise terroriste qui permet de réprimer toutes les activités de délinquance de droit commun servant à alimenter en toute connaissance de cause une activité ou un projet terroriste et dont la répression comporte une peine de confiscation au profit du fonds de secours des victimes d'actes terroristes.

Actuellement, dix enquêtes préliminaires sont en cours au parquet et trois informations judiciaires sont suivies à l'instruction à Paris sur des présomptions de financement d'activités terroristes.

Sont également actes de terrorisme par nature la provocation et l'apologie du terrorisme ainsi que la non-justification des ressources accordées à des personnes étant en relations habituelles avec une ou plusieurs autres se livrant à des actes de terrorisme.

3) Quant aux règles et aux principes généraux de la procédure, ils sont, par principe, applicables au domaine terroriste.

Ce n'est que lorsque la loi en a disposé autrement, et dans les limites qu'elle a fixées, que des normes spécifiques dérogent au droit processuel ordinaire.

Sont par conséquent applicables toutes les dispositions de droit commun relatives au contrôle permanent de l'autorité judiciaire sur l'enquête de police, notamment sur les mesures coercitives mises en œuvre par les services de police (par exemple, une perquisition).

Il convient en effet de souligner qu'en droit français il n'existe pas d'enquête policière qui ne soit pas judiciaire, ce qui signifie que dès lors qu'un service de police judiciaire (c'est-à-dire tous les services de police, à l'exception des services de renseignement) enquêtent et accomplissent des actes d'investigation, il le fait nécessairement sous le contrôle des magistrats du parquet ou d'un juge tel qu'un juge d'instruction.

C'est ainsi que, en garde à vue, le droit à l'assistance d'un avocat existe, comme dans le droit commun, même si le moment de cette assistance est différé pour garantir l'efficacité des investigations. Le magistrat de permanence à la section antiterroriste sera en revanche informé sans délai par la police du placement en garde à vue, de la même manière que dans le droit commun.

De même, les mesures les plus intrusives telles que les perquisitions, les mises sur écoute téléphonique et autres sont soumises à des conditions strictes et au contrôle de magistrats du siège, même si certaines d'entre elles sont plus souples que dans le domaine du droit commun.

En outre, en ce qui concerne la mesure la plus attentatoire aux libertés que constitue le placement en détention provisoire, si les durées de détention sont un peu plus longues dans le domaine terroriste, il est important de noter que les juges des libertés et de la détention compétents pour statuer sur les demandes de placement ou de renouvellement de détention provisoire sont les mêmes que pour n'importe quelle autre infraction. Il n'y a sur ce point aucune spécialisation de droit ou de fait de ces magistrats.

Le respect de la présomption d'innocence, le droit à un procès équitable et à un second degré de jugement s'appliquent pleinement au domaine terroriste.

Les garanties ainsi accordées aux auteurs d'infractions terroristes ne font cependant pas obstacle à l'efficacité de la lutte contre le terrorisme, dans la mesure où le système mis en place depuis 1986, et adapté par les législateurs successifs, prévoit certaines dérogations au droit commun, strictement limitées et encadrées, destinées à assurer une répression pertinente mais aussi à prévenir les attentats.

B. ... QUI COMPORTE TOUTEFOIS DES SPÉCIFICITÉS DESTINÉES À LUTTER EFFICACEMENT CONTRE LE RISQUE TERRORISTE.

1) Dans le droit pénal de fond, une infraction particulière, terroriste par nature, a été créée.

Dans le droit pénal de fond, une infraction particulière, terroriste par nature, a été créée, qui permet d'intervenir très tôt dans le processus de constitution des groupes terroristes et dans la formalisation d'un projet d'attentat ou d'une action terroriste quelconque. Il s'agit de l'infraction d'*association de malfaiteurs à visée terroriste.*

C'est là l'un des outils majeurs de la lutte contre le terrorisme en France.

Aux termes de l'article 421-2-1 du *Code pénal*, cette infraction est définie ainsi :

> « Constitue également un acte de terrorisme, le fait de participer à un groupement formé ou à une entente établie en vue de la préparation, caractérisée par un ou plusieurs faits matériels, d'un des actes de terrorisme mentionnés aux articles précédents. »

Ces articles sont ceux évoqués plus haut, contenant la liste des infractions de droit commun qui deviennent des actes de terrorisme dès lors qu'elles sont commises dans une intention terroriste particulière[2].

Cette incrimination délictuelle, complétée en 2004 par le crime de direction d'une organisation terroriste et en 2006 par le crime d'association de malfai-

---

2 4° La fabrication ou la détention de machines, engins meurtriers ou explosifs, définies à l'article 3 de la loi du 19 juin 1871 qui abroge le décret du 4 septembre 1870 sur la fabrication des armes de guerre ;
- la production, la vente, l'importation ou l'exportation de substances explosives, définies à l'article 6 de la loi n° 70-575 du 3 juillet 1970 portant réforme du régime des poudres et substances explosives ;
- l'acquisition, la détention, le transport ou le port illégitime de substances explosives ou d'engins fabriqués à l'aide desdites substances, définis à l'article 38 du décret-loi du 18 avril 1939 fixant le régime des matériels de guerre, armes et munitions ;
- la détention, le port et le transport d'armes et de munitions des première et quatrième catégories, définis aux articles 24, 28, 31 et 32 du décret-loi précité ;
- les infractions définies aux articles 1er et 4 de la loi n° 72-467 du 9 juin 1972 interdisant la mise au point, la fabrication, la détention, le stockage, l'acquisition et la cession d'armes biologiques ou à base de toxines.
- les infractions prévues par les articles 58 à 63 de la loi n° 98-467 du 17 juin 1998 relative à l'application de la Convention du 13 janvier 1993 sur l'interdiction de la mise au point, de la fabrication, du stockage et de l'emploi des armes chimiques et sur leur destruction.

teurs à visée terroriste dans le but précis de commettre un attentat susceptible de causer la mort ou de nature à provoquer des atteintes aux personnes, permet d'atteindre les organisations terroristes très en amont de leur passage à l'acte, c'est-à-dire dès les actes préparatoires de constitution d'une cellule terroriste et la collecte d'éléments logistiques ou financiers (faux papiers, armes, documentation, composants propres à fabriquer un explosif, location d'appartement et achat de téléphones portables, par exemple).

La jurisprudence n'exige pas en effet, pour qualifier l'infraction prévue et réprimée par l'article 421-2-1 du *Code pénal*, la démonstration d'un projet d'attentat ou d'une action terroriste déterminée, mais la preuve de l'existence de l'un des actes constitutifs des infractions mentionnées ci-dessus dès lors qu'elles s'inscrivent dans l'intention terroriste déjà évoquée, c'est-à-dire « intentionnellement en relation avec une entreprise individuelle ou collective ayant pour but de troubler gravement l'ordre public par l'intimidation ou la terreur ».

À cet égard, la jurisprudence de la Chambre criminelle de la Cour de cassation[3] relative aux éléments constitutifs, tant de l'association de malfaiteurs de droit commun prévue à l'article 450-1 du *Code pénal* qu'à celle relative aux dispositions de l'article 421-2-1 du *Code pénal*, considère que la loi n'exige pas que soit établi un projet de crime ou de délit précis[4].

Pour la Cour de cassation, le délit est constitué « dès lors que les circonstances de faits révèlent la volonté personnelle de chacun des auteurs d'apporter en connaissance de cause et à un titre quelconque son concours à une entreprise criminelle », étant précisé qu'il « suffit de faits concrétisant une participation personnelle effective sous une forme quelconque aux activités illicites du groupe, indépendamment de la préparation d'une action criminelle déterminée ».

Essayons de rendre notre propos plus concret en l'illustrant par *deux exemples* tirés de jugements rendus en matière de terrorisme islamiste.

Dans une première espèce jugée le 10 mai 2002, le tribunal correctionnel de Paris écrit, pour caractériser l'infraction d'association de malfaiteurs en vue de la préparation d'un acte de terrorisme :

> En tout état de cause, l'association de malfaiteurs à visées terroristes est punissable, et ses membres susceptibles d'être poursuivis de ce chef, dès que le groupement délictueux est identifié, même si les fonctions respectives de

---

3 La Cour de cassation est la Cour suprême de l'ordre judiciaire français, la Chambre criminelle étant la formation spécialisée de la Cour de cassation en matière de droit pénal et de procédure pénale.

4 Cour de cassation, Chambre criminelle, 1998-07-09, 97-84066; Cour de cassation, Chambre criminelle, 1998-07-09, 96-84724.

chacun de ses membres, inspirateurs ou exécutant, ne sont pas exactement déterminées.

Pour que la circonstance aggravante de relation de cette association avec une entreprise terroriste soit considérée comme établie, il suffit que le dessein soit formé pour atteindre l'objectif consistant à intimider une population, à troubler un état, à inspirer une peur collective.

Il n'est pas exigé que chaque membre ait été informé des activités précises envisagées par l'association: la résolution d'agir ensemble suffit, un acte préparatoire suffit, une adhésion volontaire et en connaissance de cause au groupement délictueux qui poursuit un but et est déterminé à passer à l'action suffit.

La preuve de cette résolution commune, pourra résulter des réunions, des échanges téléphoniques, de la teneur des conversations enregistrées ou de la nature des documents détenus ou échangés.

Le fait de demeurer volontairement au sein d'un groupement dont on connaît l'activité peut constituer un élément démontrant l'entente et manifestant l'adhésion au dessein poursuivi par ce groupe.

Quant au dessein lui-même, il n'est pas nécessaire qu'il soit circonscrit par un objet de commission d'un crime déterminé de façon précise. Il suffit qu'aient été recherchés par les membres du groupe, ensemble, les moyens de mettre en œuvre des activités criminelles ou certaines activités délictuelles.

En l'espèce, le tribunal précise :

La participation de O.C. « apparaît néanmoins établie par la conjonction d'éléments qui, à eux seuls, constitueraient déjà pour chacun d'eux, une forte probabilité d'implication, mais qui, par leur répétition, et par leur réunion, démontrent la réalité de sa participation positive à ce type d'entreprise ».

Ces éléments sont ensuite énumérés et détaillés par le tribunal. Il s'agit de :

- l'achat de matériel électronique en mai 1999 par le prévenu auprès d'une société.

  « Il s'agissait d'émetteurs récepteurs susceptibles d'être intégrés à des systèmes d'ouvertures de portes mais également utilisables pour agir en surface afin de commander des engins explosifs à distance par des mises à feu avec une portée maximale de 1 kilomètre en terrain dégagé et 100 à 300 mètres en milieu urbain. »

- des voyages du prévenu en Angleterre.

  Le tribunal relève qu'il a donné durant l'enquête et l'instruction, des versions contradictoires de ses déplacements à Londres durant l'année 2000 et conclut en soulignant que les lieux et les contacts établis par O. C. à Londres démontraient sa volonté de relation avec des personnes impliquées dans la mouvance islamiste radicale en particulier la mosquée de Baker Street.

- des documents saisis chez O. C. et apparaissant comme témoignant de préoccupations très ciblées. Il s'agit notamment de cassettes de leaders islamistes appartenant à des groupes activistes, cassettes traitant du djihad en Algérie, par exemple.

  Il s'agit aussi d'une carte publicitaire de l'hôtel pakistanais Al Baddar, connu comme lieu de passage des volontaires européens se rendant en stage d'entraînement militaire en Afghanistan.

- des appels émis et reçus par les trois téléphones portables trouvés en possession du prévenu.

  « Il n'a pu expliquer comment tous ces numéros, s'avéraient correspondre à des individus impliqués dans des réseaux terroristes, et permettaient de les joindre pour la plupart en Angleterre, mais aussi en Allemagne, en Algérie et au Pakistan, et, comment ils avaient pu se retrouver tous en sa possession, et, pour certains, avoir été appelés par lui entre le 18 et le 20 août 2000, époque qui correspondait précisément à son attente de la deuxième livraison de passeports ‹ thaïlandais ›. »

Le tribunal conclut ainsi :

> L'ensemble de ces éléments, les appels émis par O. C. et les numéros des extrémistes islamistes enregistrés ou détenus par lui, les documents particuliers saisis chez lui prônant, pour certains, l'action violente et émanant de deux terroristes notoires, ses voyages répétés en Angleterre correspondant à son abandon de sa vie professionnelle antérieure, ses écrits personnels évoquant le « martyr » enfin son achat en 1999 de matériel très particulier utilisable pour des mise à feu à distance auprès de la société. L'achat qu'il persiste à nier, ces éléments précisément par leur accumulation, ne laissent aucun doute quant à la participation de O. C. à une entente ou à une association de malfaiteurs à visées terroristes.

Le deuxième exemple est une affaire jugée le 6 mars 2003 relativement aux agissements du Groupe salafiste pour la prédication et le combat (GSPC), qui envisageait de poser des actions terroristes lors du déroulement du championnat Europe des Nations de football qui se déroulait en 2000 aux Pays-Bas et en Belgique. Le tribunal examine les agissements d'une personne, A. M., déjà condamné en décembre 1999 par le tribunal de Paris pour association de malfaiteurs en vue de la préparation d'un acte de terrorisme, qui est détenu à la maison d'arrêt de la Santé au moment des faits et dans la cellule duquel un téléphone portable en pièces détachées a été trouvé à la suite d'informations transmises par les services de renseignements hollandais aux services français de la DST, informations ayant entraîné l'ouverture d'une information judiciaire.

Le Tribunal écrit :

> Pour être constitué, le délit d'association de malfaiteur à visées terroristes impose que soient réunis les éléments suivants :
>
> - La participation à un groupement ou à une entente;
> - Le fait que ce groupement ou cette entente prépare un ou des actes de terrorisme, qu'il existe une résolution d'agir en commun;
> - L'existence d'un ou de plusieurs faits matériels caractérisant cette préparation d'acte de terrorisme.
>
> En revanche, il n'est pas nécessaire que l'acte de terrorisme envisagé soit déterminé et précis ni que chaque membre du groupement ou de l'entente ait été personnellement informé des actions envisagées. Il suffit que soit établie l'adhésion volontaire du prévenu au groupement dont il connaissait le dessein.

Après avoir analysé tous les contacts téléphoniques pris grâce au téléphone trouvé dans la cellule du prévenu, mais aussi ceux pris par les correspondants de A. M., le tribunal, répondant à un argument de la défense, précise:

> Il est exact qu'aucune écoute téléphonique judiciaire n'a été pratiquée dans cette procédure et qu'il ne peut donc être présenté de support matériel d'enregistrements qui n'ont pas été effectués après l'ouverture de l'information à Paris le 15 juin 2000.
>
> Il est également constant que les éléments transmis par les autorités hollandaises à la D.S.T. en juin 2000 ne seront pas communiqués et que, par voie de conséquence, les propos attribués à A. M. et à ses correspondants de Hollande dont B. A. A. entre mai et juin 2000 ne peuvent être matériellement constatés par des enregistrements qui ne seront jamais produits. Mais cette fâcheuse absence d'enregistrements ne dispense pas le tribunal de rechercher si d'autres éléments matériels et objectifs permettent ou ne permettent pas de corroborer la réalité de ces conversations et de leur contenu tels que précisés dans le rapport de la D.S.T.
>
> La production, dans cette procédure, de très nombreuses facturations détaillées déjà analysées qui objectivent la réalité des appels, leurs heures, leurs durées, leur articulation avec d'autres appels, l'identification des utilisateurs des lignes ainsi révélées comme en contact les uns avec les autres, la qualité

des utilisateurs et l'implication notable de certains d'entre eux dans des mouvements extrémistes à visées terroristes, l'exploitation des mémoires des téléphones portables de ces utilisateurs, la découverte chez certains d'entre eux de numéros de téléphone confirmant la réalité de leurs contact, tous ces éléments ne peuvent être écartés et constituent également des éléments de preuve dont, seule, l'analyse peut révéler ou non la réalité des contacts incriminés.

En outre, l'audition de certains correspondants de A. M., notamment B. A. A. a permis d'apporter des éléments utiles à la recherche de la vérité.

En l'espèce, l'analyse des mémoires des portables et surtout de toutes les facturations détaillées et leurs rapprochements ont permis de confirmer les éléments avancés par la D.S.T.

- Le 4 juin 2000 A. M. avait effectivement contacté B. A. A., à 20 h 19, durant 83 secondes;
- Le 6 juin 2000, B. A. A. avait effectivement contacté E. H.,;
- Le 9 juin 2000, A. M. avait contacté B. A. A.;
- Le 12 juin 2000, le nouveau numéro de A. M. (puce M.) est effectivement appelé par B. A. A..

Par ailleurs les utilisations de « Intercom-service » et des cabines téléphoniques alternées avec des contacts rapide, notamment les 3 et 4 juin 2000 entre D. S. et A. M., objectivent la constance et l'intensité croissante de leurs contacts et leur proximité chronologique avec les conversations « anonymes » par le canal des cabines téléphoniques et le recours aux sociétés de reroutage.

Ce recours aux société de reroutage téléphonique destiné à dissimuler l'identité du destinataire final de l'appel est illustré par l'existence de 10 numéros de ce type qui furent en contact avec les puces Mala et Menad entre le 2 et le 17 juin 2000.

De même, le changement de puces dans le portable de A. M. à quelques minutes d'intervalle est illustré par les appels passés depuis le portable de M. K. le 6 juin 2000, l'un vers la puce Mala à 19h54, l'autre vers la puce Menad à 20h09 et les appels passés le 4 juin 2000 depuis les puces Menad et Mala respectivement à 20h24 et 20h42 vers la ligne de D. S., suivis à 20h49 d'un appel de la puce Menad vers le portable de B. A. A. durant 83 secondes.

Plus loin, le Tribunal ajoute et conclut :

[...] les dates de ces rencontres, juillet 2000, et l'évolution quantitative de l'intensité et de la nature clandestine des appels passés par et vers les puces Mala et Menad entre le 3 juin 2000 et le 14 juin 2000 démontrent l'existence d'un rapport entre les deux événements qui s'accentue avec la proximité des matches.

Il n'est pas nécessaire que l'acte ou les actes de terrorisme envisagé(s) soient déterminés et précis pour que l'adhésion à l'association de malfaiteurs puisse être poursuivie.

A.M. connaissait bien les autres membres du groupement dont certains avaient été poursuivis antérieurement avec lui pour faits de même nature, et par conséquent leurs engagements dans des ententes à visées terroristes.

Or l'entente volontaire et persistante peut être caractérisée par la volonté manifeste de demeurer au sein d'une association dont on connaît, approuve et partage l'activité et le but.

Le fait qu'aucun attentat n'ait été finalement commis lors de la coupe euro 2000 peut être la conséquence de la vigilance des autorités, comme notamment le signalement effectué ici par la D.S.T.

Quant à l'existence de un ou plusieurs éléments matériels, elle résulte essentiellement de la réalité des contacts téléphoniques, de leur caractère clandestin, et des termes relatés dans le rapport de la D.S.T. (empruntés au monde du football et usuellement déjà utilisés dans un même contexte par les membres d'association de malfaiteurs à visés terroristes).

La permanence de vue, la solidarité, la résolution et le dessein commun entre A. M. et le G.S.P.C. qui ont persisté durant l'année 2000 est également confirmée par la publication d'un communiqué de H.H. au journal AL HAYAT publié le 17 juillet 2000 (et commenté par le journaliste de AL HAYAT) dans lequel H.H., sans nommer A.M. évoquait l'hostilité de la France contre l'islam et les musulmans et les humiliations des frères emprisonnés, et concluait par une menace aux autorités française qui était « responsable de ce qui découlera de ces jugements à l'encontre des frères emprisonnés ».

En effet, même si A.M. n'est pas nommé dans ce communiqué, le rédacteur de AL HAYAT a quant à lui considéré que ce communiqué le concernait et la date de ce communiqué (exceptionnel) coïncide avec l'arrestation de A.M. intervenue quelques semaines auparavant.

L'ensemble de ces éléments démontre :

- la réalité des contacts entretenus par A.M. et des personnages engagés dans les mouvements extrémistes comme les G.I.A. et le G.S.P.C.;
- le rôle central, dans ces liaisons téléphoniques, joué par A.M.;
- la volonté manifeste et très élaborée de préserver le secret et la clandestinité de ces contacts et d'empêcher l'identification et l'écoute des interlocuteurs de A.M.;
- la coïncidence entre l'intensification de ces contacts et l'approche de l'événement menacé, la coupe Euro 2000.

2) Sur le plan procédural, les particularités ou dérogations des dispositions antiterroristes concernent tant les mesures coercitives et les mesures attentatoires aux libertés que certaines techniques d'investigation spéciales.

Sans énumérer toutes ces mesures, citons tout de même les plus emblématiques.

En tout premier lieu, nous évoquerons la possibilité de « judiciariser » des renseignements, c'est-à-dire la possibilité de faire entrer régulièrement dans une procédure l'information recueillie par les services spécialisés.

Ces renseignements ainsi judiciarisés ne pourront conduire à eux seuls à la condamnation d'une personne, mais ils permettront de justifier l'ouverture d'une enquête préliminaire ou d'une information judiciaire qui, elle, réunira, s'il y a lieu, les éléments de preuve nécessaires à une condamnation.

En ce qui concerne la *garde à vue* qui a été évoquée tout à l'heure, sa durée est de quarante-huit heures en droit commun, comparativement à quatre-vingt-seize heures en matière terroriste et même à 144 heures depuis la loi du 23 janvier 2006, dans deux cas bien précis : le risque sérieux d'une action terroriste imminente en France ou à l'étranger ou les nécessités de la coopération internationale.

En outre, la personne gardée à vue ne peut s'entretenir pour la première fois avec un avocat qu'au bout de la soixante-douzième heure de garde à vue, comparativement à un entretien dès la première heure en droit commun. Elle peut ensuite revoir son avocat à la quatre-vingt-seizième puis à la cent vingtième heure. En revanche, elle a droit, comme en toutes matières, à être visitée par un médecin à chaque renouvellement.

En ce qui concerne la *durée de la détention provisoire*, elle est d'un maximum de deux ans en matière de délit terroriste, comparativement à un an pour les délits de droit commun. En matière criminelle, les durées maximales sont respectivement de trois ou quatre ans selon le quantum de la peine encourue, comparativement à deux ou trois ans en droit commun.

Il convient toutefois de préciser que ces dérogations ne sont pas propres au terrorisme, mais concernent aussi la lutte au trafic de stupéfiants. S'agissant de la durée de la détention provisoire, elles concernent aussi d'autres infractions comme celles commises en bande organisée.

C'est également le cas pour un certain nombre de techniques d'investigation qui, depuis la loi du 9 mars 2004, ont été rendues possibles pour une série d'infractions limitativement énumérées à l'article 706-73 du *Code de procédure*, dont le terrorisme fait partie. Il s'agit notamment de la possibilité d'effectuer des opérations d'infiltration, de sonoriser un lieu public ou privé et de rétribuer des informateurs.

Il s'agit aussi de la possibilité, pour le parquet, de procéder, en enquête préliminaire (c'est-à-dire avant toute saisie d'un juge d'instruction) et sur autorisation d'un juge, soit le juge des libertés et de la détention, à un certain nombre d'actes tels que des écoutes téléphoniques ou des perquisitions, qui peuvent même, à certaines conditions, être réalisées en dehors des heures légales (6 h–21 h).

Ces facultés sont très largement utilisées par la section antiterroriste du parquet de Paris qui, au 31 décembre 2006, avait 217 enquêtes préliminaires en cours, dont 42 relatives au terrorisme islamiste intégriste.

Mais c'est surtout le recours à *l'équipe commune d'enquête* qui constitue un instrument de coopération et donc de lutte contre le terrorisme, instrument particulièrement utile et efficace puisqu'il autorise l'échange instantané d'information entre autorités judiciaires d'enquête.

Cet instrument, qui figurait dans la convention cadre de l'Union européenne du 29 mai 2000 et qui a été transposé dans de nombreux États, permet de conduire des investigations avec des unités de police judiciaire composées d'officiers appartenant à deux ou plusieurs États.

Par ce moyen, l'information circule directement entre les autorités judiciaires des États, sans recours à la commission rogatoire, puisque les actes accomplis par l'équipe des enquêteurs des États prenant part à l'investigation, d'un côté ou de l'autre de la frontière, vont nourrir chacune la procédure nationale.

Cette procédure, que le parquet et la juridiction parisienne ont utilisée à plusieurs reprises, est particulièrement pertinente dans le champs du terrorisme, notamment lorsque des projets d'attentats sont en phase d'élaboration.

Le procureur chargé, sur le plan national, de la lutte antiterroriste en Espagne et nous-même avons signé, il y a dix jours, la constitution de la septième équipe commune d'enquête dans le champ du terrorisme, d'autres ayant été mises sur pied avec l'Espagne, la Belgique et l'Allemagne.

À ce premier outil de coopération internationale que constituent les équipes communes d'enquête s'ajoutent de nombreux autres, spécialement dans le domaine de la coopération européenne.

C'est le cas bien sûr du mandat d'arrêt européen, que nous avons déjà eu l'occasion d'évoquer en févier 2006 à Ottawa et que nous citons simplement pour mémoire, en disant qu'il permet la remise d'une personne, arrêtée par l'État requis, à l'État requérant dans un délai maximal de trois mois et, en cas d'urgence, en quarante-huit heures. Cette procédure concerne également les nationaux de l'État requis.

C'est le cas également d'Eurojust, institution composée de magistrats de tous les pays membres de l'Union européenne, qui constitue une plateforme d'échange d'information entre États partageant les mêmes valeurs. Eurojust intervient dans tous les domaines et pas seulement celui du terrorisme, mais son action est particulièrement précieuse dans ce champ-là.

Il arrive de plus en plus souvent que des pays tiers à l'Union européenne, comme la Suisse ou le Maroc, soient ponctuellement associés à des réunions d'échange organisées par Eurojust. Cette participation implique un minimum de confiance dans le système judiciaire de ces États tiers.

Pour terminer, nous voudrions évoquer certaines des dispositions de la dernière loi française qui traite de la lutte contre le terrorisme, celle du 23 janvier 2006, que nous avons déjà citée.

Outre les dispositions relatives à l'infraction d'association de malfaiteurs à visée terroriste et à la durée de la garde à vue dont il a déjà été question, cette loi en comporte d'autres qui ont pour objectif d'adapter les dispositifs de prévention et de répression du terrorisme à ses caractéristiques nouvelles, notamment à son caractère extrêmement mobile et à l'utilisation des nouvelles technologies.

Ces dispositifs, pour la plupart, n'ont pas pour objectif exclusif la lutte contre le terrorisme. Ils ont aussi pour but la lutte contre l'immigration clandestine, mais ces deux objectifs ont parfois des champs communs.

Ainsi, le recours à la *vidéosurveillance* des abords immédiats de bâtiments est désormais possible, après autorisation administrative, pour des personnes morales publiques comme privées, pour « prévenir des actes de terrorisme ».

Jusqu'ici, ce cas d'ouverture n'existait pas.

De même, afin de mieux prendre en compte l'existence des moyens de transport modernes, les *contrôles d'identité administratifs*, lesquels ne pouvaient depuis 1991 être effectués dans les trains internationaux au delà des vingt kilomètres suivant la frontière, peuvent désormais être réalisés jusqu'au premier arrêt au delà des vingt kilomètres, voire dans une zone de cinquante kilomètres au delà de cet arrêt.

Dans le domaine de la circulation routière, des *contrôles automatiques* des plaques d'immatriculation des véhicules avec photographie de leurs occupants peuvent être installés en tous points du territoire par les services de police, de gendarmerie ou de douanes dans le but de « prévenir et réprimer le terrorisme » (ainsi que d'autres infractions), le tout étant recensé dans des fichiers de traitement automatisés, recoupés avec le fichier des véhicules volés et le système d'information Schengen.

La loi autorise également certains agents des services de police ou de gendarmerie qui sont spécialement désignés à consulter un certain nombre de *fichiers administratifs* tels que celui des immatriculations, des permis de conduire, des cartes nationales d'identité et des passeports.

Le texte permet aussi aux mêmes services d'avoir accès aux renseignements contenus dans le *système de réservation des compagnies aériennes* (système APIS :

Advanced Passenger Information System), ainsi qu'à celles détenues par ces mêmes compagnies à l'occasion des départs (système PNR : Passengers Name Record). Seule l'information collectée à l'occasion des déplacements internationaux, hors Union européenne, est visée. Les transporteurs maritimes et ferroviaires le sont également. Cette information pourra être consultée par les seules personnes habilitées, soit dans le cadre de la lutte contre l'immigration clandestine, soit dans celui de la lutte contre le terrorisme.

Sans vouloir être exhaustif, citons encore l'obligation pour toutes les personnes qui offrent au public une connexion permettant une communication en ligne par l'intermédiaire d'un accès au réseau (cybercafés, opérateurs de « spots wifi ») de *conserver l'information sur les données techniques* de leurs clients (celles relatives aux données de connexion et à l'identification de la personne connectée, et non celles relatives au contenu de la connexion).

Sur réquisitions administratives des services de police autorisés (DST et DCRG, notamment) adressées à une personne autorisée qui est un haut fonctionnaire du ministère de l'Intérieur désigné par la Commission nationale de contrôle des interceptions de sécurité, ces données peuvent être consultées, en dehors de toute procédure judiciaire, dans le but de prévenir des actes de terrorisme, et uniquement dans ce cas.

Enfin, il faut aussi souligner la possibilité, pour le ministre des Finances, de *geler les avoirs financiers*, pendant six mois renouvelables, détenus par les personnes suspectées de terrorisme.

Si nous évoquons toutes ces procédures qui relèvent du droit administratif et très peu du domaine judiciaire, c'est d'une part parce que l'action judiciaire peut être facilitée, en amont, par le travail de prévention des services de renseignement, lequel n'est donc pas totalement dissociable du champ judiciaire. Mais c'est d'autre part parce que ces dispositions ont fait l'objet, au moment du vote de la loi, de nombreuses critiques, au motif justement que la part prise par l'administration ou les services de police agissant à titre préventif, c'est-à-dire dans le cadre d'une mission de nature administrative, devenait beaucoup trop grande au détriment de la part judiciaire. C'est le cas notamment des consultations de fichiers administratifs, auparavant réservées aux hypothèses de procédures judiciaires, et du gel des avoirs par le ministre des Finances. L'impératif de lutte contre le terrorisme ne justifiait pas, aux yeux des opposants à ce texte, autant de reculs des libertés publiques.

Ces critiques rejoignent celles qui ont tout récemment été formulées par l'association Human Rights Watch, dont la presse s'est fait l'écho et qui portent notamment sur la procédure d'expulsion française intervenant en dehors de toute procédure judiciaire, sur des critères de préservation de l'ordre public jugés trop « légers » (peu contraignants).

Contrairement à ce que laissent entendre ces critiques, ces procédures, même si elles ne sont pas soumises au juge judiciaire, gardien au terme de notre Constitution des libertés individuelles, sont toutefois soumises au contrôle d'un juge, le juge administratif, qui par la notion d'erreur manifeste d'appréciation peut invalider les procédures d'expulsion. Il n'y a donc pas absence de contrôle.

Tout est question de proportion et d'équilibre. Le Conseil constitutionnel, à l'exception d'un point mineur, n'a pas censuré les nouvelles dispositions que nous venons d'évoquer, jugeant les atteintes aux libertés justement proportionnées aux exigences de sauvegarde de l'ordre public, dans la mesure où toutes ces procédures sont entourées de garanties tenant soit à des délais de conservation limités des données collectées, soit aux possibilités de recours administratif, soit à une limitation stricte du nombre des personnes habilitées à procéder à ces mesures, à la nécessité d'obtenir des autorisations préalables etc.

Ce dispositif est d'autant plus pertinent qu'il nourrit les services de renseignements qui, nous l'avons vu plus haut, peuvent ensuite alimenter une procédure judiciaire sous forme d'un rapport de renseignements établi par un officier de police judiciaire à l'attention du procureur de la République.

En outre, il faut préciser que notre système de lutte contre le terrorisme est conçu comme un système principalement judiciaire qui, par exception et dans des domaines limités, peut relever de procédures administratives prévues pour traiter d'autres questions telles que l'immigration clandestine.

Plus le champ judiciaire, par nature plus protecteur des libertés, est large, c'est-à-dire permet d'appréhender efficacement en amont le phénomène terroriste, plus le champ administratif est corrélativement réduit.

C'est pourquoi il nous semble, mais peut-être nous démentirez-vous, qu'un équilibre acceptable a été atteint par notre dispositif d'ensemble.

Pour conclure, nous dirons que ces protestations sont saines en démocratie et permettent de garder à l'esprit que l'équilibre entre le respect des libertés individuelles et la nécessité d'assurer la sécurité de tous les citoyens contre le terrorisme est toujours fragile et nécessite de la part de tous une vigilance et une adaptation constantes.

Nous sommes certain que chacune des démocraties ici représentées par des orateurs ou des participants tente de trouver ce point d'équilibre et le fait, à sa manière, avec sa culture, son histoire, son expérience, aussi, du terrorisme.

Ces échanges que nous avons et que nous allons poursuivre jusqu'à demain nous aident à progresser parce qu'ils mettent en commun nos réflexions.

Mais il nous semble que le plus important en matière de lutte contre le terrorisme international est moins de parvenir à une unification ou à une homogénéisation de nos systèmes qu'à un renforcement très sensible de notre coopération à partir du socle de nos valeurs communes.

« Le droit est le souverain du monde », proclamait Mirabeau, et ce souverain n'est pas impuissant : en vingt ans, ce sont plus de 500 personnes qui ont été déférées devant les juridictions de jugement en France pour répondre d'accusations en matière de terrorisme islamiste intégriste.

Justice et efficacité ne sont donc pas la thèse et l'antithèse du même discours. En revanche, l'ouvrage doit être travaillé sans relâche et se nourrir de nos expériences réciproques par-delà nos différences essentielles.

CHAPTER 6

The Administration of Justice, the *Charter*, and Canada's National Security

STANLEY A. COHEN[1]
DEPARTMENT OF JUSTICE, CANADA

It did not require great prescience to predict that, once enacted, Canada's *Anti-terrorism Act* (*ATA*) would be subjected to the prolonged multifaceted challenges and sustained criticism that it has endured. This was, after all, legislation vitally affecting every Canadian—legislation involving the nation's very security. Of course, saying this takes nothing away from the important and substantial contributions to scholarly discourse in the field of national security law and policy that have appeared since 9/11. Concerned citizens are right to have questioned the propriety of the measures that their leaders contend are necessary for their protection. To be effective, national security measures necessarily actively engage and impact upon individual liberty and call into question what it means to be free in a democratic society. Wise nations will only enter this legislative bog infrequently and with great wariness.

National security concerns—certainly those of the modern variety that are disconcerting advanced democracies around the globe—are bedevilling. Ultimately, they confound our political leadership, public policymakers, and scholars alike. The intricate complexity of these issues forces one from the settled and sheltered realm of easy cases with their comfortable answers and convincing rationales into far more discomfiting precincts where doubt and uncertainty dog each twist and turn. In this area of law and public policy,

1 The views expressed herein are those of the author and do not necessarily reflect the position of the Department of Justice or its minister. A modified version of this article will also appear in a forthcoming issue of the *Supreme Court Law Review*.

irrational fears and justified terror collide and the darkening field policed by the rule of law becomes a pitched battleground. No one wishes to have to confront the kinds of appalling choices that this conflagration demands. National security imperatives hold a nation's feet to a searing fire. The dilemmas posed test a nation's resolve to adhere to the very standards of civility and due process that differentiate it from more barbarous cultures.

The challenges posed by terrorism for Canada and other global democracies are enormous; far more issues present than any single essay can address.

Can an open and democratic society take legal action in closed and secret proceedings against those who by stealth or false pretences have made their way into its midst and yet do not wish to leave? When the only viable methods of action are those that are secretive, selective, and incomplete, do the notions of governance under the rule of law, *audi alter am partum*, and fair procedure begin to fray and unravel? Can our justice system withstand the strain of such incongruity?

Must a nation, having uncovered a predatory antagonist within its territory extend shelter rather than resort to expulsion because it must not expose the individual to the prospect of torture in the state to which they must return? While determining the question of the individual's removal is it necessary or desirable to allow an international miscreant to be released into society? Is it possible to devise a form of conditional, restrained liberty for such individuals that does not itself degenerate into a form of interminable, suffocating, and ultimately unacceptable confinement?

Can a nation renounce terrorism in all its forms and yet receive and rely upon the product of torture practised by others? What constitutes state complicity in torture? Does it make a difference if the facts uncovered by torture are capable of independent verification or corroboration? Should there be a difference to a nation whether the information it receives is for purposes of intelligence rather than for use in legal proceedings within the state? Should evidence obtained by torture ever be admissible in legal proceedings? Can a rational line be drawn between lawful, albeit "coercive," interrogation and the spectacle of confessions extracted under unambiguous torture?

These are the kinds of weighty and largely unresolved issues that swirl around all modern nation-states as they struggle to come to grips with the conundrums for the administration of justice and the security of the nation that are thrown up by the realities of global terrorism.

Some tentative steps in the direction of systemic improvement have occurred recently in Canada as a result of the Supreme Court of Canada's decision in the case of *Charkaoui v. Canada (Minister of Employment and Immigration)*.[2]

2 [2007] 1 S.C.R. 350 [*Charkaoui*].

Charkaoui represented the first significant consideration by our highest Court in the post-9/11 era of the complexities and competing demands of secrecy, openness, and the evolving dynamics of national security law and practice.[3]

Charkaoui involved an attempt by the Supreme Court to fashion a procedural mechanism that would enhance the fairness of Canada's secretive security certificate procedure.[4] The Court's chosen method involved the introduction of a third party special advocate into the procedure in order to better represent the interest of affected parties.

In *Charkaoui* a unanimous Supreme Court declared the security certificate procedure of the *Immigration and Refugee Protection Act* (*IRPA*) unconstitutional and stated that the government may use confidential information in security certificate cases, only if it provides for a fairer hearing[5] involving more informed participation by the detainee and his or her counsel as required by section 7 of

3 I provide the ensuing discussion notwithstanding the fact that the version of *Immigration and Refugee Protection Act*, S.C. 2001, c. 27 [*IRPA*], that was considered by the Supreme Court in *Charkaoui* cannot be considered a new development in national security law and policy. Its procedures relative to security certificate proceedings antedate 9/11 and the enactment of the *Anti-terrorism Act*, C. 2001, c. 41 [*ATA*].

4 The security certificate procedure under *IRPA* is a process designed to determine the issue.

5 The Supreme Court concluded that the procedure under the *IRPA* for determining whether a certificate is reasonable and the associated detention review procedures infringe s. 7 of the *Charter*. The court found s. 7 was clearly engaged because the person named in a certificate faces detention pending the outcome of the proceedings and because the process may lead to the person's removal to a place where his or her life or freedom would be threatened. It concluded that *IRPA*'s impairment of the named person's right to life, liberty, and security did not accord with principles of fundamental justice. The procedure for determining whether a certificate is reasonable and the detention review procedure fail to assure the fair hearing that s. 7 requires before the state deprives a person of this right. This right to a fair hearing includes the right to a hearing before an independent and impartial magistrate who must decide on the facts and the law, the right to know the case put against one, and the right to answer that case. Although national security is a valid pressing and substantial objective, security concerns cannot be used at the s. 7 stage of the analysis to excuse procedures that do not conform to fundamental justice. The Court did not question the independence and impartiality of the judges of the Federal Court who hear these cases but it was concerned that the secrecy required by the scheme denies the person named in a certificate the opportunity to know the case put against him or her, and negatively impacted upon their ability to effectively challenge the government's case. This, in turn, undermines the judge's ability to come to a decision based on all the relevant facts and law.

Since judges of the Federal Court, when examining the reasonableness of the certificate, do not possess the kinds of sweeping powers that exist in an inquisitorial process, they may, despite their best efforts, and perhaps unknowingly, make the required decision based on only part of the relevant evidence. This deficiency can also affect the requirement that the decision be based on the law. With restricted and limited knowledge of the information put against him or her, the affected person has a hampered ability to raise legal objections relating to the evidence, or to develop legal arguments based on the

the *Canadian Charter of Rights and Freedoms*.[6] The infringements of section 7 found by the Court could not be saved under section 1 of the *Charter*[7] and thus

---

evidence. If s. 7 is to be satisfied, either the person must be given the necessary information, or a substantial substitute for that information must be found.

6 Part I of the *Constitution Act, 1982*, being Schedule B to the *Canada Act 1982* (U.K.), 1982, c. 11 [*Charter*]. On a separate issue involving detention, the Court in *Charkaoui*, above note 2, concluded that the extended periods of detention that may occur under the act did not violate ss. 7 or 12 of the *Charter*. The Court determined that although the detentions could be lengthy, there was a process for reviewing that detention and for obtaining release, and for reviewing and amending the conditions of release. A meaningful process of review would examine the reasons for detention, the length of detention, the cause of delays, and the availability of alternatives to detention. These factors must be taken into consideration in order for a review to be meaningful. *IRPA* provides a mechanism for such a review.

Another issue concerning fair procedure and fundamental justice involved detention review. The Supreme Court in *Charkaoui* found that detention pending deportation is constitutional as long as regular detention reviews are available that take into account the context and circumstances of the individual case. Prior to the *Charkaoui* decision, foreign nationals in contrast to permanent residents received a detention review 120 days after the certificate had been confirmed by the Court; permanent residents subject to a security certificate were and are provided a detention review within forty-eight hours of their being detained, and every six months thereafter. In *Charkaoui*, the Supreme Court ruled that the same rights provided to permanent residents ought to be accorded to foreign nationals.

7 The Court concluded that the certificate process could not be justified as a minimal impairment of the right to a judicial determination on the facts and the law and the right to know and meet the case. While the protection of national security and intelligence sources constitutes a pressing and substantial objective, and the non-disclosure of evidence at certificate hearings is rationally connected to this objective, the *IRPA* does not minimally impair the rights of persons named in certificates. Less intrusive alternatives developed in Canada and abroad, notably the use of special counsel to act on behalf of the named persons, illustrate that the government can do more to protect the individual while keeping critical information confidential than it has done in the *IRPA*: see paras. 66–73 and 85–87. The Court examined extensively a number of other less intrusive alternatives that demonstrate that rights could have been impaired minimally. The major alternatives that it canvassed were:

- the old SIRC process;
- s. 38 of the *Canada Evidence Act*;
- written undertakings not to disclose by counsel as was done in *R. v. Malik*; and
- the special advocate procedure utilized by the Arar Commission.

These mechanisms, the Court indicated, all illustrate that government can do more than was done in *IRPA* to protect the individual while keeping critical information confidential. The Court did not set out what mechanisms Parliament should adapt in order to create a constitutional process, rather it left it open: "Precisely what more should be done is a matter for Parliament to decide. But it is clear that more must be done to meet the requirements of a free and democratic society" (para. 87).

the Court declared that it was up to Parliament to rectify the deficiencies in the system within a fixed period of time.[8]

The decision in *Charkaoui*, with its insistence on procedural fairness in the form of a new kind of special advocate to represent the interest of affected persons in security certificate cases, did not spring forth fully formed; it did not emerge in a vacuum. The Court's views were shaped by a growing awareness of the difficulties posed by *in camera* and *ex parte* proceedings. This was not solely the result of legal proceedings shaped by (understandably) self-interested pleading in the context of single cases. There was a substantial backdrop of informed commentary and debate in parliamentary committees, academic journals, public forums, and the media.

Understood properly, the Court's decision in *Charkaoui* is a reflection of what is meant by "*Charter* dialogue," in its grandest and most positive sense.[9] At its most recent juncture his dialogue has resulted in the introduction of Bill C-3, *An Act to amend the Immigration and Refugee Protection Act (certificate and special advocate) and to make a consequential amendment to another Act.*

The Court had concluded in *Charkaoui* that the security certificate process under *IRPA* violated section 7 because it permits the use of secret material without providing for an independent agent/advocate at the judicial review stage to better protect the interest of the affected person where confidential

---

8 As noted, the Court concluded that the limit on the s. 7 right was not justified under s. 1. It is significant to note that the Court accepted that, although violations of s. 7 rights were difficult to justify under s. 1, it is not an impossible task, particularly in extraordinary circumstances where concerns are "grave and the challenges complex" (para. 66). The Court was satisfied that the protection of Canada's national security and intelligence sources undoubtedly constitutes a pressing and substantial objective. The security certificate process was rationally connected to this objective. The means chosen, however, did not minimally impair rights.

9 For the seminal discussion of the meaning of *Charter* dialogue see Peter W. Hogg & Allison A. Bushell, "The *Charter* Dialogue Between Courts and Legislatures (Or Perhaps the *Charter of Rights* Isn't Such a Bad Thing After All)" (1997) 35 Osgoode Hall L.J. 75; and see the authors' sequel, Peter W. Hogg, Allison A. Bushell Thornton, & Wade K. Wright, "*Charter* Dialogue Revisited: Or 'Much Ado About Metaphors'" (2007) 45 Osgoode Hall L.J. 1. The concept stirred much additional academic commentary and debate: see especially, the special edition of the Osgoode Hall Law Journal devoted to this topic—vol. 45, no. 1, Spring 2007, *Charter Dialogue: Ten Years Later*; and the important text by Kent Roach, *The Supreme Court on Trial: Judicial Activism or Democratic Dialogue* (Toronto: Irwin Law, 2001). The concept was initially embraced by the Supreme Court of Canada in *Vriend v. Alberta*, [1998] 1 S.C.R. 493, and *R. v. Mills*, [1999] 3 S.C.R. 668. However, the Court's stance was subsequently modified by its decision in *Sauvé v. Canada (Chief Electoral Officer)*, [2002] 3 S.C.R. 519 [*Sauvé*]. There, a divided Court nullified the inmate disenfranchisement provision of the *Canada Elections Act*. In *Sauvé* the Court's majority refused to let the concept of dialogue take it down the path of judicial deference.

information was being presented in an *in camera, ex parte* proceeding. It asserted that procedural fairness under section 7 requires a process that is fair having regard to the nature of the proceedings and the interests at stake. Security concerns can and do inform the analysis as to what is fair, but in order to conform to the principles of fundamental justice they cannot erode the essence of section 7: "The protection may not be as complete as in a case where national security constraints do not operate. But to satisfy section 7, meaningful and substantial protection there must be."[10]

While the Court concluded that the certificate process could not be justified as a minimal impairment of the right to a judicial determination on the facts and the law and the right to know and meet the case, it did not set out what mechanisms Parliament should adopt in order to create a constitutional process; rather, at paragraph 87, it left it open: "Precisely what more should be done is a matter for Parliament to decide. But it is clear that more must be done to meet the requirements of a free and democratic society."

As noted, the current response in this "dialogue" is a legislative one. It comes in the form of Bill C-3, *An Act to amend the Immigration and Refugee Protection Act (certificate and special advocate) and to make a consequential amendment to another Act.*[11] A fulsome description of what is attempted in this enactment is beyond the scope of this paper. For purposes of completeness of this discussion, what follows is merely a brief overview.

The central feature of this new legislation is naturally the inclusion of a special advocate to protect the interests of the person subject to a certificate. This Bill attempts to respond directly to the Supreme Court's ruling in *Charkaoui*, and to parliamentary recommendations. The Bill attempts to strengthen the

10 *Charkaoui*, above note 2 at para. 27. The Court did set out what constitutes a fair judicial process which is required when people are detained for significant periods of time. There must be: a right to a hearing, which in this case was satisfied; a hearing before an independent and impartial magistrate, which was satisfied in this case; and, the decision must be made by a magistrate on the facts and the law. Under the current process the evidence placed before the judge only comes from the government and thus the decision may not be based on all of the evidence available; the right to know the case against oneself; and, the right to answer that case. The Court opined that neither of these latter two principles is satisfied in the current security certificate process as the person does not know that case against them and cannot respond. The Court made it clear that the right to know the case to be met is not absolute and it confirmed that national security considerations can limit the extent of disclosure of information to the person. In some contexts, "If s. 7 is to be satisfied, either the person must be given the necessary information, or a substantial substitute for that information must be found. Neither is the case here" (para. 61). Acting alone, the judges' active efforts are not an effective substitute for informed participation.

11 Assented to 14 February 2008 [*IRPA amendment Act*].

certificate process while maintaining Canada's ability to safeguard confidential information, the theory being that in doing so, it would maintain Canada's ability to protect the safety and security of Canadians.

In *Charkaoui* the Supreme Court had insisted that the government could do more to protect the interests of the affected individual and suggested that the process could be rectified by the inclusion of a special advocate possessing sufficient attributes of independence and neutrality who could safeguard the individual's interests. In saying this, the Court was not blind to the difficulty in balancing the government's need to safeguard information against the individual's right to know the case against them.

Under the current process, it is the judge who determines relevance and weight of confidential information based on government submissions. It is the judge who challenges and probes the government's confidential information and makes a determination based on this information as well as on the submissions made in the open hearing. The new amendments modify this arrangement by empowering a special advocate to challenge and contest the government's claims to confidentiality.[12] The special advocate is assigned the role of contesting the minister's claim that the disclosure of the information would be injurious to national security or would endanger the safety of any person. The special advocate in closed proceedings is allowed to cross-examine witnesses and challenge the relevance, sufficiency, and weight of the information presented. The special advocate's role is defined so as to protect the interests of the permanent resident or foreign national in a proceeding when information or other evidence is heard in the absence of the public and of the permanent resident or foreign national and their counsel. The special advocate is *not* a party in these proceedings and the relationship between the special advocate and the permanent resident or foreign national is *not* that of solicitor and client.

---

12 *Ibid*. The role of the special advocate is defined in s. 85.1:

> **85.1** (1) A special advocate's role is to protect the interests of the permanent resident or foreign national in a proceeding under any of sections 78 and 82 to 82.2 when information or other evidence is heard in the absence of the public and of the permanent resident or foreign national and their counsel.
>
> (2) A special advocate may challenge
>
> (*a*) the Minister's claim that the disclosure of information or other evidence would be injurious to national security or endanger the safety of any person; and
>
> (*b*) the relevance, reliability and sufficiency of information or other evidence that is provided by the Minister and is not disclosed to the permanent resident or foreign national and their counsel, and the weight to be given to it.
>
> (3) For greater certainty, the special advocate is not a party to the proceeding and the relationship between the special advocate and the permanent resident or foreign national is not that of solicitor and client.

Under the new scheme, the special advocate as well as the affected person is provided with an unclassified summary of the confidential information to assist in preparation for the closed hearing. Prior to seeing confidential information the special advocate is expected to meet with the affected person in order to discuss his or her case. Once appointed, the special advocate is empowered to meet with the person as many times as necessary *prior* to seeing the confidential information.

After this initial phase, the special advocate receives the confidential information on which the case is based. Once provided with and having seen the confidential information, these advocates are then precluded from communicating with anyone about the proceedings and the material disclosed during the remainder of the proceeding, unless specifically authorized to do so by the judge. It will be up to the judge to determine, on a case by case basis, if, when and how further communication may or may not be achieved.

As the closed proceedings progress, the special advocate possesses the ability to contest the government's claim to confidentiality. Success in so doing can result in either the declassification of documents, or in the production of new judicial summaries of information that is expected to be of assistance to the detainee and their counsel, thereby allowing them to raise better and more effective arguments in the open hearings.

The theory underlying this new regime is that, as matters go forward, the special advocate will be better positioned to raise arguments that the information presented by the government is irrelevant or insufficient and for reasons such as these should be given little or no weight or consideration. The assumption is that this arrangement will be superior to the predecessor arrangement wherein the judge alone was left to test the evidence. If the legislation operates in this manner, this revised certificate process should better protect the interests of the affected person by potentially revealing and providing more useful information through a more robust method for testing the sufficiency of the state's case.

Will this be the last word on this matter? Almost certainly not. Critics will argue that the legislation still hobbles the defendant, inadequately protects the right to counsel and precludes an adequate exchange of information for the purposes of full answer and defence. The proposed law has already been roundly criticized[13] on the basis that it is based on the "heavily flawed" special advocate

13 A comprehensive study on and critique of the special advocate process has already appeared: Craig Forcese & Lorne Waldman, *Seeking Justice in an Unfair Process: Lessons from Canada, the United Kingdom and New Zealand on the Use of "Special Advocates" in National Security Proceedings*, study commissioned by the Canadian Centre for Intelligence and Security Studies, Carleton University, August 2007, online: University of

system used in national security deportation appeals in the United Kingdom.[14] Constitutional challenges to the new regime are virtually inevitable.

The substantial question of torture will remain. It is appropriate to question whether a nation can renounce terrorism in all its forms and yet receive and rely upon the product of torture practised by others and ask what constitutes state complicity in torture.[15] Other related questions remain to be addressed concerning whether it makes a difference if the facts uncovered by torture are capable of independent verification or corroboration or if there should be a difference to a nation whether the information it receives is for purposes of intelligence rather than for use in legal proceedings within the state and whether

---

Ottawa Faculty of Law (Common Law Section) http://aix1.uottawa.ca/~cforcese/other/sastudy.pdf at 41. See also their newspaper commentary: Craig Forcese & Lorne Waldman, "Canada Doesn't Need a Star Chamber" *National Post* (25 October 2007).

14 See the critique by Human Rights Watch: Joanne Mariner, "Canada: Parliament Should Amend Bill on Special Advocates: Letter to Members of Parliament" (18 November 2007), online: Human Rights Watch www.hrw.org/english/docs/2007/11/28/canada17435.htm.

15 In this regard the question arises of where, if anywhere, the line is to be drawn between intelligence gathering and the collection of evidence for use in criminal proceedings. The 2005 House of Lords decision in *A(FC) v. Secretary of State for the Home Department*, [2005] UKHL 71, addressed the issue of whether the SIAC (Special Immigration Appeals Commission) could receive evidence that had been or may have been procured by torture by officials of a foreign state (without the complicity of the British authorities). In this decision the Court was unanimous in holding that courts must refuse to admit such evidence. However, some of the judges went further and commented on "the executive's ability to take into account information procured by torture." For example, Lord Brown stated (at para. 161):

> Generally speaking it is accepted that the executive may make use of all information it acquires: both coerced statements and whatever fruits they are found to bear. Not merely, indeed, is the executive *entitled* to make use of this information; to my mind it is *bound* to do so. It has a prime responsibility to safeguard the security of the state and would be failing in its duty if it ignores whatever it may learn or fails to follow it up. Of course it must do nothing to promote torture. It must not enlist torturers to its aid (rendition being perhaps the most extreme example of this). But nor need it sever relations even with those states whose interrogation practices are of most concern. So far as the courts are concerned, however, the position is different. Generally speaking the court will shut its face against the admission in evidence of any coerced statement (that of a third party is, of course, in any event inadmissible as hearsay); it will, however, admit in evidence the fruit of the poisoned tree. The balance struck here ("a pragmatic compromise" as my noble and learned friend Lord Bingham of Cornhill describes it at para 16 of his opinion) appears plainly from section 76 of the Police and Criminal Evidence Act 1984. There is, moreover, this too to be said: whereas coerced statements may be intrinsically unreliable, the fruits they yield will have independent evidential value.

evidence obtained by torture will ever be admissible in legal proceedings.[16] This new legislation has an important provision regarding torture[17] that declares:

> 83 (1.1) For the purposes of paragraph (1)(*h*), reliable and appropriate evidence does not include information that is believed on reasonable grounds to have been obtained as a result of the use of torture within the meaning of section 269.1 of the *Criminal Code*, or cruel, inhuman or degrading treatment or punishment within the meaning of the *Convention Against Torture*.

However, the substantial questions posed above may still require judicial clarification and amplification.

---

16 Also unaddressed is the fundamental issue of what does and does not constitute torture. I have asked whether a rational line can be drawn between lawful, albeit "coercive" interrogation and the spectacle of confessions extracted under unambiguous torture. The complexities of this issue are explored by President Aharon Barak on behalf of the Supreme Court of Israel (sitting as the High Court of Justice) in H.C. 5100/94; H.C. 4054/95; H.C. 6536/95; H.C. 5188/96; H.C. 7563/97; H.C. 7628/97; and H.C. 1043/99, consolidated decision at *Judgement on the Interrogation Methods applied by the GSS*, online: Jewish Virtual Library www.jewishvirtuallibrary.org/jsource/Politics/GSStext.html. The *Convention against Torture and Other Cruel, Inhuman or Degrading Treatment or Punishment*, G.A. res. 39/46, annex, 39 U.N. GAOR Supp. (No. 51) at 197, U.N. Doc. A/39/51 (1984), 1465 U.N.T.S. 85 [*CAT*], Article I reads:

> 1. For the purposes of this Convention, the term "torture" means any act by which severe pain or suffering, whether physical or mental, is intentionally inflicted on a person for such purposes as obtaining from him or a third person information or a confession, punishing him for an act he or a third person has committed or is suspected of having committed, or intimidating or coercing him or a third person, or for any reason based on discrimination of any kind, when such pain or suffering is inflicted by or at the instigation of or with the consent or acquiescence of a public official or other person acting in an official capacity. It does not include pain or suffering arising only from, inherent in or incidental to lawful sanctions.

An additional question that may be litigated in future is whether there is a meaningful distinction between torture and other cruel, inhuman, or degrading treatment or punishment. In *Lai*, the FCA does not make such a distinction, concluding that neither form of activity should be regarded as producing credible or trustworthy evidence: see *Lai v. Canada (Minister of Citizenship and Immigration)*, 2005 FCA 125 at para. 95.

17 *IRPA amendment Act*, above note 11. The new legislation allows the judge to receive into evidence "anything that, in the judge's opinion, is reliable and appropriate" (s. 83(1)(*h*)). The committees had recommended adding the word "reliable" out of concern that information obtained by means of torture might otherwise be taken into evidence. The House of Commons Standing Committee on Public Safety and National Security further modified the provision to make it clear that reliable and appropriate evidence does not include information that is believed on reasonable grounds to have been obtained as a result of the use of torture within the meaning of s. 269.1 of the *Criminal Code*, or the use of cruel, inhuman, or degrading treatment or punishment within the meaning of the *CAT*, *ibid*. (*IRPA amendment Act* at s. 83(1.1)).

In more general terms, what will prevail will be the normal and sometimes dramatic ebb and flow of events: the tides of academic, journalistic, bureaucratic, judicial, and parliamentary discourse and debate, as well as the strategic machinations, challenges, and political developments that must occur in a vibrant democracy when large issues of state are at play.

Concerns about national security butt up uncomfortably against the margins of *Charter* protection. Terrorism challenges civilized values.

Our *Charter* proclaims the values that we cherish and affirms the rights and freedoms that we deem to be "fundamental." But it is also a document that speaks to life in the real world. Thus, the *Charter* not only guarantees rights. It also recognizes that rights are not unbounded; there must be limits on rights. The legal response to terrorism necessarily involves rights and their limitation.

It would be passing strange if our *Charter*'s ability under section 1 to preserve those limits that are demonstrably justifiable in a free and democratic society was, on the one hand, capable of sustaining legislative action enjoining hate speech[18] or imposing indefinite detention on dangerous offenders[19] while, on the other hand, being unsupportive of or unresponsive to measures that were thought necessary by Parliament to safeguard the nation's security.

The rough beast that slouches toward civilized nations exacts a cost from them in terms of the preparation for its arrival. To address terror, we must safeguard our communities, and, to a certain extent, this means that some limits on freedom must be contemplated. The dilemma here is that there is also another danger lurking—we must not, in the name of national security, sanction the subversion of our liberties.

That said, in the criminal law, and *a fortiori* in national security law, we must reserve some space for justifiable exceptions and worst case scenarios. This does not mean that we can or should create exceptions that swallow the rule but, speaking realistically, we must recognize the necessity to create reasonable areas of exception. True threats to national security and real terrorism *are* exceptional. They call for difficult policy choices, and demand real safeguards and truly effective oversight and accountability. These are crucial choices. Thus, they must be the best ones that we can devise.

Mr. Justice Binnie remarked in *Bagri* that "[t]he danger in the 'war on terrorism' lies not only in the actual damage the terrorists can do to us but what we can do to our own legal and political institutions by way of shock, anger, anticipation, opportunism or overreaction."[20]

---

18 *R. v. Keegstra*, [1996] 1 S.C.R. 458.

19 *R. v. Lyons*, [1987] 2 S.C.R. 309.

20 *R. v. Bagri*, [2004] 2 S.C.R. 248 at para. 116 [*Bagri*].

Avoiding these pitfalls—not to overreact; being measured in our responses to great provocations—are among the great challenges facing civilized nations today. It was Justice William O. Douglas who remarked that "upholding constitutional rights at times of national stress is 'one of the chief distinctions' that sets a liberal democracy apart from the 'totalitarian regimes.'"[21] Justifiably, in this era of global terror, we expect our independent judiciary to maintain fidelity to the rule of law while fostering these values. In cases like *Bagri*, *Juliet O'Neill*,[22] or the prosecution of Momin Khawaja,[23] our judges have wrestled with large, intractable dilemmas of law and public policy. The results of their labour hold enormous implications for the integrity of the Canadian polity.

The question of whether our new national security laws better protect us or whether they merely arm the state authorities with more powerful means to reduce our freedoms and damage our democracy has been a constant in the debate over liberty and security in this country since the twin towers fell.[24] Several critics, of course, have suggested that Canada's response to 9/11 has been marked by haste, unnecessary law-making, and overreaction. Such criticisms are a sign of a healthy and functioning democracy. There is need in perilous times to constantly assess the received or conventional wisdom.

Indeed, only six years after 9/11, it appears that we may already be entering a revisionist era in national security law reform. It is not necessarily that it is believed that the so-called war on terror has been won, but, rather, some believe

---

21 *Terminiello v. Chicago*, 337 U.S. 1 (1949).

22 *Canada (A.G.) v. O'Neill* (2005), 198 C.C.C. (3d) 143 (Ont. S.C.J.) [*O'Neill*].

23 See *R. v. Khawaja* (2006), 214 C.C.C. (3d) 399 (Ont. S.C.J.), leave to appeal to S.C.C. refused 5 April 2007 [*Khawaja*], involving the motive requirement in the *ATA*'s definition of "terrorist activity."

24 This chapter makes no claim to being a comprehensive survey of all *Charter* developments in national security law and policy. It does not, for example, deal with the issue of the judicial release of security certificate detainees. Neither does it address, other than in a peripheral manner, the controversial issue of the removal of individuals from Canada to places where they might face the possibility of torture. Canada is, of course, a signatory to the *CAT* (above note 16) and denies complicity in torture, but the issue remains a live one in the aftermath of the controversial exceptional circumstances exception recognized in the case of *Suresh v. Canada (Minister of Citizenship and Immigration)*, [2002] 1 S.C.R. 3. Torture and Canada's putative or alleged role and actions in relation to it also has very much been a contentious and live issue in two recent inquiries: the Commission of Inquiry into the Actions of Canadian Officials in Relation to Maher Arar (online: http://epe.lac-bac.gc.ca/100/206/301/pco-bcp/commissions/maher_arar/07-09-13/www.ararcommission.ca/eng/index.htm) [Arar Commission]; and the ongoing Internal Inquiry into the Actions of Canadian Officials in Relation to Abdullah Almalki, Ahmad Abou-Elmati, and Muayyed Nureddin (final report released 21 October 2008, available for purchase from Federal Publications Inc., online: Federal Publications www.fedpubs.com/subject/govern/iacobucci_inquiry.htm) [Iacobucci Inquiry].

that it might be politic at this juncture to declare victory.[25] James Fallows, a respected commentator, did exactly this in September 2006 in a detailed and nuanced *Atlantic Monthly* article entitled "Declaring Victory."

Other commentators make even more dramatic claims. Professor John Mueller, in his recent book *Overblown*, discusses the phenomenon of "terrorist anxiety" enveloping the American nation and the development of a "false sense of insecurity." It is the thesis of Mueller's book "that our reaction against terrorism has caused more harm than the threat warrants—not just to civil liberties, not just to the economy, but even to human lives. And our reaction has often helped the terrorists more than it has hurt them."[26]

Mueller, like other commentators, does not doubt that real terrorism is indeed a serious enemy of political democracy. Nations around the globe have been properly concerned about the dangers terrorism poses. Most have moved to provide greater latitude to intelligence gathering and other self-protective, preventive state action in the hope that doing so will assist the task of the early detection and prevent terrorist activity. However, the calibration of the balance between liberty and security is neither easy nor simple to strike. The danger lurks that the cure may prove more destructive than the malady.

Some might argue—emphatically, I do not—that in the war against terrorism we can afford to jettison due process. Not so long ago, Justice Ian Binnie provocatively cited the maxim "[l]et ten go free rather than one innocent be punished" to spur public discussion, and asked, as another jurist has: "why should any of them go free lest the state be destroyed by terrorist acts?" Binnie's basic query was "how does one get the balance right between our traditional criminal law position of ten to one, and the new equation suggested by Lord Brooke of, in effect, one to nothing?"

Canada has a refined and sophisticated system of checks and balances that encourages the kind of democratic discourse involving the public, the press, and our elected representatives that is the lifeblood of a truly free society. Ideally, after the enactment of rights-encroaching measures, the judiciary, through judicial review, will act as a check on governmental or police abuse or excess. No legislation can completely ward off overzealousness in application or abuses such as discriminatory or lawless behaviour. The essential soundness of Canada's institutional arrangements is the ultimate guarantor of its ability to preserve its fundamental values. Parliament, as is its duty, must subject coercive or intrusive measures to searching, meticulous, and skeptical scrutiny. It must realize

---

25 See Max Rodenbeck, "How Terrible Is It?" *New York Review of Books* (30 November 2006).

26 John E. Mueller, *Overblown: How Politicians and the Terrorism Industry Inflate National Security Threats, and Why We Believe Them* (New York: Free Press, 2006).

that increasing security may exact a cost in terms of lost liberty but that such tradeoffs need not be inevitable. Where tradeoffs are required, there should be a requirement that they be proportionate to the gravity of the situation being addressed and the objective pursued. This is not a zero-sum game.

In Canada, from the very earliest moments of our post-9/11 law-making exercise, substantial voices, including those of Kent Roach, Don Stuart, and David Paciocco, were raised suggesting that our then existing laws were more than sufficient to protect Canadians from those who would do them harm.[27] This critique has now infused the litigation challenges that have been mounted against many of the provisions of the *ATA*.

For example, *Khawaja*, a case that is well known primarily for its invalidation, at the Ontario Superior Court level, of the *ATA*'s controversial "motive requirement,"[28] actually fired a much broader legal broadside at the *ATA*. Momin Khawaja had asserted multiple claims of insufficiency primarily involving allegations of unconstitutional vagueness and overbreadth pertaining to an array of substantive provisions of the kind to which I have just referred.[29]

---

27 See, for example, Kent Roach, "The Dangers of a *Charter*-proof and Crime-based Response to Terrorism" in Ronald J. Daniels, Patrick Macklem & Kent Roach, eds., *The Security of Freedom: Essays on Canada's Anti-terrorism Bill* (Toronto: University of Toronto Press, 2001) at 131; Don Stuart, "The Dangers of Quick Fix Legislation in the Criminal Law: The Anti-terrorism Bill C-36 Should Be Withdrawn," *ibid.* at 205; David Paciocco, "Constitutional Casualties of September 11: Limiting the Legacy of the Anti-Terrorism Act" (2002) 16 Sup. Ct. L. Rev. (2d) 185.

28 For commentary on this case see Kent Roach, "Terrorism Offences and the *Charter*: A Comment on *R. v. Khawaja*" (2007) 11 Can. Crim. L. Rev. 271 [Roach]. Justice Rutherford of the Ontario Superior Court of Justice struck down the so-called motive requirement that is part of the *ATA*'s "terrorist activity" definition. Ironically, the deletion of proof of a "political, religious or ideological purpose" means that the defendant, Khawaja, has essentially sacrificed his rook. Commentators suggest that he has theoretically weakened his defences, making it easier for the Crown to establish his liability. (*Khawaja*, above note 23.)

29 As regards the instructing or leadership offence challenge, this terrorism provision is potentially at risk due to conflicting decisions that have been handed down concerning the invalidity of the analogous organized crime provision (s. 467.13 of the *Criminal Code*). Justice Holmes of the British Columbia Supreme Court found fatal *Charter* deficiencies in the organized crime provision in *R. v. Accused No. 1*, [2005] B.C.J. No. 2702 (S.C.). Here the court found the boundaries of the term "criminal organization" to be both impermissibly vague and overbroad with respect to the instructing offence in s. 467.13, one of whose elements is that the accused be a member of a criminal organization. Although the court invalidated s. 467.13, it did not invalidate either the definition of criminal organization or the other offences that employ this definition. Because the accused individual's membership in a criminal organization does not constitute an element of the latter offences, the court argued that the lack of precision in defining the boundaries of a criminal organization does not produce a constitutional issue. This allowed the court to claim that its ruling is consistent with *R. v. Lindsay* (2004), 70 O.R. (3d) 131 (S.C.J.) [*Lindsay*].

These claims, quite stunning in their own way, were all found to be unwarranted by Mr. Justice Rutherford.[30]

The core observation of the court's vagueness and overbreadth analysis — which the court found to be indistinguishable in this case — is that the provision's definition of a group "does not require a nexus between the characteristic of the group which causes it to be a group and the serious offence activity in which it engages." *Ibid.* at para. 82. As a result, "there may be individuals within the group who do not personally engage in or subscribe to the . . . main activities of the group." *Ibid.* at para. 69. It is therefore possible that the criminal organization definition would apply to "a group that exists because of a purpose or feature completely unrelated to crime [but] nonetheless ha[s] as one of its main activities serious crime." *Ibid.* at para. 81. The court also found that the "only form of limitation in relation to 'group' appears in the words 'however organized,' *ibid.* at para. 75, and that the other elements of the instructing offence fail to limit the definition of "criminal organization."

The court thus found that the criminal organization definition inadequately delineates a zone of risk with respect to an element of the instructing offence. *Ibid.* at para. 103. A typical instance of impermissible vagueness would occur in applying s. 467.13 to a "person [who] may be fully aware of the existence of a group that devotes itself to serious crime but unaware that he or she may be considered part of that group . . . especially . . . where that person engages in crime at the periphery of the serious crime to which the group is dedicated." *Ibid.* at para. 105. Finally, although the court held that s. 467.13 could be saved by reading the term "group" restrictively, it refused to do so because Parliament clearly intended a broad reading, and because doing so would unnecessarily affect ss. 467.11 and 467.12, as well as other procedural matters.

By contrast, the Saskatchewan Court of Queen's Bench in *R. v. Smith*, [2006] S.J. No. 184 (Q.B.), upheld convictions under ss. 467.12 and 467.13. The court, in explicit disagreement with *R. v. Accused No. 1* (above, this note), upheld the challenged provisions. The court held that it accepted the analysis of Fuerst J. in *Lindsay*, *ibid.*, and therefore upheld the challenged provisions. Unlike Holmes J., the Saskatchewan court saw no relevant distinction in analysis and evaluation of "whether or not a 'criminal organization' as defined in s. 467.1 exists, and whether the accused is 'one of the persons who constitute a criminal organization.'"

30 The legal challenge in *Khawaja* repeatedly cites unconstitutional vagueness and overbreadth in questioning the validity of the Act's definition of "terrorist activity" (s. 83.01), the material support provision of the Act (s. 83.03 providing property or services for terrorist purposes), the commission, participation and facilitation offences (ss. 83.18, 83.19 & 83.2) as well as the leadership or instructing offence. Justice Rutherford considered and dismissed the vagueness and overbreadth challenges under s. 7 of the *Charter* to both the definition of terrorist activities and to the various offences. He concluded that the reference to actions being committed "in whole or part" for political and religious objectives was not vague and that the intended harms defined in ss. 83.01(1)(b)(ii)A–E are "all clearly undesirable, adequately comprehensible and not at all surprising objectives of criminal sanctions": *Khawaja*, above note 23 at para. 18.

Justice Rutherford dismissed Khawaja's vagueness arguments concluding that the legislative provisions provided fair notice to the accused and sufficiently restrained law enforcement discretion. In his view the law provided an intelligible standard for legal debate and complete precision was not an achievable goal.

In the aftermath of the enactment of the *ATA*, some critics of Canada's legislation contended/lamented that it had been "*Charter*-proofed" and complained that the effort that went into making the legislation *Charter*-compliant was ill considered and misguided. The contention was that *Charter* standards should not be confused with policy wisdom; the *Charter* establishes essentially minimum standards for assessing whether legislative policies are fundamentally just and cohere with fundamental values.

This may be fair comment, but what is important to recognize, is *not* that an effort went into *Charter*-proofing the legislation (the expression "*Charter*-proofing" is colloquial political language), but rather that a concerted effort was made to ensure that Canada's response to 9/11 was a *proportionate* response.[31] This effort of constructing proportionate legislation (and I am speaking here of "proportionality" as that term is used in *Charter* jurisprudence) was, of course, a human exercise, one that, like all complex human endeavours, could not be expected to meet a standard of perfection. In any event, this complaint of *Charter* invincibility has begun to fade away as it has become apparent that even the best efforts to make this kind of national security legislation pass the litmus test of *Charter*-viability will not always succeed.[32] In point of

---

With regard to Khawaja's argument that the law was overbroad because, *inter alia*, the offences and the definition of terrorist activities they could be applied to lawyers or those providing necessary services, Rutherford opined that "a good lawyer can almost always create a hypothetical circumstance that might arguably be caught within the reach of a provision and that arguably should not be caught . . . ." Citing the Supreme Court's jurisprudence in cases such as *R. v. Heywood*, [1994] 3 S.C.R. 761 and *Ontario v. Canadian Pacific*, [1995] 2 S.C.R. 1031 he reasoned (at paras. 25–26) that such cases should be left to "case by case determination . . . with a view to avoiding absurd results."

31 Proportionality, as that term is used in the context of the *Charter*, was attempted in the *ATA*, above note 3, in several ways, including: strictly defined limits on new powers; special authorization and designation requirements that incorporate direct political accountability; and extensive provisions for judicial supervision and ministerial review. The *Act* as a whole was made subject to a full parliamentary review within three years of its enactment. Also, specific annual reporting requirements for the Attorney General of Canada, the Solicitor General, and their provincial counterparts were inserted into the legislation with regard to the use of certain of the new powers. The powers of investigative hearings and preventive arrest were made subject to a demonstrably effective sunset clause that mandated expiry after five years unless renewed. Finally, existing oversight mechanisms that were already part of the law, such as civilian oversight of law enforcement, continued to apply.

32 Kent Roach voiced initial criticism of the *ATA*, *ibid.*, on the basis that it had been "*Charter*-proofed" but has now modified his stance on this point, noting that the legislation has not proven to be bullet-proof: "the *Charter*-proofing of Bill C-36 has not turned out exactly as planned . . . parts of Bill C-36 have taken more of a *Charter* beating" and "Just because something is consistent with the *Charter* does not mean that it constitutes wise

fact, important aspects of the *ATA* have met with constitutional rebuke. Such reverses as have occurred have led some observers to contend, perhaps in their own exaggerated fashion, that the *ATA* is now "in shreds."[33]

The *ATA*, of course, was not a single discrete enactment; it was an "omnibus act" amending numerous existing statutes and creating one entirely new one. Its viability can be assessed in the light of certain restraining criteria involving safeguards, review, and oversight that were employed in its design.[34] It is not special pleading to suggest that the *ATA* has performed, not perfectly, but well when evaluated against these standards, especially when also considering the nature of Canada's initiative in comparison with the steps taken by other democratic countries in their fight against terrorism.

The two recent reports issued by the House and Senate committees charged with conducting a three-year review of the *ATA* are remarkable in terms of their overall endorsement (albeit subject to a vigorous two-person dissent in the House Report) of the basic soundness of the approach adopted in crafting Canada's response to the catastrophic events of 9/11.[35]

Both parliamentary reports supported the continuation of all of the existing legislation, including even the controversial and now expired investigative hearings procedure and the preventive arrest/recognizance with conditions provisions. This is not to suggest that these committees did not offer up a conscientious critique of many aspects of the *ATA*, for they did; or, that they did not put forward numerous thoughtful recommendations for amendment and reform of existing laws as they were charged with doing by the terms of the *ATA* itself, for they did.

---

or effective security policy": Kent Roach, "Is There a Tyranny of the *Charter* in Criminal Justice and Security Policy?" (2007) Policy Options 94 at 97.

33 Wesley Wark, "A Judge Editorializes on Terrorism: Parts of an Act Introduced after 9/11 Lie in Shreds after Ruling" *Ottawa Citizen* (26 October 2006).

34 These included: tailoring affecting the scope of the measures; sunset clauses affecting the most controversial provisions (compelled questioning and preventive arrest); mandatory parliamentary reviews; conformity with international laws; the nature of the safeguards provided; and, the availability of judicial review.

35 See House of Commons, Subcommittee on the Review of the *Anti-terrorism Act, Review of the Anti-terrorism Act Investigative Hearings and Recognizance with Conditions Program: Interim Report of the Standing Committee on Public Safety and National Security* (October 2006), online: House of Commons www2.parl.gc.ca/committeebusiness/ReportsResponses.aspx?Cmte=SECU&Language=E&Mode=1&Parl=39&Ses=1; and Senate, Special Senate Committee on the *Anti-terrorism Act, Fundamental Justice in Extraordinary Times: Main Report of the Special Senate Committee on the Anti-terrorism Act* (February 2007), online: Senate of Canada www.parl.gc.ca/39/1/parlbus/commbus/senate/com-e/anti-e/rep-e/rep02feb07-e.htm.

Having said this, let us evaluate this suggestion that the *ATA* is being dismembered. There have, of course, been cases that have seen elements of the *ATA* invalidated.

In cases such as *Vancouver Sun*,[36] *Bagri*,[37] *O'Neill*,[38] *Khawaja*,[39] and *Toronto Star Newspapers Ltd. and Kassim Mohamed v. The Queen*,[40] legislative elements of the Act have been struck down or significantly qualified. In a related development concerning the security certificate process under *IRPA* (a measure that was not part of the *ATA*), in the *Charkaoui* case,[41] the *Charter* was successfully invoked in order to call into question the secrecy of these proceedings and compel Parliament to consider the future participation in them of some form of special advocate.

A significant proportion of these adverse rulings have involved the notion of state secrecy and the tension that exists between this concept and the open court principle.

A. THE TENSION BETWEEN STATE SECRECY AND THE OPEN COURT PRINCIPLE

In the *Vancouver Sun* case, the Supreme Court held that the open court principle is a fundamental characteristic of judicial proceedings that should not be presumptively displaced in favour of an *in camera* process. Thus, subject to judicial discretion, there is now a presumption of openness regarding the holding of an investigative hearing. The Supreme Court drew a distinction between openness in the context of *applications* for a hearing as opposed to openness in the investigative hearing itself.[42]

---

36 *Vancouver Sun (Re)*, [2004] 2 S.C.R. 332.

37 *Bagri*, above note 20.

38 *O'Neill*, above note 22.

39 *Khawaja*, above note 23, involving the motive requirement in the *ATA*'s definition of "terrorist activity." For commentary on this case, see Roach, above note 28.

40 [2007] 4 F.C.R. 434 (Fed. Ct.).

41 *Charkaoui*, above note 2.

42 Other developments have also occurred pertaining to the significance of the open court principle as it relates to the administration of justice. See now, the Federal Court's recently released determinations concerning the *CSIS Act*'s provisions requiring that warrant applications must be heard in private. The court in 2006 decided that the *Act* must be interpreted in a fashion that is consistent with jurisprudence favouring open courts. While warrant applications must remain secret, questions of law and other collateral matters need not necessarily be shielded. The determination of disclosure will depend on whether the analysis and discussion "could have the effect of informing of methodologies utilized for obtaining information in a covert fashion": *Canadian Security Intelligence Service*

Another case involving the tension that exists between this state secrecy and the open court principle was that of *R. v. Ribic*.[43] This case called into question the constitutional adequacy of the new procedures devised in reforms to section 38 of the *Canada Evidence Act* (*CEA*) that were accomplished with the passage of the *ATA*.[44]

The amendments to section 38 of the *CEA* effected by the *ATA* established new pre-trial, trial, and appellate procedures. These amendments attempted to provide a means for contentious national security evidentiary issues to be resolved at an early stage in the process. The new rules sought to prevent any disclosure of sensitive information before the government is afforded an opportunity to address the issue.[45] While clearly improving the government's ability to protect sensitive, potentially injurious information from disclosure, these initiatives also endeavoured—admittedly, not without criticism or complaint—to promote the ability of affected parties to access and use information relating to international relations or national defence or national security, in a manner consistent with their fair trial rights.[46]

Act (Re), 2008 FC 300 at para. 55. See also *Canadian Security Intelligence Service Act (Re)*, 2008 FC 301 re: limitations on the extraterritorial application of the *CSIS Act*, Canadian Security Intelligence Services Act, R.S.C. 1985, c. C-25.

43 See *Ribic v. Canada (A.G.)*, 2003 FCA 246, 320 N.R. 275 [*Ribic*, cited to N.R.].

44 One of the difficult challenges that Canada faced in the post-9/11 security environment was how to provide adequate disclosure to those facing criminal charges or other proceedings initiated by the state (such as immigration removal) without jeopardizing intelligence sources or information received from the nation's allies. (In this regard, see the discussion below at footnotes 46 and 47.) The reforms in the *ATA* (above note 3) that sought to address these challenges included a substantial revision of s. 38 of the *CEA* (*Canada Evidence Act*, R.S.C. 1985, c. C-5). The primary focus of the reform exercise was on how to deal with information that is potentially injurious to international relations, national defence, or national security in proceedings where that information is expected to be adduced before a court, person, or body having jurisdiction to compel the production of information.

The reforms addressed, *inter alia*, the judicial balancing of interests that must occur when the disclosure of information in proceedings would encroach on a specified public interest (such as injury to international relations, national defence, or security). This balancing process contemplates empowering the court to protect the fair trial rights of the accused by the making of necessary remedial orders, and, where no other remedy will suffice, this can even include the granting of a stay of proceedings.

45 For an example of how the procedures established under the *CEA* (*ibid.*) revisions have been applied in the context of a public inquiry see the rulings that have been made respecting national security confidentiality in the proceedings of the Arar Commission, above note 24, dated 29 July 2004, 23 November 2004, and 20 December 2004, online: http://epe.lac-bac.gc.ca/100/206/301/pco-bcp/commissions/maher_arar/07-09-13/www.ararcommission.ca/eng/11g.htm.

46 In considering whether to order the disclosure of information that would be injurious to international relations, national defence or national security, the Federal Court, when

In the *Ribic* case, for example, the Federal Court of Appeal conducted a lengthy examination of the new procedures.[47] The Court of Appeal dismissed Ribic's *Charter* challenge to the new procedures. It held that no unconstitutional breach of the accused's rights to make full answer and defence or to his fair trial *Charter* rights had been occasioned. The accused's application for leave to appeal this decision to the Supreme Court of Canada was refused.

Ribic, however, should not be read as a definitive indication that the section 38 *CEA* procedures are pristine or beyond improvement.

More recently a related ruling on section 38 was handed down by the Chief Justice of the Federal Court in *Toronto Star Newspapers Ltd. and Kassim Mohamed v. The Queen*, involving a constitutional challenge brought by the *Toronto Star* to those portions of the section 38 *CEA* scheme that impose restrictions on proceedings and court records to protect sensitive information from disclosure. The *Toronto Star* successfully argued that there was no valid reason why it could not gain access to the "private" as opposed to the *ex parte* portion of court record. None of the documents in private sessions are intended to contain secret information. Lutfy C.J. held that the relevant provisions of

---

considering a matter, must balance the interest in disclosure against the public interest in non-disclosure. The court under the amended procedure has the ability to choose from a variety of options regarding the disclosure of the information, including the use of summaries and agreed statements of facts.

47 The factual background to the case is as follows: Ribic, the accused, was a Canadian citizen who joined Serb forces in Bosnia and was involved in a hostage-taking incident that led to his prosecution under the *Criminal Code*. In his trial before a judge and jury in the Ontario Superior Court of Justice, the defence sought to call two witnesses who were members of the Canadian Armed Forces deployed in Bosnia as part of the United Nations Protective Force in 1995. Those two witnesses gave Notice to the Attorney General of Canada, pursuant to s. 38 of the *CEA*, above note 44, that the evidence they could give might include sensitive information. The Attorney General did not authorize disclosure of the information, so the accused applied to the Federal Court.

In 2003, the Federal Court judge prohibited the two witnesses from testifying at the criminal trial. However, the Federal Court appointed counsel for the Attorney General, independent from the prosecution, to conduct extensive interviews with the two witnesses *in camera*, on the basis of questions provided by counsel for the accused, but in the absence of the accused or his counsel. The Federal Court judge then made an order authorizing disclosure of the transcripts of the interviews of the two witnesses, edited to remove sensitive information. The judge also held that the edited transcripts could be introduced in evidence at the criminal trial as if the two witnesses had testified under oath and in lieu of their *viva voce* testimony.

In upholding this decision, the Federal Court of Appeal found that there was no breach of the accused's rights to make full answer and defence or to a fair trial under the *Charter*, above note 6. As noted above, the accused's application for leave to appeal to the Supreme Court of Canada was refused. *Ribic*, above note 43.

the *CEA* violate the principle of judicial openness protected under section 2(*b*) of the *Charter* and could not be justified as a reasonable limit under section 1 of the *Charter*. He held that the impugned provisions went beyond what is minimally required to safeguard secret information and therefore trench unduly on the open court principle.

In a subsequent development, in another challenge brought by Momin Khawaja,[48] the Chief Justice of the Federal Court had occasion to consider the validity of that portion of the section 38 procedure involving *ex parte* hearings. In proceedings under section 38 of the *Canada Evidence Act*, the Attorney General of Canada has the right to make representations to a judge of the Federal Court in the absence of the party seeking the disclosure of secret information. Chief Justice Lutfy considered whether in a case where the party seeking access to the secret information is an accused facing serious criminal charges, the right of the Attorney General of Canada to make these *ex parte* representations offends the principles of fundamental justice, the right to a fair and public hearing and the open court principle enshrined in the *Charter*. He concluded ultimately that the procedure with its built-in safeguards did not occasion constitutional offence. This decision was ultimately confirmed on appeal to the Federal Court of Appeal.[49]

In dismissing Mr. Khawaja's challenge, Lutfy C.J. held that even where the party seeking access to the secret information is an accused facing serious criminal charges, the right of the Attorney General of Canada to make *ex parte* representations does not offend the principles of fundamental justice, the right to a fair hearing and the open court principle enshrined in the *Charter*. The Chief Justice stated that the right to know the case to be met cannot be absolute. He observed that Canadian statutes often provide for *ex parte* or *in camera* hearings, in which judges must decide important issues after hearing from only one side and noted that there is no principle of fundamental justice that the Crown and the defence must enjoy precisely the same privileges and procedures. This does not mean that fairness must be sacrificed at the altar of efficiency. Rather, where the national security context makes it impossible to adhere to the principles of fundamental justice in their usual form, adequate substitutes must be found.

In analysing Mr. Khawaja's situation in contextual terms, the Chief Justice found that section 38 provides a number of substantial substitutes for the information that ensure a fair process, including that: the party seeking disclosure may request the opportunity to make representations in the absence of any other

48 See *Khawaja v. Canada*, 2007 FC 463.

49 *Khawaja v. Canada*, 2007 FCA 388 [*Khawaja* 2007].

party; the judge has the discretion to appoint a security-cleared *amicus curiae*; a judge may provide a substitute for the redacted information by authorizing disclosure under conditions most likely to limit injury to national security; parties may appeal to the Federal Court of Appeal and to the Supreme Court of Canada; and, the judge in the criminal proceeding has a range of options to protect the right to a fair trial, including staying the criminal charges.

As noted, this aspect of Khawaja's case was recently considered on appeal by the Federal Court of Appeal where the decision of the Chief Justice was affirmed, albeit by a divided bench taking divergent routes in order to reach the same ultimate conclusion.[50] In *Khawaja v. Canada*,[51] the Federal Court of Appeal confirmed the conclusions but not necessarily all of the reasoning of Lutfy C.J. concerning the constitutionality of the *CEA*'s *in camera*, *ex parte* procedure under section 38.11.[52]

Section 38 of the *Canada Evidence Act* has also been the locus of an expected litigation controversy growing out of the Supreme Court of Canada's decision in *Charkaoui*.[53] The issue involves the legality or propriety of the Federal Court's appointing an *amicus* or special advocate to assist the Court in its *ex parte* and *in camera* deliberations.[54] The roots of this issue extend much further back in the Federal Court's jurisprudence than simply the SCC decision in *Charkaoui* would indicate. In any event the controversy has now crystallized in an extradition decision rendered by Mosley J. of the Federal Court in January of 2008.

In *Khadr v. Canada (Attorney General)*, Mosley J. ordered the appointment of a security-cleared *amicus curiae* for the purpose of attending the *ex parte* proceedings, viewing the secret information and testing the government's position.[55] His reasons cite a variety of compelling contextual circum-

---

50 See *ibid*. The concurring opinions all came to the same conclusion, but were less clear than the Chief Justice in the court below had been concerning the applicability of s. 7 to the issues posed.

51 *Ibid.*

52 The FCA determined that s. 7 was not infringed by this legal regime, as "... the features of subsection 38.11(2) do not fall below the level of fairness required in section 7 of the *Charter*.": *ibid*. at para. 31.

53 *Charkaoui*, above note 2, discussed below.

54 In this regard note that the Attorney General of Canada has submitted in both the *Khawaja* and *Khadr* (*Khadr v. Canada (A.G.)*, 2008 FC 46 [*Khadr*]) cases that the Federal Court judge presiding over s. 38 proceedings has the discretion to appoint an *amicus* where is it necessary to assist the court.

55 *Khadr*, *ibid*. The case concerns extradition proceedings involving the United States. The s. 38 issue has arisen by reason of the national security information at issue in the proceedings.

stances[56] justifying his resort to this inherent jurisdiction to appoint an *amicus curiae* to assist the court in its deliberations.[57] The procedures governing the role and conduct of this *amicus* adopted by Mosley J. in making this order were very much in line with those that are endorsed by the government and were recently considered by Parliament in enacting Bill C-3, *An Act to amend the Immigration and Refugee Protection Act (certificate and special advocate) and to make a consequential amendment to another Act*.[58]

Disclosure of evidence is a recurring dilemma in cases involving fair trial rights, secrecy, and national security concerns. These concerns were the focus of another recent Federal Court of Appeal decision involving the prosecution of Momin Khawaja. Once again, the matter arose in the context of the *CEA* proceedings relative to the Khawaja anti-terrorism prosecution. In *Canada v. Khawaja*[59] the Court of Appeal largely endorsed the approach of Mosley J. to the issue of disclosure noting that the judge "was cognizant of his obligation to authorize disclosure in the form that is most likely to limit injury to 'international relations or national defence or national security' resulting from disclosure."[60] (Mosley J., in balancing the national security interest in secrecy against the

---

56 These factors included importantly the fact that evidence relied upon by the United States in support of the extradition may have been obtained through torture and illegal detention.

57 Justice Mosley declined the opportunity to rest his order on the alternative basis that the appointment of an *amicus* can be a constitutional requisite under s. 7. This question remains unsettled in light of the FCA decision in *Khawaja* 2007, above note 49.

58 Discussed below.

59 2007 FCA 342.

60 *Ibid.* at para 10. Writing for the unanimous court, Létourneau J.A. stated:

> [10] It is obvious to me that the judge has concluded that public interest in disclosure of the information outweighs the public interest in non-disclosure. However, the judge was cognizant of his obligation to authorize disclosure in the form that is most likely to limit injury to "international relations or national defence or national security" resulting from disclosure: see subsection 38.06(2).
>
> [11] Balancing the public interest in a fair trial, which includes the right to full answer and defence, and the public interest in protecting injurious information from disclosure, he was of the view that disclosure of a descriptive summary of the documents containing the information at issue would protect the right to a fair trial and result in minimal impairment of international relations, national defence or national security. That summary is contained in Schedule A.
>
> . . .
>
> [13] The judge was dealing with a substantial number of documents. He showed a very good knowledge of the working of section 38 of the Act and of the jurisprudence applicable to it. It is reasonable to infer that the errors are not errors of law resulting from a misconception of the law, but errors of fact reviewable on the palpable and overriding error standard.

public interest in disclosure, had ordered the release of some previously undisclosed secret material held by the Crown in the case.)

Secrecy and openness—the recurring and important themes of the post-*ATA*/post-9/11 era—were also considered from a somewhat different perspective in the *O'Neill* case. Juliet O'Neill, an *Ottawa Citizen* journalist, took the RCMP to court to quash the sealing orders pertaining to an abusive search of her premises for evidence of the identity of a source who allegedly leaked Arar-related classified documents to her. She recently succeeded in both her abuse claim and her challenge to section 4 of the *Security of Information Act* (the controversial "leakage" provision that was the Act's sole holdover from the *Official Secrets Act*) based on claims of unconstitutional vagueness and overbreadth. The case involved the sealing of information away from the public eye and illustrates the chilling effect of national security claims and secret classifications on the open court principle.

B. CONCLUSION

This review of the notions of secrecy and openness as they affect the administration of justice and of the evolving dynamics of national security law and practice buttresses the claim that national security law and policy cannot and should not be regarded as static or frozen. It must develop and be shaped by *Charter* standards and by the signal importance that our *Charter* jurisprudence places on events and circumstance (in essence, context). In addition, an obvious impetus to change or reform is provided by the evolving jurisprudence. The example furnished by the continuing controversy surrounding the future role and status of special advocates in so-called secret proceedings (and crystallized in the decision in *Charkaoui*,[61] discussed above) is illustrative of the point that I am seeking to make here.[62]

The cases that I have discussed in this article all reveal a judicial reluctance to accept the balance struck in our national security laws between openness and secrecy. At first blush, demands for secrecy in the general administra-

The Court of Appeal reviewed the alleged errors in disclosure at an *ex parte* hearing. It was satisfied that they should be corrected. Therefore, a minimally modified Schedule A was substituted for the one prepared by the judge.

61 *Charkaoui*, above note 2.

62 As previously noted, I provide this discussion notwithstanding the fact that *IRPA*, above note 3, should not be considered a new development in national security law and policy. Its procedures relative to security certificate proceedings antedate 9/11 and the enactment of the *ATA*, above note 3.

tion of justice seem an affront to the kind of openness to which flourishing democracies aspire. But no society can function with complete transparency. The security of the state can be compromised by the disclosure of sensitive information essential to its well-being. For this reason, virtually all nations have laws proscribing such activities as espionage and leakage; and they also adopt a variety of practices in an effort to safeguard state secrets and other confidential information. Although the importance of openness and secrecy cannot be gainsaid, an inevitable tension between them exists in all democratic societies.

People too often read the cases discussed herein for what they have struck down or qualified. Too little attention is paid to what the courts have sustained and to our independent judiciary's reasons for why they have upheld so much of what has been enacted. Those who suggest that, because of these decisions, the *ATA* is now "in shreds" would do well to return to the cases and examine them through this lens.

My point in this review is that Canada's experience with national security law reform should *not* be viewed with alarm. The centrepiece of Canada's endeavours, the *Anti-terrorism Act*, thus far has largely withstood concerted attack from many quarters because it is, in relative terms, moderate and restrained; our judiciary has resisted the bellicose contention that the mere invocation of the term "national security" should result in judicial absolution, as well as the histrionics of those who believe that any departures from a traditional justice template represents a grave and mortal danger.

That said, we should always reserve space for doubt and skepticism where claims are made for the arrogation of new exceptional powers to the state. We should not become locked into a paradigm of reflexive thinking. Also, there is nothing static or ineradicable in the current reality. It is appropriate to ask whether the threat of terrorism is receding and to adjust our laws as appropriate.

The major question facing us today is *not* whether terrorism constitutes an existential threat to our free societies. In an age of nuclear and biochemical warfare, it is always theoretically possible to view it as such. The real question is whether it is such a threat *now* and into the foreseeable future.

It is not possible for life to be shorn of all danger. Free societies, by virtue of the very freedom and openness that they cherish, are vulnerable to the predations of those who would do them harm. Coping with political extremism and global terrorism and the dangers and the risks that they pose is the unfortunate reality that we are obliged to confront in the twenty-first century. Perhaps a "new normal" now exists but it is not necessarily a permanent one. The threat of global terrorism, although serious, should not and cannot be allowed to become a paranoid and paralyzing fixation at a time when the world must confront the equally or even more daunting challenges of poverty, disease, and environmental degradation.[63]

In this, as in every area of complex public policy, not every idea is a good idea. As I have said, the danger lurks that the cure may prove more destructive than the malady. Unfortunately, and hence the need for constant vigilance, the calibration of the balance between liberty and security is neither easy nor simple to strike.

---

63 Here I am paraphrasing sentiments expressed by James Fallows in "Declaring Victory" *The Atlantic Monthly* (September 2006).

CHAPTER 7

Common Law and Statutory Provisions Relating to National Security

THE HONOURABLE SIR ANDREW COLLINS
JUDGE, ADMINISTRATIVE DIVISION, HIGH COURT OF JUSTICE, ENGLAND AND WALES, UNITED KINGDOM

Since the advent of parliamentary government in England and Wales, the common law—or perhaps I should say the judges—has not sought to intervene when national security has been said to be the justification for particular actions by the executive. That at least used to be the approach, but recently there have been indications that national security will not always provide a complete answer for the executive. These indications have largely resulted from the *Human Rights Act* which established as part of our domestic law the rights embodied in the *European Convention on Human Rights* and which have nothing to do with the common law.

The common law has been applied to ensure that persons affected by executive action are treated fairly and, if necessary, statutory provisions are construed so as to provide for such fairness. But when national security was raised, the courts have said that they would and could not intervene. Thus in *R. v. Secretary of State for the Home Department Ex parte Hosenball*[1] we find Lord Denning, M.R. saying:

> Our history shows that, when the state itself is endangered, our cherished freedoms may have to take second place. Even natural justice itself may suffer a set-back.

Lord Denning went on to assert that, while in "some parts of the world" national security had on occasions been used as an excuse for all sorts of

1 [1977] 1 W.L.R. 766 (E.W.C.A.(Civ. Div.)).

infringements of civil liberty, that had not occurred in England. I am afraid I am not as confident as he seems to have been that that has been or is likely to continue to be the case if the courts apply a "hands off" approach.

The case that has been most often cited to indicate the correct approach of a court is *The Zamora*.[2] That was an appeal to the Judicial Committee of the Privy Council from a decision of a Prize Court which concerned the seizure and condemnation as prize of a neutral ship with a cargo of copper. Requisition by a belligerent power could only be exercised lawfully if it could be established that the cargo or vessel was urgently required for use in connection with the defence of the realm, the prosecution of the war or other matters involving national security. In considering that limitation on the exercise of the power, Lord Parker of Waddington said this:

> The judge ought as a rule to treat the statement on oath of the proper officer of the Crown to the effect that the vessel or goods are urgently required for [such] use . . . as conclusive of the fact. . . . Those who are responsible for the national security must be the sole judges of what the national security requires. It would be obviously undesirable that such matters should be made the subject of evidence in a court of law or otherwise discussed in public.

It is worth noting that Lord Parker did not say that the statement must always be treated as conclusive and on the facts of the case the Judicial Committee decided that the requisition was not justified since the evidence did not go so far as to show that the copper was urgently required. It is also worth remembering that this was a decision in time of war when the safety of the realm was in serious danger.

Apart from its invocation in making decisions directly affecting individuals by restricting their freedoms in some fashion, national security has been invoked to prevent the production of evidentiary material which is relevant in civil or criminal proceedings. In 1942, in *Duncan v. Cammell Laird*,[3] the House of Lords decided that if a government department objected to production of material, that objection should be upheld since the Crown could be trusted to give discovery in the interests of fairness and justice. That trust was misplaced and the decision was not followed in Scotland or other common law jurisdictions. The superiority of the law of Scotland, Canada, Australia, New Zealand, and the United States of America was recognized in a case in 1964. The rule has gone and the present position, following the decision of the House

2 [1916] A.C. 77 (P.C.).

3 [1942] A.C. 629 (H.L.).

of Lords in *Conway v. Rimmer*,[4] is that refusal of disclosure can only be upheld if the Crown can establish that it is in the public interest, which includes national security, to maintain the secrecy of such material.

In criminal cases, the principle that an accused must know what is being alleged against him and must have made available to the court any material which might help him to show that he is innocent has created real problems. The obvious one is where information has come from an informant and to disclose that would put the informant's life at risk. The problem is particularly acute in dealing with alleged terrorists. Some of the material that can be used to show involvement in terrorist activities will result from covert surveillance or informants. To disclose this to the defendant may well risk the life of an informant or disclose matters that will put the ability to gather information and so protect citizens from the risk of terrorism in jeopardy. It would clearly be contrary to the interests of national security to disclose it.

Since in England and Wales there are statutory bars to the use of evidence obtained by intercepting telephone calls, it has proved difficult to prosecute some alleged terrorists. This has led to alternative means of trying to deal with them. Under the *Prevention of Terrorism Act 2005*, control orders which contain obligations such as curfews, access to homes by police with powers to search, residence within particular areas and other such restrictions can be imposed if the Home Secretary has reasonable grounds for suspecting that the individual in question is or has been involved in terrorism-related activity. The court must decide on the material put before it once the order has been made whether it should continue in being.

In 1997, a tribunal known as the Special Immigration Appeals Commission (SIAC) was created by statute. This was to deal with appeals by individuals who were to be removed from the United Kingdom on national security grounds. Since it was recognized that much of the material relied on might not be disclosable to the appellant, the Act provided for the appointment of what are known as special advocates to represent the interests of the appellant and to consider and test on his behalf evidence that could not be given openly because to disclose it to the appellant would be contrary to the public interest.

It was thought, following a decision of the European Court of Human Rights in *Chanal v. United Kingdom*[5] that the special advocate system derived from Canada. In so believing, the court was misled, although I understand something which might have been thought to have some relevance existed at a level below the courts. The system has been applied to control orders and can

4 [1968] A.C. 910 (H.L.).

5 (1996) 23 E.H.R.R. 413.

be used in criminal cases. It has also been approved in connection with hearings before the Parole Board when information that the prisoner should not receive may be used to object to his application for parole.

The system obviously leaves the individual against whom an order is made at a disadvantage. It is the experience of those who deal with these cases, both in SIAC and in relation to control orders, that the public interest will prevent the individual concerned knowing much of the material relied on against him. The state must disclose all that it can in open material and the individual will make such defence as he can. At that stage, the special advocate can receive instructions from him or those representing him and discuss his case with him. The closed material will then be served on the special advocate who thereafter cannot communicate with the individual or his representatives without the leave of the court. He can, however, receive information from the individual but it must be unsolicited. There is then a procedure whereby the special advocate requests that there be further disclosure and, if there is a refusal, a judge must decide. The principle that must be applied is that, while nothing must be disclosed contrary to the public interest, which in context will usually be because national security will be damaged but may be because an informant or other agent may be put at risk, there must be as much disclosure as possible.

The system cannot produce perfect fairness and equality of arms. It also has the disadvantage that it takes time to carry out the process. If there is further disclosure, the individual may be able to put forward additional grounds for defending himself. There is also an obligation on the state to look through all material available to it to see whether there is anything that may be exculpatory. It can do this the more satisfactorily when it sees more of the grounds of defence and these may become clearer following additional disclosure. We have found that it can take months before a hearing can take place which is, to say the least, unfortunate when a control order, which lasts for twelve months but can be renewed, continues in force in the meantime.

While recognizing the shortcomings, I believe the system is the best that can be devised to balance the need to protect individuals from being subjected to restrictions on or deprivation of their liberty and the need to protect citizens from the risk of terrorism.

Since I delivered my address at the International Conference on the Administration of Justice and National Security in Democracies, the House of Lords has delivered judgments that consider whether, in the context of control orders, the special advocate system can provide the necessary fairness for individuals. The majority decision was that it usually would, but there might be cases (albeit it seems they are likely to be exceptional) where the right to a fair hearing could not be achieved because the individual did not know and so could not deal with crucial matters alleged against him. I am afraid that I do not think that the decision was at all helpful nor did it give those who had to deal with these cases much assistance in deciding whether there would without disclosure—which might be impossible to achieve because it would clearly be contrary to the public interest to make it—be an absence of fairness. If no fair hearing could be achieved, the decision meant that the order would have to be quashed even if it were apparent to the court that the result would be a serious risk to the safety of the state. The House of Lords did not look at the closed material or the closed judgment. That in my view was most unfortunate since, if they had, they would have seen how the system worked in practice.

There has been a further decision of the House of Lords in *Secretary of State v. A.F.*[6] This has seriously limited the effectiveness of the special advocate procedure by making clear, following a decision of the European Court of Human Rights in *A. v. U.K.*, that a person subjected to a control order must be given sufficient information of the allegations against him to enable him to give effective instructions to meet them. Only thus will a fair hearing that complies with Article 6 of the *European Convention on Human Rights* be afforded him. Article 6 does not apply to immigration decisions and so the special advocate procedure may still apply, without the need for disclosure to the extent required by *A.F.*'s case to SIAC proceedings. We are in the process of seeing how the system can work in dealing with alleged terrorists who cannot be prosecuted because evidence cannot be produced in public because of national security or risks to the life of informants.

I believe that there is no reason to reject the use of special advocates. They are still needed to deal with closed material disclosure of which is not required to enable a proper defence to be raised by the controlled person. How their use will develop remains to be seen.

---

6 [2009] 3 W.L.R. 74 (H.L.).

PART THREE

CONDUCTING AND REPORTING NATIONAL SECURITY PROCEEDINGS

CHAPTER 8

Terrorism Trials

THE HONOURABLE IAN BRUCE JOSEPHSON
JUDGE, SUPREME COURT OF BRITISH COLUMBIA, CANADA

A terrorism trial can place considerable demands on the ability of the judicial system to cope. That was the case with the Air India trial. To the credit of the Court Services branch of the Attorney General's ministry, it responded by providing the considerable funding necessary to construct a courtroom unequalled in North America to meet these demands.

The security concerns were significant. Our head sheriff, Ross McKenna, through a committee system involving all the players in this trial, began planning long before the trial. They also acquired courtroom technology that brought huge efficiencies to the trial itself. Taking advantage of technological developments was another matter however. There is great inertia in the judicial system. We are slow to change, and that's not always a negative thing. When we began the trial, I had some senior defence counsel telling me, almost with a sense of pride, that they didn't know how to turn on a computer, let alone use one. Some senior Crown counsel, even though they had their own technician available to utilize the technology, at first steadfastly refused to do so. So, without for a moment being critical, this was far from an instant love affair between counsel and technology in evidence presentation.

The technology can be intimidating for the judge as well, at least initially. I am no techie. I tend to clutch to court traditions like a security blanket. But let me encourage you to make the effort. There's lots of assistance for you out there—costs are coming down, and the results can be remarkable.

Turning to the courtroom itself, the designers turned a sow's ear of an office space into a silk purse of a courtroom. This had been office space on the ground floor of the courthouse in Vancouver. They ended up with a remarkably functional courtroom. Counsel usually examined witnesses and made submissions from the evidence presentation station. However, there were microphones in the ceiling that could pick up their remarks from the counsel table.

There were well-hidden video cameras that focused automatically on whoever was speaking. All counsel could connect in the courtroom to the Internet and email. The monitor depicting exhibits was very low profile. For the jury, there was one monitor for every two jurors. When one of the three accused pled guilty, the remaining abandoned the jury trial and re-elected to be tried by judge alone.

The video and sound feed from the courtroom went to the public area behind the security glass through three large monitors facing them at the back of the courtroom. That included the exhibits, so the public had as good a view as did the judge and counsel of the exhibits as the evidence unfolded, including objects, documents, photographs, and videos. They could also see the touch-screen marks and highlighting placed on the exhibits by counsel and the witness.

This same video and audio feed went to the press gallery room in a separate building, with strict conditions as to its use. This minimized the traffic of media people entering and exiting the courtroom in their quest for the juicy bits. The feed also went to an overflow courtroom and to an office in my own chambers. Finally, it went to counsels' offices in the courthouse adjacent to the courtroom itself so that some could work while keeping an eye on proceedings. When an issue came up, those in the back could rescue counsel in the courtroom with a quick message via computer.

In addition to monitoring sound and video, and fixing computer glitches, a court technician beside the witness box kept a minute-by-minute running account of what was happening and when. His record contained links to the audio as heard in the courtroom. The adjacent clerk, Mary Lewish, did an incredible job of managing the exhibits. Her record contained links to the exhibits.

The evidence presentation station could handle everything from CDs to DVDs to VHS, as well as documents and small objects. A scanner, on which could be placed both documents and objects, produced a sharp image on the monitor, which could then be handled like other digital exhibits. Counsel or the witness could then identity any portion of the image.

We were facing some fourteen hundred exhibits with tens of thousands of pages of paper, diagrams, and photographs. The Crown provided these intended exhibits on CDs prior to trial. They were uploaded into our system after ensuring their accuracy by comparing them to the original hard copy documents.

They were then pre-marked with exhibit numbers, to be formalized in the trial itself.

Using the evidence presentation station, counsel or the technician could call up an exhibit with a mouse click. The image appeared on everyone's screen. Using various colour codes, either counsel or the witness could mark the image using their finger or a plastic stylus. For example, an expert identified a portion of the aircraft in the area of the blast, with diagrams identifying portions of the aircraft found after the crash and where they would have originated on the aircraft. Each piece was designated a Target number. We spent many hours looking at diagrams such as this, usually marked by an expert witness in attempting to explain his opinion. When the witness was finished with a particular exhibit, a hard copy was printed then and there and marked as an exhibit. That was slightly cumbersome. But now there is inexpensive software enabling a copy of the marked-up screen to be entered as a digital exhibit immediately and printed later when convenient.

Evidence of photographs, documents, objects, and videos was presented in this fashion. Later, whether in direct or cross, exhibits could be called up in seconds with a mouse click, as I could also do when working on the judgment.

One of the objects put on the scanner and imaged onto our monitors was a mock-up of the bomb that detonated and killed two baggage handlers in Narita, Japan. All, including those in the public gallery, could view the exhibit, including magnifications of some portions, and the markings of the expert witness on the image. Portions of any image could be quickly and easily highlighted or magnified.

I mentioned the reluctance of some counsel to utilize this technology. As the trial progressed, however, most counsel came to see the advantages and efficiencies offered by the technology. While perhaps not exactly embracing it, they came to take advantage of it.

Let me give you one example. Judges will have experienced this many times. The Crown counsel I mentioned who left the technology sitting there unused had a witness hold up a photograph from a large binder and had him point to a particular location where something of some significance had occurred. The witness held up the binder in the air with the photograph towards us and pointed vaguely to something. Everyone, including me, strained to get some idea of the location being identified. Crown counsel then repeated the usual mantra: "For the record, the witness is pointing in the lower lefthand corner of the photograph near and to the left of what appears to be something or other and just above what appears to be a thingamabob." If counsel had put the image up on the monitor, the witness could have quickly marked the location on the monitor and all would have been instantly and permanently clear.

By mid-trial, both Crown and defence counsel came to realize that it was unwise not to take advantage of this technology, and they did so with relative ease. At trial's end, some even offered their submissions on CDs, with links to exhibits or transcripts for ease of reference as one moved through the submission.

Speaking of documents and to offer you one example, I was informed that the Crown counsel dealing with considerable banking records of one person was of the opinion that what took one day would have taken four days with binders and hard copies.

I was surprised and disappointed by the failure of the bomb-location experts to use better technological methods of conveying their very complex theories regarding the location of the bomb and the manner of the break-up of the aircraft, two strongly interrelated issues. They were two of the world's leading experts and they disagreed vehemently about just about everything. If the defence expert's evidence raised a reasonable doubt about the location of the bomb by a matter of four to five feet, the Crown's theory was lost. A simple CAD computer program would have allowed them to present a visual depiction of the manner of the aircraft's break-up. Instead, I was given descriptions like: "target 204 folded outwards, upwards and aft from the aircraft." When I asked what that meant, I witnessed this expert flapping his arms in some incomprehensible manner endeavouring to convey how this one target folded away from the aircraft. It appeared that he was attempting to get airborne himself. It was extremely difficult evidence to follow for that and almost every other target being described.

Down sides to the technology? What exhibits you watch and how long you watch them in the courtroom is in the control of others, unless you intervene of course. There is certain comfort in having a hard copy binder before you. You can flip and compare or linger on exhibits of interest. Despite this disadvantage, when the day is done, you have complete access to those exhibits as quickly and easily as you please. While trials are more efficiently run and result in great savings in one pocket, the other pocket must first pay for the technology and, for greatest efficiency, have a technician there to assist in running it. So there is a direct upfront cost with fuzzier soft returns that cannot easily be calculated.

Let me give you a very small demonstration of a few other capabilities we had.

A daily record was kept by clerk Mary Lewish. It was quick and easy if you needed to refresh your memory. An audio record of the proceedings was also kept. The technician kept a running account of the witness and the subject matter.

I'm told that, generally speaking, the cost of this technology is dropping and there is hope that it will be more readily available in future. I'm just waiting for technology that has a button reading "Write Judgment." I'll hit that and go off and play with Judicom.

Understandably, the practice for evidence presentation is slow to change. Many, including myself, are simply more comfortable with the traditional approach and worry about the unknown. But we must be open to reasonable change. As Chief Justice McLachlin recently pointed out, litigation is becoming increasingly costly and out of reach of ordinary people. For that reason, judges as a group have been constantly striving for many years to develop practices and procedures that bring efficiencies to reduce that cost. Technology has an important role, I would suggest, in achieving that goal.

However, technology is far from being the "end all, be all." The Chief Justice had the wisdom and foresight to authorize me to hire two younger but experienced counsel to act as counsel to the court. Frankly, I don't think I could have managed without them. Keep this in mind if you are assigned to a large complex trial. Their work allowed me to do the things a trial judge is paid to do—make considered decisions promptly. I was able to respond to the at times flurry of applications without interrupting the flow of the trial too often. They relieved me of the drudgery of summarizing the day's evidence and assigning it to the major issues identified in the Summation software for later recall. They relieved me also of the drudgery of summarizing the facts and positions of the parties in the many rulings. They were invaluable in another way. Colleagues are very generous with their time in discussing difficult issues, but their own plates are often very full. It was a great luxury for me to have two very bright counsel, my counsel, in the courtroom who heard both the evidence and the submissions. We had some great debates. It brought back some fun to the law and greatly reduced the burden on me.

There is one other important factor in managing a long complex trial. You remember the old saying that the key to a long life is to choose your parents well? The key to a well-managed trial is to choose your counsel well. Of course you can't do that and it's entirely a matter of good or bad fortune. Once the third accused, Mr. Reyat, fell away with a guilty plea, I was left with senior experienced counsel who worked endless hours out of court with senior Crown finding solutions to mountains of disclosure issues and the like. Their efforts saved endless weeks of courtroom drudgery on very difficult and sensitive issues. As well, they ironed out mountains of admissions to speed the trial. I had had suspicions that counsel for Mr. Reyat was going to stick with a jury, drag out the trial as long as possible (three years rang in the air), and dare the Crown to try and keep a jury together for that length of time.

I've been asked what the impact had been on me as the trial judge. The enormity of the alleged crime is always on your mind and the burden of being the trial judge can be burdensome. You are faced with teams of counsel for each accused, dealing with various aspects of the case. My chambers were built adjacent to the courtroom on the ground floor. They put in one-way bullet-proof glass, so thankfully, I could at least look out onto the world. Yes, there were times that the workload felt overwhelming. But, with the help of my two counsel, and with regular trips to the judge's coffee room to enjoy the support, encouragement, and wit of my colleagues, the moments of near panic would pass.

How essential judicial independence is to our judicial system was never made more clear to me. The pressures were significant, but I was free to do exactly what my judicial conscience led me to do. The Honourable John Major is now free to go where I couldn't. We are indeed fortunate that such a distinguished legal mind agreed to accept that heavy responsibility.

CHAPTER 9

Media Reporting on National Security Judicial Proceedings

THE RIGHT HONOURABLE LORD HUTTON[1]
CHAIR, INVESTIGATION INTO THE CIRCUMSTANCES SURROUNDING THE DEATH OF DR. DAVID KELLY, UNITED KINGDOM

There are a number of separate issues that can be considered when discussing media reporting on national security judicial proceedings, and I hope that it will provide a framework for this discussion to refer very briefly to some of them in the context of English law.

One issue relates to the problem that arises when a defendant is charged with a terrorist offence and the prosecution, as part of its case, wishes to rely on evidence based on intelligence, which in the interests of national security it would be harmful to reveal. In the case of *R. v. H and others,*[2] Lord Bingham said:

> The problem of reconciling an individual defendant's right to a fair trial with such secrecy as is necessary in a democratic society in the interests of national security or the prevention or the investigation of crime is inevitably difficult to resolve in a liberal society governed by the rule of law.

The European Court of Human Rights in Strasbourg has accepted that in a democracy some operations must be conducted secretly if they are to be

1 Introductory remarks by Lord Hutton prior to a round table discussion on this subject at the International Conference on the Administration of Justice and National Security in Democracies, Ottawa, 12 June 2007, by a panel of journalists constituted by: Stewart Bell, *National Post*; Yves Boisvert, *La Presse*; Jean Chichizola, *Le Figaro*; and, Charlie Savage, *Boston Globe*

2 [2004] 2 A.C. 134 at 151C (H.L.).

conducted effectively and in *Klass v. Federal Republic of Germany*,[3] the Court said:

> Democratic societies nowadays find themselves threatened by highly sophisticated forms of espionage and by terrorism, with the result that the State must be able, in order effectively to counter such threats, to undertake the secret surveillance of subversive elements operating within its jurisdiction.

One way of protecting highly sensitive intelligence information is for the trial court to appoint a security-cleared special counsel to represent the defendant and to protect his interests insofar as he can, without that counsel communicating to the defendant the nature of the intelligence that the prosecution wishes to use to support its case.

It is interesting to note that in *Chahal v. UK*,[4] the European Court referred with approval to the procedure followed at that time in Canada in immigration cases and said, at paragraph 131:

> The Court recognises that the use of confidential material may be unavoidable where national security is at stake. This does not mean, however, that the national authorities can be free from effective control by the domestic courts whenever they choose to assert that national security and terrorism are involved. The Court attaches significance to the fact that, as the intervenors pointed out in connection with Article 13, in Canada a more effective form of judicial control has been developed in cases of this type. This example illustrates that there are techniques which can be employed which both accommodate legitimate security concerns about the nature and sources of intelligence information and yet accord the individual a substantial measure of procedural justice.

And in paragraph 144 the Court stated:

> Under the Canadian Immigration Act 1976, a Federal Court judge holds an *in camera* hearing of all the evidence, at which the applicant is provided with a statement summarising, as far as possible, the case against him or her and has the right to be represented and to call evidence. The confidentiality of security material is maintained by requiring such evidence to be examined in the absence of both the applicant and his or her representative. However, in these circumstances, their place is taken by a security-cleared counsel instructed by the court, who cross-examines the witnesses and generally assists the court to

---

3 [1978] 2 E.H.R.R. 214 at para. 48.

4 [1997] E.H.R.R. 413.

test the strength of the State's case. A summary of the evidence obtained by this procedure, with necessary deletions, is given to the applicant.

In England, as Lord Bingham emphasized in *R. v. H and others* the overriding requirement is that the defendant should have a fair trial, and in some cases the judge may decide that disclosure of intelligence information to the defendant is essential in the interests of a fair trial. If the judge so rules this may lead to the prosecution deciding that the case be discontinued rather than that it proceed with the consequence that the intelligence will be revealed to the defendant.

Another issue that arises is how do courts strike a proper balance between the right of a government to keep secret the workings of its intelligence agencies that must to a very considerable extent operate in secret if they are to work effectively, and the right of free expression, which lies at the heart of a democratic society and which is exemplified by the right of the press to report on matters of public interest.

This issue was considered in *R. v. Shayler*,[5] where it was described as a clash between two competing aspects of the public interest:

> On the one hand there is the assertion by the appellant of the public interest in freedom of speech and the exercise of that freedom by those who give information to the press so that the press may publish it and comment on it for the public benefit. On the other hand there is the reliance by the Crown on the public interest in the maintenance of the secrecy of the work of the security service so that it can operate effectively to protect national security. Both interests are valid and important and it is for the courts to resolve the clash of interests and to decide how the balance is to be struck.

This issue had earlier been discussed at great length in the cases relating to the book entitled *Spycatcher*, written by Mr. Peter Wright, a former member of the British security service, MI5, that contained an account of alleged irregularities in MI5, and alleged unlawful activities carried out by the members of that organization. In the case of *Attorney General v. Guardian Newspapers (No. 2)*,[6] Lord Goff said:

> In cases concerned with Government secrets, as appears from the judgments of two Chief Justices—of Lord Widgery CJ in *Attorney-General v Jonathan Cape Ltd* [1976] QB 752,770, and of Mason CJ (then Mason J) in *Commonwealth of Australia v John Fairfax & Sons Ltd*, 147 CLR 39,51–53—it is

5 [2003] 1 A.C. 247 at 289G (H.L.).

6 [1990] 1 A.C. 109 at 283C (H.L.).

> incumbent upon the Crown, in order to restrain disclosure of Government secrets, not only to show that the information is confidential, but also to show that it is in the public interest that it should not be published. . . . The reason for this additional requirement in cases concerned with Government secrets appears to be that, although in the case of private citizens there is a public interest that confidential information should as such be protected, in the case of Government secrets the mere fact of confidentiality does not alone support such a conclusion, because in a free society there is continuing public interest that the workings of government should be open to scrutiny and criticism. From this it follows that, in such cases, there must be demonstrated some other public interest which requires that publication should be restrained.

In the *Spycatcher* case, the House of Lords held that because the worldwide publication of *Spycatcher* had destroyed any secrecy as to its contents, and copies of the book were readily available to any person who wished to obtain them, continuation of the injunctions previously granted against certain newspapers in the United Kingdom was not necessary. But in his judgment Lord Keith said:

> I regard this case as having established that members and former members of the Security Service do have a lifelong obligation of confidence owed to the Crown. Those who breach it, such as Mr Wright, are guilty of treachery just as heinous as that of some of the spies he excoriates in his book.[7]

In the *Shayler* case, the defendant, a former member of the security service, was charged with disclosing without lawful authority documents or information relating to security and intelligence matters contrary to sections 1 and 4 of the *Official Secrets Act 1989*. He argued that the prohibitions imposed by that Act and his prosecution under it infringed his right under Article 10(1) of the *European Convention of Human Rights* to impart information about the security service without interference by public authority. He further submitted that the infringement was more serious because the information that he disclosed was given by him to the press, and the freedom of the press to receive information of public interest and to publish it was one of the great bulwarks of democracy. These arguments were rejected by the House of Lords which held that by reason of the special position of members of the security services, and the highly confidential nature of the information that came into their possession, the interference with their right to freedom of expression contained in the 1989 Act was not greater than was required to achieve the legitimate object

7 *Ibid.* at 264G.

of acting in the interests of national security. Accordingly, sections 1 and 4 of the 1989 Act came within the ambit of the qualification in Article 10(2) of the *European Convention of Human Rights* that permitted interference with the right to freedom of expression given by Article 10(1) of the *Convention*, and were not incompatible with Article 10(1).

A further issue is the extent to which the claim of public interest in respect of important security or intelligence matters protects the media if it publishes a report relating to such matters that constitutes a serious attack on the integrity of politicians and public servants and the report is subsequently shown to be unfounded. A related question is whether it makes a difference if the reporter making the report has not acted with reasonable care.

In England there have been three recent cases that bear on the question of the protection given by the claim of public interest, although they were not cases relating to security or intelligence matters. The cases are *Reynolds v. Times Newspapers Ltd.*,[8] in the House of Lords, *Bonnick v. Morris*,[9] in the Judicial Committee of the Privy Council, and *Jameel v. Wall Street Journal Europe*,[10] in the House of Lords.

In the *Reynolds* case, the plaintiff, a prominent politician in the Republic of Ireland, sued Times Newspapers for defamation and the newspaper relied on the defence of qualified privilege in that it had reported on political matters of public importance. In his judgment Lord Nicholls, with whom Lord Cooke and Lord Hobhouse agreed, stated that the case concerned the interaction between two fundamental rights: freedom of expression and protection of reputation. He laid emphasis on the great importance of freedom to impart and receive information in a democracy and the importance of the role of the media in communicating information on political matters. But Lord Nicholls also stressed the importance of the protection of reputation in a democratic society and stated that it is in the public interest that the reputation of public figures should not be debased falsely.

He went on to state that the crux of the appeal lay in identifying the restrictions that were fairly and reasonably necessary for the protection of reputation. He said that in the case of statements of opinion on matters of public interest, it was sufficient for the protection of reputation to require that such statements should not be actuated by malice, but as regards defamatory imputations of fact, the position was different and more difficult. In the absence of any additional safeguard for reputation, a newspaper, anxious to be first with a "scoop,"

8 [2001] 2 A.C. 127 (H.L.) [*Reynolds*].
9 [2003] 1 A.C. 300 (P.C.) [*Bonnick*].
10 [2007] 1 A.C. 359 (H.L.) [*Jameel*].

would in practice be free to publish seriously defamatory misstatements of fact based on the slenderest of materials. Therefore some further protection for reputation was needed if this could be achieved without a disproportionate incursion into freedom of expression.

In a later part of his judgment Lord Nicholls referred to a number of matters to be taken into account in deciding whether the defence of qualified privilege had been established, and concluded that the report of which the plaintiff complained was not one which was protected by that defence. Lord Nicholls also made it clear that in his judgment it was not a disproportionate incursion into press freedom to require reasonable care from investigative reporters in order to protect the reputation of public figures from defamatory imputations of fact and he said:

> The common law does not seek to set a higher standard than that of responsible journalism, a standard the media themselves espouse. An incursion into press freedom which goes no further than this would not seem to be excessive or disproportionate.[11]

In the subsequent case of *Bonnick*, Lord Nicholls said:

> Stated shortly, the *Reynolds* privilege is concerned to provide a proper degree of protection for responsible journalism when reporting matters of public concern. Responsible journalism is the point at which a fair balance is held between freedom of expression on matters of public concern and the reputations of individuals. Maintenance of this standard is in the public interest and in the interests of those whose reputations are involved. It can be regarded as the price journalists pay in return for the privilege. If they are to have the benefit of the privilege journalists must exercise due professional skill and care.[12]

In the *Jameel* case, a Saudi Arabian businessman and the trading company of which he was president and general manager, brought proceedings for defamation against the publisher of the *Wall Street Journal Europe* in respect of an article published in that newspaper. The defendant did not plead the defence of justification and therefore the judge directed the jury that if they found the article defamatory of the claimants, they should assume it to be untrue. The defendant sought to rely on a defence of qualified privilege that protected responsible journalism when reporting matters of public concern and this defence was upheld by the House of Lords. It ruled that the defence of qualified privilege claimed by the defendant derived from the general obligation of a

11 *Reynolds*, above note 8 at 202E.

12 *Bonnick*, above note 9 at 309F.

publisher to communicate important information on a matter of real public interest that the public had a general entitlement to receive, and that where the court considered that the public interest criterion was met the publisher was required to satisfy the test of responsible journalism by showing that reasonable steps had been taken to verify the publication.

In *Jameel* as in *Reynolds*, the House of Lords made it clear that the defence of qualified privilege based on public interest would not arise if the reporter had acted without due care. As the Court of Appeal stated in *Loutchansky v. Times Newspapers Ltd (Nos. 2/5)*[13]: "'Carelessness, impulsiveness or irrationality' would cost a journalist dear in the evaluation of his claim to privilege under several of the *Reynolds* factors."

The final matter to which I would like to refer relates to the law of contempt where there is a clash between two rights, the right of the media to freedom of expression and the right of the defendant to a fair trial, and there are differences of approach to this issue in various jurisdictions. In England in earlier years the attitude of the courts had been that any report or comment in the press that could be regarded as endangering the fair trial of a defendant should not be permitted, and any such report or comment was at risk of being treated as a contempt of court as tending to obstruct or prejudice the administration of justice. But in the past forty years there has been a change of approach and, although in clear cases of serious prejudice the courts will still act to protect the right of a defendant to a fair trial, there has been a greater readiness by the courts to trust the good sense of jurors not to be swayed by what they may read or see in the press or other parts of the media.

In 1969 in *R. v. Kray*,[14] Lawton J. stated:

> I have enough confidence in my fellow-countrymen to think that they have got newspapers sized up just as they have got other public institutions sized up, and they are capable in normal circumstances of looking at a matter fairly and without prejudice even though they have to disregard what they may have read in a newspaper.

In the later case of *Re The Telegraph*,[15] Lord Taylor L.C.J. said that in deciding whether matters published in newspapers would cause a substantial risk of prejudice to a forthcoming trial a court should credit the jury with the will and ability to follow the judge's direction to decide the case only on the evidence that was put before them. The court should also bear in mind that the staying

---

13 [2002] Q.B. 783 at 807F (C.A.).

14 [1969] 53 Cr. App. R. 412 at 414.

15 [1994] Cr. App. R. 91.

power and detail of publicity, even in notorious cases, was limited and that the nature of a trial was to focus the jury's minds on the evidence placed before them rather than on matters outside the courtroom.

PART FOUR

IMPLICATIONS OF TORTURE AND COERCION

CHAPTER 10

Adjudicating National Security: Ethics, Counter-Terrorism, and the Administration of Justice

ANGELA GENDRON

CANADIAN CENTRE OF INTELLIGENCE AND SECURITY STUDIES, CARLETON UNIVERSITY

How do the courts adjudicate between individual and collective rights in national security cases? When those responsible for public safety call for "adjustments" in the balance to give priority to community rights, civil libertarians argue that it is precisely when the world is in turmoil that we should hold fast to our liberal ideals and not allow the state to undermine democracy's freedoms. What *moral* rules ground our thinking?

> It is all too easy for us to respond to such terror in a way which undermines commitment to our most deeply held values and convictions and which cheapens our right to call ourselves a civilised nation ... the Government, even in times when there is a threat to national security, must act strictly in accordance with the law.[1] (Cherie Blair, Barrister)

But there is a middle path between these two polarized positions: rather than weighing public safety against individual rights, we might do better to see them both as interdependent parts of the critical political-cultural infrastructure on which democracies depend. The importance of one right does not diminish the importance of the other. The challenge then is to find ways

1 Cherie Booth (Blair), barrister, "The Role of the Judge in a Human Rights World" (Address to The Malaysian Bar, Malaysia, 26 July 2005) online: The Malaysian Bar www.malaysianbar.org.my/human_rights/the_role_of_the_judge_in_a_human_rights_world_cherie_booth_qc.html . See also *The Times [London]* (27 July 2005).

within the rule of law that will enable us to be both more effective against those who threaten us *and* preserve the civil values that define us.

In this first section the conflict between personal liberties and community safety is discussed in terms of the corresponding moral dilemma and the contention that without exceptions to the rule, the Constitution (or the rule of law) must break. The second section applies moral theories to the issue that is most contentious with respect to human rights: can there ever be moral justification for torture?

A. THE DEMOCRATIC DILEMMA: INDIVIDUAL LIBERTY AND COMMUNITY SECURITY

Democratic societies define themselves by the values and principles they hold dear. The rule of law and due process are paramount in supporting the conditions necessary for a free society, and democratic societies in turn have an intuitive sense of what it is to act morally: to act in accordance with "what is right." If the actions of any democratically elected government are perceived to be undermining those values, then it risks losing its authority and legitimacy.

> [W]e only win people [to our position] if our policy is not just about interests but about values, not just about what is necessary but about what is right.[2]
> (Tony Blair, former UK Prime Minister, 2006)

As members of a liberal-democratic society, we accept constraints on our individual rights in order that the state can fulfill its obligations to provide various "collective" goods, the most important of which is public security. Security is a precondition of freedom because individual rights are meaningless without it; but equally, no society where the civil and political rights of individuals are insecure, can call itself a democracy.

Furthermore, in distinguishing between public and private morality, we accept that some actions carried out by public agents contravene normal moral rules but they may have to be tolerated to maintain a stable, flourishing, and free society. The extent to which we tolerate an erosion of civil liberties will largely depend upon our perception of the magnitude, gravity, and imminence of the threat. Since the state is responsible for threat assessments it is in a

---

2 Tony Blair, "Speech on the Middle East" (Address to the World Affairs Council, Los Angeles, 1 August 2006), online: Number10.gov.uk: The Official Site of the Prime Minister's Office www.number10.gov.uk/Page9948. See also *Der Spiegel* (3 August 2006).

position, should it so choose, to exaggerate the threat (from precautionary or other motives) in order to win public support for its emergency legislation.

Over time, the law comes to embody the values of society and its sense of right and wrong. In the discourse between politics and morality, it often acts as the intermediary between their conflicting demands: in effect, it represents a compromise between what is desirable and what is possible. In political democracies, leaders must justify and seek approval for their policies: what the state is morally obligated to do is limited by what is politically possible, and what is politically possible is itself affected by moral considerations. In discussing the relation between law and morality, Lon Fuller[3] draws the distinction between the *morality of duty* and the *morality of aspiration*.

Emergencies require nations and leaders to make heroic decisions which in hindsight may prove either to have been justifiable or an overreaction. It is a time when the measures taken are likely to be ones we would avoid if we could because, just as hard cases make bad law, so emergency measures put morality itself at risk. When our deepest values and collective survival may be threatened, adhering to the high moral ground may compromise both our capacity to counter threats to public safety and defend our democratic freedoms and way of life. At such times, can moral constraints have any hold upon us?

Britain's Attorney General Lord Goldsmith thought they could and should, even with respect to those suspected of the most vicious terrorist outrages:

> There should be in modern society no outlaws; no people to whom the law does not apply who can ignore its constraints and to whom therefore anything can be done. They should be bound by the law and held rigorously to account in accordance with the law when they do not uphold it—but the law should not treat them as non-persons either.[4]

The task of judges then is to apply the law and uphold the fundamental rights of even those suspected of horrific atrocities. But holding "rigorously to account" terrorists who break the law by planning and perpetrating mass slaughter in furtherance of revolutionary ambitions can prove difficult under the *Criminal Code*. The nature of current threats requires proactive measures designed to *prevent* attacks, rather than traditional law enforcement procedures that *react* to the perpetration of a crime. When the threat of irreparable damage and loss of life necessitates preventive action, it may not be possible to gather sufficient evidence to obtain a conviction in a criminal court of law

---

3 See Lon L. Fuller, *The Morality of Law* (New Haven: Yale University Press, 1969).

4 Former UK Attorney General, Lord Goldsmith, reported in "Law Must Apply to Terror Suspects" *Daily Express [London]* (23 February 2006).

to prove an "intention" to commit mass murder or show that an actual attack was planned.

> Terrorists who could cause "irreparable damage on a hitherto unknown scale" evade prosecution because admissible court evidence cannot be gathered, or avoid deportation because they could be in danger in their home countries.[5] (Former British Home Secretary, John Reid)

A decision by the Court of Appeal in the UK overturned the sentences of five young Muslims on grounds that while they had been "intoxicated" by propaganda, this did not amount to "the commission, preparation or instigation" of terrorist acts.[6] The five had gathered and exchanged radical propaganda of the sort used to groom those who go on to commit acts of suicide terrorism.

When does the fantasy of becoming a martyr slip into the reality of criminal preparation? By making the distinction between proof and accusation, Lord Phillips' decision won respect but it also generated anger: while it was hailed as demonstrating the strengths of democracy by upholding individual liberties, the government's efforts to remove from society those whom it had assessed as posing a danger to the community appeared to have been frustrated. The decision was later overturned by the House of Lords which found that: to secure a conviction, the prosecution was not required to show that a defendant had had a terrorist purpose for collecting or recording information of a kind likely to be useful to a terrorist or possessing a document or record containing information of that kind.[7]

It is this perceived inability to hold terrorists "rigorously to account" which has given rise to concerns about the emphasis on individual rights when public safety is at risk. There is a perception that the legal system fully protects the rights of those believed to be responsible for terrorist outrages but is unable to offer equal protection to the lives and rights of their intended victims. Dissatisfaction with the efficacy of the ordinary criminal justice process for the legal pursuit of terrorists has spawned proposals for a new adjudicatory framework in the United States; administrative orders and investigative detentions in the UK and France; and, in Canada, preventive detentions and investigative hearings.

The sense that justice is no longer equal for everyone, or that it favours some more than others, has led to anger and frustration on both sides of the divide: while security authorities have been incensed by the judicial overthrow of

5 Cited in Nigel Morris, "Reid Attacks Judges Who Hamper Life and Death Terrorism Battle" *The Independent [London]* (10 August 2006) [Reid].

6 UK Court of Appeal decision in the case of Irfan Raja, Awaab Iqbal, Aitzaz Zafar, Usman Malik, and Akbar Butt, reported in *The Daily Telegraph [London]* (14 February 2008).

7 *Zafar and Ors v. R*, [2008] EWCA Crim 184.

public safety legislation on human rights grounds, human rights activists have been equally concerned that special anti-terrorism measures are bypassing the criminal justice system which they regard as enshrining democracy's core values. They argue that "it is not a question of 'the innocent public' versus the terrorists, but rather 'the innocent public' versus other members of the innocent public wrongly suspected of terrorism."[8]

Lord Justice Laws succinctly summarized the moral dilemma:

> [Confronted by the "grave and present threat" of terrorism] the state faces a dilemma: If it limits the means by which the citizens are protected against the threat of terrorist outrage to the ordinary measures of the criminal law, it leaves a yawning gap. It exposes its people to the possibility of indiscriminate murder committed by extremists who for want of evidence could not be brought to book in the criminal courts. But if it fills the gap by confining them without trial it affronts "the most fundamental and probably the oldest, most hardly won and the most universally recognised of human rights": freedom from executive detention.[9]

A moral dilemma requires a choice to be made between two (or more) options, each of which entails moral harm. Any decision in favour of one will inevitably incur the moral hazards of the other. The preference of those charged with responsibility for public safety was articulated by former British Home Secretary John Reid in August 2006: "Sometimes we may have to modify some of our freedoms in the short term in order to prevent their use and abuse by those who oppose our fundamental values and would destroy all of our freedoms in the long term."[10]

This is the "lesser evil" that charts a middle course between the claim by pure civil libertarians that no violations of rights can ever be justified, and a purely pragmatic or consequentialist position that judges the curtailment of individual freedoms by their effectiveness. Any adjustment to individual rights entails moral harm but the lesser evil is justifiable only because it is the least harmful option and other means would be insufficient or unavailable. Michael Ignatieff cites as an example the United Kingdom's derogation from its commitments under the *International Covenant on Civil and Political Rights* in 2001 after enacting legislation regarding the detention of terrorist suspects from overseas who could not be returned to their countries of origin because

8 Dr. Eric Metcalfe, "Human Rights: Individual Freedom versus Security" (2007) 6(5) RUSI Homeland Security & Resilience Monitor 18 [Metcalfe].

9 *A and Others v. Secretary of State for the Home Department*, [2004] EWCA Civ 1123 at para. 155, Laws L.J.

10 Reid, above note 5.

of the risk of persecution or torture: "Faced with two ways of jeopardizing the human rights of suspects, it chose the lesser form."[11]

On the other hand, the response of a human rights activist, who rejects the notion of trading liberty for increased security, focuses on the element of entitlement: "Human rights are not about giving terrorists freedom to carry out attacks on innocent civilians, they are about the freedoms that people who live in a free society are entitled to demand from their government."[12]

Those who have the responsibility for national security are likely to give less weight to the consequences of an incremental reduction in civil liberties than to the incremental benefits they associate with enhanced security measures. It is they who will be held accountable for any failure to safeguard the public. Conversely, those who are primarily concerned with protecting civil liberties can be expected to oppose even a modest concession out of concern that a "temporary" measure introduced as a necessity in times of emergency, may eventually become permanent.

The impasse, which arises from conflicting individual and collective rights, is commonly spoken of as a "balance" in which more of one necessarily entails less of the other. More accurately, it should be recognized that since a liberal-democracy is defined by both personal and political freedoms, a reduction in either necessarily diminishes the whole.

While a temporary "adjustment" to individual rights in favour of enhanced security may be possible within the rule of law, it nevertheless entails a moral harm that can only be justified as a means of avoiding a greater one. Given the nature of contemporary forms of terrorism, the adjustment is likely to become long-lasting and therefore it is all the more important to ensure that the imminence and gravity of the threat fully warrants the preventive measures proposed.

How should we deal justly with those who openly reject our democratic values and corresponding legal and moral norms, those who acknowledge no obligations to the societies in which they live, nor feel bound by its laws? Lord Goldsmith was in no doubt, but even if we accept the necessity of maintaining the high moral ground in the struggle against extremists, it provides no refuge from the necessity of making hard practical decisions. When goals or values come into conflict, there is no formula that can tell us what to do. In the face of a moral dilemma, difficult choices must be made. What is needed is a rational

---

11 Michael Ignatieff, *The Lesser Evil: Political Ethics in an Age of Terror* (Princeton, NJ: Princeton University Press, 2004) at 50 [Ignatieff].

12 Metcalfe, above note 8 at 18–19.

procedure for weighing competing claims in order to arrive at a moral view that will guide action and minimize the moral harm.

Unfortunately, in a climate of fear and uncertainty, the danger to democracies is that we may overreact and derogate from basic human rights commitments, or underestimate the adversary's intentions and capabilities and allow idealism, naïveté, or complacency to assist those who threaten us. In national security cases, idealism and the desire to do what is right comes up against pragmatism and the need to find practical solutions for preserving both democratic values and security. We must find ways to be creative and innovative in using the law to do so. There is no place for absolutism.

1) Tensions between the Political and Judicial Branches of Government

While there may be a societal consensus about absolute values, the relationship between those values and the rights that express them is contentious. Different individuals and groups have different values and principles. These guide action toward achieving what is deemed to be good. When the promotion of a particular set of values brings one group into conflict with another that has very different ideals, reconciling the two requires principles that can be endorsed by both. However, if the debate has become polarized and there is an absence of consensus, judges are required to resolve the impasse by adjudicating competing rights claims.

Tensions between the political and judicial branches of government have arisen in national security cases precisely because of a perception that the law's insistence on respect for individual rights is in disregard of community rights. Judges are required to take account of both, but in times of emergency their attempts to uphold the law are sometimes perceived by the public and the executive as frustrating public safety measures.

In the wake of the July 2005 London bombings, Britain's former Prime Minister Tony Blair observed that "the traditional court processes do too much to protect the rights of the accused while proving 'utterly useless' in protecting the ordinary citizen on the street."[13]

And a former UK Conservative Opposition Leader, Michael Howard, declared in 2005 that "judicial activism seems to have reached unprecedented levels in thwarting the wishes of Parliament."[14]

---

13 *Daily Telegraph [London]* (23 March 2006).

14 "Howard Rounds on Activist Judges" *The Times [London]* (10 August 2005).

Judicial review bodies have the power to invalidate laws adopted by legislators who are elected by and accountable to the people, as indeed they have done with respect to post-9/11 anti-terrorism legislation. In 2004, a ruling of the UK Law Lords declared parts of Britain's anti-terrorism legislation to be "disproportionate" to the threat and invalid on human rights grounds. The ruling led to the introduction of administrative control orders which the government declared to be necessary to manage the immediate risk.

Executive criticism of judicial decisions in national security cases has consequently questioned whether the power of judicial review is consistent with the democratic principle that governments derive their authority from collective consensus and consent: although the independence of the judiciary is a principle of democracy, it has been argued in Britain that the judiciary should be more subservient towards Parliament given that Parliament is responsible for *making law* and the judiciary's role is to *apply and interpret it.*

> While judges have a legitimate role in challenging ministers if they implement laws differently from parliament's intentions, they do not have the right to gainsay the will of an elected parliament or overturn its decision.[15] (David Blunkett, former UK Home Secretary)

> If, under pressure of events, politicians introduce laws to protect public safety which restrict civil liberties to an unnecessary extent, then the judges have not only a right but a duty to say so.[16] (Lord Goodhart, senior human rights lawyer, 2005)

The introduction of the *Human Rights Act* in 1998 led to an increase in judicial activism (or interference as some have described it) by drawing judges into areas of political controversy. The Act has been described as "fast becoming the law of unintended consequences,"[17] which casts a shadow over every court in the land and provides succour to terrorist suspects.

---

15 Blunkett, while acknowledging that judges have a legitimate role in challenging *ministers,* said if they differ from Parliament's intentions, and "if the judiciary were saying 'We think that parliament was wrong and therefore the democratic vote is wrong,' I think that is a different matter.... We obviously have the right to go back to parliament and to say 'We, the sovereign body who are elected, are the only ones in the end who are answerable for the protection of security and stability in our country. We will make the decision.'" See "Blunkett Warns Judges over Anti-terror Plans" *The Guardian* (8 August 2005) [Blunkett].

16 Lord Goodhart, cited in "Guilty! Senior Judges Accuse Politicians over Terror Laws" *The Independent [London]* (11 August 2005).

17 "The State, the Judges, the Terrorists" *Sunday Times [London]* (29 April 2007).

racy's undoing. But on what basis do we give priority, even temporarily, to one rather than the other in the face of imminent physical threats from terrorism or corrosive and insidious attack on our democratic institutions and ideals?

Terrorism has obliged democratic societies to think carefully about the values and principles that define them and consider to what extent they would be prepared to curtail, suspend, or dilute individual rights in order to preserve public safety. In the global and long-term struggle against violent extremism we are facing an ethical dilemma:[27] we must choose between two alternatives, both of which have harmful consequences.

Since the use of torture in democracies is one that illustrates this dilemma in the starkest possible terms and, despite a legal ban, continues to be a contentious issue, the next section looks at the ethical arguments that are used on both sides of the debate in an attempt to determine whether there is a *moral* argument that can support resort to torture in exceptional circumstances.

B. RESORT TO TORTURE

1) Legal Prohibition

The use of torture is the most extreme example of the issue of conflicting rights. A clear prohibition in the name of human dignity comes up against a utilitarian case grounded in national security. International laws: the *Geneva Conventions*, the UN *Convention against Torture and Other Cruel, Inhuman or Degrading Treatment or Punishment*, the *European Convention on Human Rights*, and the *International Covenant on Civil and Political Rights*, make it clear that the ban on torture is absolute, even in times of war:

> No exceptional circumstances whatsoever, whether a state of war or a threat of war, internal political instability or any other public emergency, may be invoked as a justification of torture.[28]

All democratic societies accept, in principle, that the prohibition is indeed absolute and that there should be no exceptions whatever the consequences may be. This is said to be an iconic value—the essence of what it is to be a liberal-democratic society. Torture is seen as the ultimate abuse of political authority against individuals who, at the time of the abuse at least, are disarmed

27 Ignatieff, above note 11 at Chapter 2.

28 *Convention against Torture and Other Cruel, Inhuman or Degrading Treatment or Punishment*, G.A. res. 39/46, annex, 39 U.N. GAOR Supp. (No. 51) at 197, U.N. Doc. A/39/51 (1984), 1465 U.N.T.S. 85 [*CAT*], art. 2(2).

and helpless. Nevertheless, governments also recognize that while torture is an unqualified evil, it might also save many lives: we cannot torture because of who we are, yet the first duty of a liberal-democractic government is to protect its citizens. That is the ethical dilemma.

But can the very survival of democratic society itself legitimize committing an ultimate violation to human dignity? This question is especially pertinent to Israel, a state that has faced a constant and continuing threat to its existence. Following a decade-long debate in legal and security circles about the legitimacy of torture, the Israeli Supreme Court ruled in 1999 that it was illegal. In a landmark ruling, Justice Aharon Barak noted that the destiny of democracy is that not all means are acceptable to it:

> At times democracy fights with one hand tied behind her back. Despite that, democracy has the upper hand, since preserving the rule of law and recognition of individual liberties constitute an important component of her security stance. At the end of the day, they strengthen her and her spirit, and allow her to overcome her difficulties.[29]

Even if we *could* use "both hands" as it were—if there were no moral or legal constraints—it is not at all clear that we could subsequently claim that illegal targeting and torture had enabled us to eradicate the threats and was therefore justified as a temporary moral harm. Both Israel and Spain concede as much. Judge Balthazar Garzon acknowledged that counter-terrorism actions by elements of Spain's security forces, which exceeded both the limits of the rule of law and basic morality, were counterproductive: the costs to civil society, in terms of its own self-image and place in the wider community of civilized nations, have outweighed any benefits.[30]

The prohibition on unacceptable means locates the strength of a democracy in its willingness to enshrine individual liberties within the rule of law. But the issue concerning any departure or adjustment of human rights protections is not just a matter of legitimacy but of *morality*. Intuitively, or through a process of reasoning, we know that certain conduct is not right. Equally, we may also sense that in certain *exceptional* circumstances, the use of force in preventive interrogation may be *morally*, if not legally, justified.

Should the claims to human rights and dignity of the terrorists prevail over the security interest, and right to life, of the majority? The state is likely to

29 H.C. 5100/94, *The Public Committee against Torture in Israel v. The State of Israel*, 53(4) P.D. 817 at 845.

30 Judge Baltasar Garzon, "Civil Law Approaches to National Security in Spain" (Address to the International Conference on the Administration of Justice and National Security in Democracies, Ottawa, 12 June 2007).

claim that security is a value that trumps all others and that since it has the responsibility to protect, it also has a legal and moral duty to use all means necessary, subject to proportionality and last resort, to obtain information that might be critical in saving hundreds if not thousands of lives. Even in captivity, terrorists may remain potentially dangerous to the public because the knowledge they possess may pose a mortal threat.

Conversely, David Rodin contends that democratic societies *are* willing to accept the enhanced risk that may be the cost of "not resorting to torture" and expect those who govern by their authority to promote and protect this foundational democratic value as a prime duty. When states fail to do so, it is because moral concepts are prone to abuse: "morality has failed to take proper cognizance of politics and its astonishing capacity to subvert, abuse, and manipulate moral categories."[31]

2) Practical Considerations and Compromises

While it is axiomatic that political democracies "don't do torture"—that they accept the legal prohibition—the line between torture and less coercive methods of interrogation is far from settled. Do disorientation and disinformation techniques count? Furthermore, some democratic governments that eschew the practice of torture themselves deport detainees to other countries that do, under the protection of Memoranda of Understanding.[32] In certain circumstances Canada can deport suspected terrorists even without such assurances on the grounds that their presence may constitute an imminent threat. The admissibility of evidence "possibly" obtained by torture is specifically prohibited by international law,[33] but the difficulty of determining the provenance of any information leaves admissibility open to legal interpretation, and in many jurisdictions there is nothing prohibiting its use for *investigative* purposes.

The ambiguities that allow these and other controversial practices to continue are deplored by some as an abuse of state power but accepted by others as

31 David Rodin, *War and Self-Defence* (Oxford: Clarendon Press, 2002) at 196.

32 The British Government is also trying to make deportations possible without such assurances. It has asked the European Court of Human Rights to set a precedent ruling that the risk of torture faced by Mohammed Ramzy has to be weighed against the security risk faced by the host country; see "Observations of the Governments of Lithuania, Portugal, Slovakia and the United Kingdom," *Ramzy v. The Netherlands*, no. 25424/05, Eur. Ct. H.R. (21 November 2005).

33 The *CAT* and the *Convention for the Protection of Human Rights and Fundamental Freedoms*, 4 November 1950, 213 U.N.T.S. 221 at 223, Eur. T.S. 5 [E.C.H.R.], ratified by all European Union member countries and the United States, ban the admission in court of evidence possibly obtained under torture.

pragmatic compromises necessitated by national security and therefore morally justifiable. Widespread support for practices that fall short of torture but that contravene the spirit of prohibition suggests that the debate is far from over. There is certainly a constituency for the view that in certain extremely limited situations, a *moral* case for treating terrorists or suspected terrorists unjustly can be made: "there is nothing unjust nor morally repugnant about ensuring the survival of our society."[34]

Given these ambiguities, it is judges who, in interpreting the law and filling the gaps, must "weigh the balance of probabilities." It is they who must adjudicate between conflicting requirements in the public interest. What is legal is not necessarily ethical, but in reaching their decisions judges are influenced indirectly by moral rules that govern the rightness of actions and reflect the values to which a society is committed.

3) The Extreme Case

The *moral* case for torture, despite an absolute legal prohibition on its practice, is usually invoked in the "ticking bomb" situation. Professor Alan Dershowitz[35] formulated the following moral dilemma: a captured terrorist knows the location of a ticking bomb that threatens hundreds of innocent lives; the only way to prevent the mass murder is to torture the terrorist into disclosing the bomb's location; there is no time for reflection; a decision must be made. Does the noble end of saving innocent lives justify the ignoble means of employing torture?

US Supreme Court Justice Antonin Scalia has publicly stated his opinion that interrogators should be allowed to inflict pain to obtain critical information which is crucial to society, such as the location of a bomb about to explode or the plans or whereabouts of a terrorist group. He conceded that it was difficult to determine when coercive measures should come into play, which measures constitute "torture," and whether those that are not permitted with respect to punishment under the criminal law would be prohibited by the Constitution (in an emergency situation): "Is it really so easy to determine that smacking someone in the face to find out where he has hidden the bomb that is about to blow up Los Angeles is prohibited by the Constitution?"[36]

---

34 Dan Saxon, "Philosophy in a Time of Terror: Searching for an Appropriate Jurisprudence" (2005) 4 J. Hum. Rts. 73 at 79 [Saxon].

35 Alan M. Dershowitz, *Shouting Fire: Civil Liberties in a Turbulent Age* (Boston: Little, Brown and Co., 2002) at 470.

36 The Associated Press, "Scalia Accepts Infliction of Pain to Get Key Information" *Los Angeles Times* (13 February 2008), citing comments made by Justice Antonin Scalia (12 February 2008) on *Law in Action*, BBC Radio 4.

Just as hard cases make bad law, so "artificial cases might make bad ethics" according to Henry Shue who questions whether it is possible to draw conclusions for ordinary cases from the extraordinary ones of philosophers.[37] Nevertheless, he concedes that in a precise case such as Dershowitz describes, torture would be morally justifiable. However, any state official or law enforcement officer who believes that such an act would be the least available evil and defies the legal ban on grounds of necessity or self-defence, should be required to justify themselves to claim any legal defence. Moral principles prohibit attacking the defenceless, but the terrorist who planted the bomb is not defenceless; he has the means to avoid the abuse.

4) Moral Theories

The question of whether moral theories can help guide actions, particularly in times of emergency, is germane to the issue of torture. In political democracies, we derive our moral commitment to the protection of basic human rights from various traditional philosophical and legal foundations.

Kant sought moral salvation in the power of human rationality alone, believing that there must be universal moral laws governing the social world. Kierkegaard championed individual choice. David Hume placed emphasis on the passions. Bentham and Mill developed utilitarianism, a moral rationality that employed a "utility calculus" as the basis of decision-making and from which consequentialism has developed. Twentieth-century philosophers developed other moral theories focusing on intuition and emotivism and, more recently, philosophers have applied "virtue theory" to modern questions of morality concerning war, self-defence, and torture.[38] All have been found wanting. Resort to an Aristotelian account of the "virtues" that ancient Greeks considered essential to living a happy and ethical life is perhaps a sign that our moral concepts are suffering from fatigue and a failure to provide a clear guide to action when under pressure.

These and other philosophical and legal theories have influenced the different weights that people assign to certain values and the rights that express them. Kant believed that we are all moral equals, but rather than claiming that we all have equal *rights*, he stressed that we all have equal *duties or obligations.* Treating people as *ends* rather than *means* is a categorical imperative. Natural

---

37 Henry Shue, "Torture," in Sanford Levinson, ed., *Torture: A Collection* (Oxford: Oxford University Press, 2004) [Levinson].

38 Alasdair MacIntyre, *After Virtue: A Study in Moral Theory* (Notre Dame, IN: University of Notre Dame Press, 1981) [MacIntyre].

rights theorists claim that each and every human life has a distinct and equal inherent value,[39] and they associate equality with the idea of justice. The rights to which they refer have been enshrined as *human rights* in public documents, partly to ensure that they are not violated. John Rawls, a leading proponent of natural rights, argues that only "times of extreme crisis" could justify deviating from the values protecting the natural rights of persons[40]—grounds that democratic governments worldwide have cited to justify anti-terrorism measures in the post-9/11 security environment.

Democratic societies place a priority on acting justly, of treating people equally—even those who are our adversaries.[41] But what constitutes "justness" when dealing with those whose moral values and principles of justice are very different and, in some respects, contrary to our own. Those whose own sense of "justice" allows no respect for others and treats democracies' political values as weaknesses that can be used against us? Rawls defined justness in terms of "fairness"[42] but fundamental divergences in the values of different societies, or even within a particular society, inevitably mean that there will be little agreement on what is just or fair, especially when a society faces threats to its security.

From a Kantian perspective, the ban on torture is an unconditional duty in every circumstance, trumping all other values, including the right to life and the survival of the world. This is the position of moral absolutists who refute the notion that there could be any moral justification to use persons as means rather than ends. Consequences can have no bearing on "right action." Doing what is good, or having "a good will" is valued for itself and not for any outcome that it accomplishes.

In the real world, however, the position of moral absolutists would become both practically and morally untenable when the risk was not of *one* death but millions. For example, if the ticking bomb was a chemical or nuclear device and its activation might result in wide-scale slaughter and physical destruction. And similarly, while ideas of rights, consequences, duties, and aspirations lie at the heart of the debate about the inviolability of human rights, any claim that they should trump majority preferences on the basis of democratic or other principles is empty without reference to the corresponding duties that give meaning to those rights.

---

39 *International Covenant on Civil and Political Rights*, 19 December 1966, 999 U.N.T.S. 171, arts.9–14 at art. 10.

40 John Rawls, "Fifty Years after Hiroshima," [Rawls] in Samuel Freeman, ed., *John Rawls: Collected Papers* (Cambridge, MA: Harvard University Press, 1999) [Freeman] at 572, cited in Saxon, above note 34.

41 John Rawls, "Justice as Fairness," in Freeman, *ibid.* at 72.

42 *Ibid.* at 70.

> My concern is to change the climate of rights so that people appreciate that with rights go responsibilities. ... And society cannot deliver rights unless others accept their responsibilities.[43] (Jack Straw, Lord Chancellor, the United Kingdom)

Such responsibilities or duties have been referred to as the "business end" of justice in that they formulate the ethical and political requirements of our democratic societies.[44] Many of those who proclaim the inviolability of rights are strong on ideals and aspirations, but short on the costs and demands (or consequences) of respecting those rights.

Justice Richard Posner has said that moral theory "does not provide a solid basis for moral judgments."[45] His comment mirrors the philosophical claims of Alasdair MacIntyre who argues that most contemporary moral theorizing is of little relevance because it lays too much stress on reason, and too little on people and the contexts in which they live their lives.[46] An emphasis on the precise and logical structure of moral arguments is worthless if it fails to provide a guide to right action in the midst of the social chaos and moral havoc of everyday human life. But if moral theory provides no *practical* guide, how should we decide on the issue of torture.

5) Moral Decision-making: Idealism and Consequentialism

In any debate concerning conflicting rights, those for whom moral values and right conduct are *intrinsically* obligatory and admirable, having a merit in themselves quite apart from any good that they might bring about, are *idealists*. Theirs is a *morality of aspiration*: an intuitive desire to adhere to the moral high ground and defend those values that represent the best to which human beings aspire. Moral *absolutists* reject any compromise of values to avoid a particular undesirable outcome but accept that society will be at greater risk as a consequence because the means it has to defend itself will be more limited. *Pragmatic* idealists, however, are more likely to consider whether, in order to save lives or ensure survival, it may be justifiable to sacrifice or suspend certain

43 Jack Straw, in an interview with Joshua Rozenberg, Legal Editor, reported in "Brief Encounters" *Daily Telegraph [London]* (14 February 2008), in connection with a proposal to have a "non-justiciable" Bill of Rights and Responsibilities.

44 Onora O'Neill, *A Question of Trust: The BBC Reith Lectures 2002* (Cambridge: Cambridge University Press, 2002) at 31–34.

45 Richard A. Posner, "The Problematics of Moral and Legal Theory" (1998) 111 Harv. L. Rev. 1637 at 1638. See also Dworkin, above note 19 at 75.

46 MacIntyre, above note 38, cited in Vardy & Grosch, above note 18 at 94.

values even while endeavouring to act as much in accordance with their ideas of what is right as possible.

At the other end of the moral continuum are the *realists* or consequentialists. Theirs is a morality of *outcomes*. They place less emphasis on right conduct and more on the importance of making practical, utilitarian choices that have the consequences desired. At one extreme of the realist spectrum, morality is divorced from decision-making. More usually, realists define morality narrowly in terms of a *duty* to adhere to those rules that are essential to social living and that reduce uncertainty and irrationality in human affairs. With respect to the abridgment of human rights, the "good" that is to be achieved or maximized is public security and the criteria for decision-making, cost-benefit analysis.

6) The Moral Case against Torture: Idealism

Idealists are *primarily* governed by ideas and intuitions about what is moral and constitutes right conduct, rather than which actions achieve desirable outcomes. A concept of shared humanity requires them to treat all persons justly and not merely as means to an end. Those who behave inhumanely are still entitled to a basic equality of treatment, even if, as Michael Ignatieff so graphically points out: "the rights of the beheader may be honoured more than those of the beheaded."[47] Ignatieff, a pragmatic idealist, believes that authorities interrogating terrorist suspects should be allowed to engage in disinformation or disorientation techniques—short of physical or psychological pain.

Idealists assert that a majoritarian justification for torture amounts to a failure to respect the inviolability of human life. Taking the life of an adversary in self-defence may be justified but inflicting pain and indignity on another human being is not. Idealists' aversion to torture is rooted in an intuitive knowledge that morally, it is neither acceptable nor worthy of human beings and strategically is likely to be counterproductive. Torture is a practice that ultimately leads to the destruction of the trust necessary for one human being to live among others; it inflicts moral damage not only on its victims but on those agents who are tasked to carry it out.

7) The Case for Torture: Realism

Realists or consequentialists justify actions on grounds of "necessity" if they produce desired outcomes or consequences. They are concerned more with consequences than conduct but accept that morality matters as a social construct

47 Ignatieff, above note 11 at 34.

that eases relationships within a community. They do not deny the value of human beings, but, with respect to resort to torture, the motivation to save innocent lives is stronger. Their morality of duty requires the protection of potential *victims* as well as preservation of the rights of terrorists.

Some realists believe that an absolute prohibition on torture, even in a ticking bomb situation, is a morally indefensible position that reflects the disinclination of idealists to "dirty their hands" or compromise their ideals in order to prevent harm to others. Most realists nevertheless concede that the negative consequences of legalizing torture in emergency situations outweigh the potential benefits: "Among legal academics, a near consensus has emerged: coercive interrogation must be kept 'illegal,' but nonetheless permitted in certain circumstances."[48]

Richard Posner has given several examples that demonstrate the need to balance costs and benefits when deciding whether torture is justifiable.[49] He argues that this balancing test avoids the possibility that, even in extreme circumstances, the end may not justify the means because the end, while a good one, may not be as valuable as the means are costly.

Realists believe that the greatest threat to civil liberties comes from continuing successful acts of mass-casualty terrorism: "those who love liberty must therefore be at the forefront of efforts to prevent terrorism, even if such efforts require some compromise of the maximalist civil liberties paradigm."[50] This does not mean replicating the immorality of the adversary, but it may mean compromising temporarily the high moral standard to which we aspire. This is the "lesser evil" position that tolerates one moral harm in order to avoid a greater one.

While the positions set forth above do not do justice to the depth of arguments that support them, they capture the essence of the debate. Idealists are prepared to accept a greater level of risk in order to avoid sacrificing democracy's bedrock moral values; realists are concerned that adhering too strictly to human rights commitments will undermine the capacity of democratic governments to act effectively and *ethically* in preserving human life and defending liberal democracy. A failure to protect society may lead to catastrophic consequences for humankind and the demise of democratic government.

The moral arguments against torture are quite separate from any doubts that both idealists and realists have regarding the efficacy of torture as an

---

48 Eric A. Posner & Adrian Vermeule, "Should Coercive Interrogation Be Legal?" (2006) 104 Mich. L. Rev. 671 at 673.

49 Richard Posner, "Torture, Terrorism and Interrogation," in Levinson, above note 37 at 291–98.

50 Alan Dershowitz, "How to Protect Civil Liberties" *The Spectator [London]* (30 August 2006).

information-gathering tool.[51] Many critics of torture argue that it is *ineffective* as well as repugnant. Given that democratic governments support an absolute *legal* ban on torture, the debate as to its use only continues in the context of whether there can ever be circumstances that would justify a *moral* case. Resort to torture would be a last resort, used only for preventive purposes and against a person whom it is highly likely has the information required. The veracity of the information obtained may nevertheless be suspect, but it is all that may save us from catastrophe.

8) Common Ground

While there are more "absolutists" on the issue of torture than on any other measures that abridge human rights, in the real world idealism is usually tempered by realism and vice versa in the search for a way out of the impasse that arises from conflicting values. Idealists who adhere to the moral high ground recognize that practical decisions must still be made and have no wish to preside over the demise of democracy because of a failure to mount an appropriate defence. They may be prepared to accept measures, as a last resort, that temporarily abridge individual rights provided they are convinced that they are necessary and proportional to the dangers threatening the safety of the community. Realists as well as idealists support an absolute legal prohibition on torture but the threshold for a moral case that might justify or excuse an official resorting to torture illegally is likely to be lower because realists believe there is less moral harm involved.

Both sides of the divide are aware that the practice of torture in a democracy has detrimental and corrosive effects on those who carry it out as well as to the society that they seek to protect. Realists are as committed to the ideals of democracy as idealists, but the two diverge on how best to preserve democratic societies that are threatened. A departure from democratic values risks the charge of moral bankruptcy and hypocrisy and removes the advantage of the moral high ground which in itself may increase the threats. Although moral absolutists are prepared to trust in the strength of their ideals alone, pragmatic idealists and realists alike are less sanguine. Both "sides" acknowledge the moral hazards of torture but for idealists that cost is paramount, whereas for realists, costs may be outweighed in certain circumstances by the benefits of "harms prevented."

> Yet reason and careful moral reflection also teach us that there are times when the first and most important reply to evil is to stop it. There are times

51 Darius Rejali, "5 Myths about Torture and Truth" *Washington Post* (16 December 2007).

when waging war is not only morally permitted, but morally necessary, as a response to calamitous acts of violence, hatred, and injustice. This is one of those times.[52]

9) Legislating for Extreme Circumstances

What moral principle could justify the death penalty for past individual murders and at the same time condemn non-lethal torture to prevent future mass murders?[53] (Alan Dershowitz)

Alan Dershowitz,[54] a strong advocate of civil liberties, believes it to be inevitable that in the face of continuing mass-casualty terrorism, there would be public demand for extraordinary preventive measures that would violate moral and legal norms. On the basis that "bad times make bad law" he argues that it is better to debate the issues and agree what response will be appropriate ahead of the emergency. He has proposed that the use of torture should be legislated to regulate the precise conditions under which resort to torture would be justified in an emergency. It would remove from the individual investigator the moral hazard of acting illegally in the public interest and seeking retrospectively to be excused criminal liability.

Those who oppose codifying the use of torture into a legal framework do so not only because of the practical difficulties relating to definitions and thresholds, but out of concern that once legalized, the provision could eventually lead to the practice of torture for non-preventive purposes (retribution and punishment); in circumstances that are not truly exceptional; or against ordinary criminals. Israel is the only country in modern times to have openly allowed "moderate physical pressure" as a "last resort," but in 1999, citing the "slippery slope" argument, Israel's Supreme Court ruled that torture could never be justified, even in the case of a ticking bomb. Kant too used the slippery slope objection in justifying his opposition to espionage in a time of war asserting that any justification was negated by the likelihood of the practice being continued into peacetime.

Dershowitz's proposal that we should legitimize resort to torture in specific situations is the product of both moral and practical thinking. Like the laws

52 Enola Aird, *et al.*, "What We're Fighting For: A Letter from America" (14 February 2002), online: InfoUSA: United States Department of State: Washington File http://usinfo.org/wf-archive/2002/020214/epf407.htm.

53 Alan M. Dershowitz, *Why Terrorism Works: Understanding the Threat, Responding to the Challenge* (New Haven, CT: Yale University Press, 2003) at 148.

54 Alan Dershowitz, "Tortured Reasoning," in Levinson, above note 37 at 257–80.

of war, the objective was to impose a moral framework on the use of force and abuse of power in preventive interrogations that he believed were inevitable in an extreme emergency. For most participants the negative effects of derogating from an absolute legal ban is sufficient grounds for rejecting the idea, but even proponents of natural rights accept, as does John Rawls, that while "[t]here is never a time when we are free from all moral and political principles and restraints," there may be extraordinary circumstances when these principles and restraints must be bent or even occasionally broken.[55] The US Constitution itself contemplates significant abridgments of individual liberties during grave national emergencies.[56]

There is an element of pious pragmatism in the current situation. The commitment to an absolute legal ban on torture is qualified by the hope that, *in extremis*, a civic-minded law enforcement officer will resort to torture illegally if this is the only means of safeguarding a society (which values civil liberties). Rather than legislate the possibility of torture and remove the moral hazard from individual investigators, as Dershowitz suggests, torture is declared to be wrong but the individual who does it from a feeling of necessity or in self-defence is released from criminal liability.

However, given concerns (supported by some research)[57] that legislating the use of evil means for good ends seems inevitably to promote evil acts (the unintended negative consequences of "slippage"), the current stand is understandable if not excusable. Democracies do not want to invite the opprobrium associated with any derogation from an absolute ban, nor do they want to take steps that might create a broader-based constituency for the practice.

C. CONCLUSION

We cannot know in advance how we would respond to a ticking bomb situation but Dershowitz, among others, has urged that we consider the options before the emergency is upon us. If new rules, strategies, and tactics to deal effectively and fairly with dangerous new realities are needed, then serious nonpartisan debate on the use of coercive interrogation techniques should inform our decisions. The tendency of civil libertarians to view any discussion of the issue as somehow diminishing or weakening the effect of absolute prohibition

55 Rawls, above note 40 at 572.

56 *Padilla v. Rumsfeld*, 352 F.3d 695 at para. 68 (2d Cir. 2003).

57 Vladimir A. Lefebvre & Jonathan David Farley, "The Torturer's Dilemma: A Theoretical Analysis of the Societal Consequences of Torturing Terrorist Suspects" (2007) 30 Studies in Conflict & Terrorism 635.

and opening the way for a legalized system, only allows entrenched assumptions to go unchallenged. Oliver Wendell Homes believed that free speech facilitated the "correction" of weak ideas.[58] Impartial and scholarly analysis may well serve to strengthen the case for absolute prohibition while rectifying the current situation in which those who support legalization are villified.

There is no empirical evidence to indicate that the peoples of democratic societies place greater value on due process than any potential benefits that might be gained from allowing "unacceptable" practices in extreme circumstances. In fact, two surveys conducted by the British Broadcasting Corporation and the Pew Research Centre[59] indicate that a significant minority of those polled in 2006 supported the use of torture to combat terrorism. Whether, and to what extent these results provide any meaningful indicator of how people might actually react in specific situations is debatable. However, we do have examples in history where idealism and a rigid adherence to the law and individual rights have undermined the capacity of government to exercise effective authority when necessary. Nevertheless, it is all too easy to overreact in times of turmoil in ways that are themselves a threat to the stability of democratic societies. Rights claims must be given a fair hearing, but we must also consider the costs to our society of preserving those rights. Governments have a moral duty to protect *both* the rights of individuals and those of society, and must frame legislation accordingly.

Ultimately, it is a judgment call: it is for the judiciary to assess the evidence in the light of the law, and the law in the light of society's collective right to security and individual rights to equitable justice. Is the conflict between values as described in the abstract indeed tragic, or can a clarification of their actual substance allow us to find a way out of the impasse? The jury is out with respect to the appropriate balance between individual and community rights in an emergency situation; but in the final analysis, it behooves society to decide where the moral line should be drawn before an emergency threatens.

---

58 G. Edward White, "Justice Holmes and the Modernization of Free Speech Jurisprudence: The Human Dimension" (1992) 80 Cal. L. Rev. 391.

59 "Terrorism and Civil Liberty: Is Torture Ever Justified" *The Economist* (20 September 2007). The article refers to a BBC survey of 27,000 people in twenty-five countries in October 2006 that revealed that more than one out of three people in nine of those countries, including America, considered a degree of torture acceptable if it saved lives. Opposition was highest in most European and English-speaking countries. Another poll in 2005 by the Pew Research Centre found that nearly half of all Americans thought the torture of suspected terrorists was sometimes justified.

CHAPTER 11

Torture and Evidence in Criminal Matters

THE HONOURABLE YORICK ALER
JUDGE, COURT OF APPEAL, THE HAGUE, THE NETHERLANDS

The issue of "the use of evidence obtained in countries known to use torture" raises fundamental questions, for example, with regard to the tense relation between the fight against terrorism—or organized crime—and law enforcement, on one hand, and due and fair criminal procedures, on the other. In my opinion, the role of the judiciary in guaranteeing human rights is also at stake, just as the need to preserve the integrity of the judicial process is. As someone who always studied and worked in the field of criminal law I would like to focus on that aspect and would not venture myself in the field of civil law or questions on deportation or extradition and the perspective of Article 3 of the *Convention against Torture* (*CAT*). The formulation of the theme indicates also that we talk about statements of witnesses made under "suspect" circumstances in other countries, that is, countries that are not under the jurisdiction of the prosecuting state. Another starting point for me is that there is no involvement in any way of the latter state in the creation of those suspect circumstances. I won't speak about "real or material" evidence, such as blood, hair, or DNA material, obtained by inhuman treatment.

As far as my own experience is concerned, I have been confronted only once with these problems. In the first Dutch criminal case concerning terrorism, which took place in Rotterdam with the codename *"Eik"*—that means: *Oak*, the file contained a statement of a witness that was taken from him in a certain country in the Middle East under the circumstances referred to above. Needless to say, strong doubts may arise to make use of that statement, even though there is no doubt about its reliability. But what to do if that statement is a crucial element in the chain of evidence? And what if, as a consequence of leaving it out, you have to acquit the accused? That is at last the fundamental decision we are talking about. Fortunately, that dilemma didn't occur in our case. During the criminal procedure the witness was transferred to France and laid down a new statement in which he complained about the harsh treatment he suffered making his statement in the country concerned. Furthermore the defence in our case got the opportunity to question the witness in France and to challenge the statement he made. We had no problem in using that last statement (which was much less detailed than the first one). A point of discussion nevertheless is whether there are problems from the point of view of "fruit of a poisonous tree." Another aspect of the Rotterdam *Oak* case is related to our problem, namely, the possibility that intelligence described before as "suspect" was used in starting the investigations in the Netherlands against this terrorist group.

I will leave for what they are, questions of the burden of proof of torture treatment and the procedural "translation" and consequences of that point, and the question of when one should speak about torture, when ill-treatment has attained the minimum level of severity required to fall within the scope of *CAT*, Article 1(1).

The prohibition of torture is absolute: "No exceptional circumstances whatsoever, whether a state of war or a threat of war, internal political instability or any other public emergency, may be invoked as a justification of torture" (*CAT*, Article 2). I may also quote the European Court of Human Rights (ECHR):

> Even in the most difficult circumstances, such as the fight against terrorism and organised crime, the *Convention* [i.e., *The European Convention on Human Rights* (*ECHR*)] prohibits in absolute terms torture and inhuman or degrading treatment or punishment, irrespective of the victim's conduct [meaning "the victim of torture"]. Unlike most of the substantive clauses of the *Convention*, Article 3 makes no provision for exceptions and no derogation from it is permissible under Article 15 § 2 even in the event of a public emergency threatening the life of the nation.[1]

Article 15 of the *CAT* reads as follows: "Each State Party shall ensure that any statement which is established to have been made as a result of torture shall not be invoked as evidence in any proceedings, except against a person accused of torture as evidence that the statement was made." According to this article, the question of the use of statements obtained by torture seems simple

1 *Jalloh v. Germany*, no. 54810/00, [2007] 44 E.H.R.R. 32 at para. 99 [citations omitted].

to answer. It is very difficult for me to imagine the situation in which the use of any evidence in the form of a statement obtained by torture or other cruel or degrading treatment could be acceptable. Nevertheless from that starting point I would like to add the following observations. In my opinion the real problem may not be the use of the tainted statement itself but the use of new evidence—statements or "real" evidence—that is obtained by that route.

The use of a forced confession or statement by the suspect is—given the presumption of innocence—(also) incompatible with the right to remain silent and not to incriminate oneself. Moreover the European Court and our own Dutch Supreme Court make perfectly clear that the use of a statement of the defendant under coercion or oppression is also incompatible with a fair procedure under *ECHR*, Article 6, or the *International Covenant on Civil and Political Rights*, Article 14, since we are talking about a generally recognized international standard. Taking into account the fundamental, absolute, and non-derogable character of the right that is at stake, I couldn't imagine that distinction could be made between statements made under torture in the country that is prosecuting and third countries. Under all circumstances this use is prohibited.

Is there any reason to come to another conclusion in the situation in which the statement of a witness is concerned? Could that statement be used as evidence despite the fact that it was obtained by torture? Let's go back to my *Oak* case. Apart from *CAT*, Article 15—is it acceptable that a coerced statement obtained from any country, for example in the Middle East, without any involvement of Dutch authorities, is used as proof in a Dutch court? I was unable to find arguments strong enough to accept that, taking into account the—in my view—overwhelming arguments making clear that that use should not be accepted. I mention shortly and in a quite arbitrary sequence:

- The character of the prohibition, which could be said to enshrine "one of the fundamental values of the democratic societies of the Council of Europe." I already quoted the ECHR in *Jalloh*. Should there be distinction between that treatment of the suspect or of a witness, or between torture and other forms of cruel or inhuman treatment?
- A second aspect concerns the reliability of the statement and the (lack of) possibility to question and challenge the witness, especially when he or she remains in the foreign third country where that statement was made. In my opinion it is in this respect quite irrelevant that the prosecution also is unable to do so.

In my opinion there are also aspects of integrity of government and the administration of justice involved:

- When the prohibition of torture enjoys the highest normative force recognized by international law and States should suppress and discourage the practice of torture or other cruel, inhuman, or degrading treatment or punishment, could these same States use the (direct) fruits of torture for evidence?
- *CAT,* Article 4, demands that States ensure that all acts of torture are criminal offences, "punishable by appropriate penalties which take into account their grave nature." This implicates that the individual officer who commits this crime—as "an enemy of all mankind"—is punishable. It is also a crime for which secondary universal jurisdiction should be established, as Article 5(2) states, including the obligation of a State to prosecute if it does not extradite, according to "*aut dedere aut punire.*" What to think about the State that, on the one hand, tries the perpetrator of torture who is present in a territory under its jurisdiction and, on the other hand, uses the statement obtained by that torture in another procedure and thus implicitly authorizes torture? Moreover, that would give problems in relation to the obligations of *CAT,* Article 2.

I realize that a foreign State will not be very impressed by the exclusion by the judiciary of another State of statements made in their country, but our primary interest is to preserve the integrity of the judicial process in our own country.

Finally, I'd like to make some observations on the fruits of the poisonous tree. I'd like to stress that these observations are strictly personal and that my thinking on this subject raised more questions than I could answer.

Imagine the situation wherein the police receive information that terrorists are preparing an attack and have a cache of weapons in a specific location. Would it be acceptable if the police refrained from taking any action as this information has most probably been obtained by torture? I would expect no one to say: So let it be. In my opinion, the terrorists can't complain successfully that the action against them started on an illegal footing, providing that the police—acting as we expect—were in no way involved in the torture itself. If and when the terrorists were to be prosecuted for the possession of the weapons that were actually found, should the exclusionary rule find application? I don't think so.

What, however, would be the opinion if it was by torture of the defendant that the information had been obtained and substantiated? Or the case that he or one of his accomplices was subjected to torture or to the use of psychopharmacologic means by our own security services, and mentioned the place where the ticking bomb was waiting? Can or should we then make a distinction between the victim of torture and other perpetrators in answering the question on the legitimacy of a criminal prosecution on the basis of the fruits of that action in the form of "real" evidence? And what about the arrest of the co-conspirators named after torture? Isn't there a limit where we should say: we understand and accept the use of strong violence under these circumstances, but we can't use the fruits of that violence as evidence in a criminal procedure, and we as a society should accept that too.

In concluding I quote some—thought-stimulating—considerations on that subject by Lord Hoffmann:

> As for the rule that we do not necessarily exclude the "fruit of the poisoned tree," but admit relevant evidence discovered in consequence of inadmissible confessions, this is the way we strike a necessary balance between preserving the integrity of the judicial process and the public interest in convicting the guilty. And even when the evidence has been obtained by torture—the accomplice's statement has led to the bomb being found under the bed of the accused—that evidence may be so compelling and so independent that it does not carry enough of the smell of the torture chamber to require its exclusion. But that is not the question in this case. We are concerned with the admissibility of the raw product of interrogation under torture.[2]

The criterion "is the evidence carrying enough of the smell of the torture chamber?" is appealing, although I'm afraid to admit that my nose becomes rather sensitive in such cases.

Technically, the *Dutch Code of Criminal Procedure*, Article 359a, provides for the consequences in the case that a criminal investigation is not conducted properly. As one of the consequences, the obtained material could be excluded from evidence, for example, because of the illegal search of a house or of the luggage of a person. Having said that, you will not be surprised that such consequence is usually reserved for the situation where the suspect was the victim of the illegal action and the omission took place in the course of the criminal investigation for which he is prosecuted. Illegal actions of third parties are generally not relevant as long as the police or the prosecution service is not in any respect involved in such action. Then there has been no "public interference."

From this point of view there is little reason to worry about questionable evidence, provided the rights of the accused himself were not violated.

I hesitate to accept this solution as "it is just like that." After all: other interests than those of the suspect are also at stake. In my opinion we should also consider the role of the judiciary in guaranteeing human rights, for example,

2 *A and others v. Secretary of State for the Home Department*, [2005] UKHL 71 at para. 88.

in the perspective of the provisions of the *CAT*, and the need to maintain the integrity of the judicial system. The fundamental character of the prohibition of torture might impel a court to leave the fruits out of consideration, just to avoid infection or contamination of the integrity of the judicial procedure. In that respect one could possibly learn from the *Rome Statute of the International Criminal Court*, Article 69(7). According to that paragraph, not only is evidence inadmissible that is obtained by means of a violation of the *Statute* or internationally recognized human rights, if the violation casts substantial doubt on the reliability of that evidence, but also if "the admission of the evidence would be antithetical to and would seriously damage the integrity of the proceedings."

So I think we should find a balance that, on the one hand, takes into account the fundamental character of the prohibition and the obligation of States and their organs to suppress and discourage the practice of torture, and, on the other hand, has an adequate eye for the importance of law enforcement and the fight against terrorism and the repression of serious criminal offences. Finding that balance is so complicated that I realize, once again, one of the most attractive aspects of reaching a judicial decision is that one does it in concert with one's colleagues.

By taking up the position that under strict, codified conditions, torture should be legalized, Professor Gendron incited an interesting discussion.[3] If I understand her correctly, her point of view is based on the assumption that protection of societies' interests and counter-terrorism require so and justify these measures. In reaction thereupon the following:

As a judge, I was raised with Montesquieu's famous words that a judge is nothing more than an interpreter of the law: "*ni que la bouche de la loi.*" According to these words and, for that matter, also according to my own legislation, I am not allowed to judge upon the intrinsic moral values of the law. Having said so, I have to get off my chest that I am not at all enthusiastic about Professor Gendron's proposal.

As I mentioned earlier: the prohibition of torture is absolute. The ban of torture represents a fundamental moral value in democratic societies, and the conventions, such as the *CAT*, leave no room whatsoever for exceptions, not even under circumstances that constitute a direct threat to the continuation of a state. Furthermore, governments have, according to that convention, the obligation to penalize torture in a way in which the seriousness of this offence

3 Angela Gendron, "Adjudicating National Security: Ethics, Counter-Terrorism and the Administration of Justice" (Address to the International Conference on the Administration of Justice and National Security in Democracies, Ottawa, 12 June 2007); see Chapter 10.

is expressed. Do we really want to set aside the *CAT* in order to legalize torture? And is legalization of torture the only way to take into account the interest of protection of society and counter-terrorism?

In my opinion we have to bear in mind that executive authorities, such as the police and national security services, tend to seek the limits set by the law for their competencies in carrying out their duties. Legalizing torture implies a serious loss of grip on these authorities and services. How could we ever say: "You, torturer, have crossed the limits of your competencies (as set out by society and legislator) and you will now have to face a severe punishment for your actions." That doesn't seem like an attractive perspective: not to the authority concerned, nor to the human rights situation in the country involved.

I think it would be better if we would acknowledge and reluctantly accept that there are exceptional situations in which we will not be able to uphold the absolute prohibition of torture, although we should. In such a situation, or "case of emergency," the exclusionary rule of *CAT*, Article 15, should be fully applied. However, the torturer who is being prosecuted could be absolved from criminal liability on the ground that his actions were excusable by the extreme situation in which they were committed. I acknowledge: the officer torturing in such an alleged situation of emergency does run a risk of being prosecuted. But is it not a consequence of being an officer of police or of a national security service that he should accept that society keeps a close watch on his acts and if those acts can pass muster? *Quis custodiet ipsos custodes*?

I recollect, in conclusion, something that my old teacher in criminal law, Enschedé, once said to me: he who wants to lay down in legislation anything in the field of criminal competences that is justifiable, creates so many abstract rules—that (possibly) will be interpreted too broadly—that this eventually will suffocate the rule of law.

CHAPTER 12

Deportations with Assurances: A United Kingdom Court's Perspective

THE HONOURABLE SIR DUNCAN OUSELEY
CHAIR, SPECIAL IMMIGRATION APPEALS COMMISSION, UNITED KINGDOM

A. INTRODUCTION

International conventions and the constitutional provisions of various countries forbid the removal of foreign nationals to their country of nationality if there they would face torture or cruel, inhuman, or degrading treatment.

Under the *European Convention on Human Rights* (*ECHR*), which is the relevant international convention binding the United Kingdom and enforceable at the suit of individuals, removal is now forbidden if there are substantial grounds for believing that there is a real risk that the individual would face torture or cruel, inhuman, or degrading treatment. There is, however, no express provision in the *ECHR* to that effect. The European Court of Human Rights, in what to me was the judicial arrogation of a power truly belonging to the legislature or to the treaty-making powers of the executive, decided that certain Articles of the *ECHR* should be read as imposing indirect responsibility on the removing country for acts done in the country of nationality. It ruled, and has recently upheld its earlier 1996 decision in *Chahal v. UK* to the same effect, that, in imposing such indirect responsibility, no account is to be taken of any risk, however severe, which the individual may pose to the human rights or well-being of those living in the country on which he may have chosen to impose himself, even if deliberately to harm it.

Those foreign nationals who pose the major current threat to national security are extremist Islamists mostly from North Africa and the Middle East. Such individuals have posed and in many of their countries continue to pose threats to the stability and future of national regimes. In such countries and for such individuals, the use of torture is or has been commonplace whether to obtain confessions, incriminating statements, intelligence, or even for punishment, notwithstanding that those countries are party to international conventions or have domestic legislation that prohibits such treatment. An Islamist extremist deported to those countries would often be at a real risk of a breach of his human rights and so his removal would be prohibited, absent other factors.

After 9/11, the UK government examined the prospect of seeking specific bilateral agreements with countries to which it hoped to return at least some such foreign nationals. These agreements would control how those returned would be treated.

Attempts to reach agreement with Egypt had failed, but the London bombings of July 2005 provided a real impetus to the UK government's endeavours to deport foreign nationals who were a threat to national security. Nationals of Algeria and Jordan were arrested with a view to their deportation as the negotiating process was under way. Later that year, Libyan nationals were likewise arrested.

Their appeals against deportation were heard by the Special Immigration Appeals Commission (SIAC), which I then chaired.

There were almost always two separate but not unrelated issues: Did the individual pose a threat to national security? Would that individual be at risk of torture on return? The SIAC heard some evidence on both those issues in the absence of the individual and his legal advisers, but with Special Advocates present to represent his interests and to question witnesses. This process was not devised to limit the availability to the individual or court of evidence that had hitherto been openly available, but to permit judicial decision-making in an area that had hitherto been the exclusive preserve of the executive—but without depriving the executive of the opportunity of relying on relevant material, open disclosure of which could not properly be expected.

In addition to "closed" evidence about the national security case, "closed" evidence about the diplomatic and political background was very useful and in each case has reinforced the conclusion we came to. In fact there is usually nothing which the individual could add in relation to such closed material anyway because this fuller and frank material would be beyond his knowledge.

B. ALGERIA

The upshot of the negotiations was an Exchange of Letters between the UK and Algerian governments that contained very general provisions about the way in which those deported would be treated. The UK government said that

Algeria at the highest level had undertaken to safeguard the well-being of those deported. This general assurance would be supplemented in each individual case with information or assurances tailored to that individual, depending on whether he had been convicted of offences there or would face charges on return. The UK government did not obtain any agreement for NGO or diplomatic monitoring of those who were to be detained or tried on return. There was instead a diplomatic contact point, with the British Embassy in Algiers, for the individual and the immediate family of those returned and not detained on arrival, and in practice used by the immediate family of those returned and detained. There was an oral assurance from the President that no person returned from the UK would be executed if convicted on a capital charge.

Y, the first Algerian case dealt with by the SIAC, had been convicted twice *in absentia*, and sentenced to death and to life imprisonment on terrorist-related charges. He would normally face a retrial on return if he appealed against his earlier conviction. Assurances were given as to certain trial processes, that his human dignity would be respected, and in less clear terms, that he could benefit from an amnesty. SIAC later concluded, after an appeal against its first decision was allowed in relation to the applicability of an amnesty provision, that his trial would not be so unfair as to preclude removal and that he would not be tortured in custody.

A number of Algerian appeals have now been heard and the SIAC has concluded that the appellants can be returned safely, even where they will face trial on serious charges. The later cases have had the benefit of practical experience of the way in which the Algerians treated four men who returned, having abandoned their appeals, three with the benefit of assurances given to the UK.

Powerfully influential in these decisions were the political changes in Algeria: the ending of the civil war, the reduction in violence and torture, the process of an amnesty that had led to the release of 2,000 Islamists, including some regarded as very serious terrorists. Also, the growing diplomatic, intelligence, commercial, and legal ties between Algeria and the UK provided incentives for it to adhere to rather than breach the assurances and to do so to develop relations with European countries other than France. These factors were all objectively supportive of the genuineness and effectiveness of the assurances.

C. JORDAN

The main Jordanian case concerned the notorious Abu Qatada, also known as Othman. The UK government negotiated a Memorandum of Understanding with the Jordanian government, and terms of reference for monitoring by an identified monitoring body which agreed to undertake the task. It is not a well known NGO; the better known NGOs refused to participate in the process. But it is being trained and supported with assistance from the UK government. The Memorandum of Understanding provides for the UK and Jordan to comply with international human rights obligations and covers certain aspects of trial and detention. There is a side letter that deals with the death penalty, without being an explicit exclusion of it, but the general attitude towards its use in a UK deportation case was made clear at a high level.

Othman had been convicted in his absence on serious but not capital terrorist offences. He would be retried and probably convicted again and would probably spend a long time in prison. We rejected the contention that he risked being rendered to the United States of America or into its hands. The case of Arar was considered. We concluded that he did not face a real risk of being charged with a capital offence or of execution were he to be convicted of one, although there were still executions in Jordan.

Once again, the issue of safety on return did not turn simply on the existence and terms of the Memorandum of Understanding. The situation in Jordan differed from that in Algeria: it remained the case that torture of Islamists, especially of those facing charges, was commonplace and unlike in Algeria there had not been a significant reduction in the level of incidents. There had not been a recent political change of real significance to bring that about. There was no program of reconciliation with those who, as Islamists, regarded the Jordanian regime as un-Islamic and to be overthrown.

It was agreed by Othman's own expert that, even without the Memorandum of Understanding, this particular individual would not face a real risk of torture in the period up to the conclusion of his retrial. There were two reasons for this: he was a well-known figure and his return, court appearances, and retrial would be followed closely by the media and by his numerous supporters, whether because of his Islamist views or simply because he was seen as standing up to the West. He was also a Palestinian from the West Bank, and that gave him a further group of supporters whom those in authority would not wish to inflame. The authorities' desire for stability would ensure that it remained in their interest to avoid allegations that Othman had been tortured. We accepted that analysis. There were also other institutions that would enable his position to be raised publicly: there was a degree of press freedom, a degree of freedom of assembly for those critical of the government, and a Parliament that was not wholly toothless. We also considered that there were no real risks of torture after this early, if quite lengthy, period was over.

But we also took the view that that was reinforced by the Memorandum of Understanding and the monitoring body: the obligations of the Memorandum of Understanding ran in harmony with the self-interest of the Jordanian regime. The very good long-standing relations between the UK and Jordan, their range and depth over the years, provided for a relationship in which the Jordanians would actively seek to comply with their new bilateral obligations, and the range of relationships gave the UK leverage in a variety of ways if there were concern about the treatment of Othman.

We heard a great deal of evidence about how Othman's retrial would be conducted before the State Security Court, which for a number of reasons could not be considered an independent court. There were assurances about detention, access to lawyers, prompt determination of the legality of detention, time for preparation for trial; these were general, rather than specific to Othman, and were supplemented by a very general provision about a fair and public trial before an independent judiciary. In the end the question of the fairness of the trial and the degree to which any unfairness might preclude deportation in the light of the inchoate jurisprudence of the European Court of Human Rights became the main focus of the case. We concluded that the deficiencies in the fairness of the trial would not be so severe as to prevent removal.

This decision was appealed by Othman, to the Court of Appeal, which allowed his appeal and said that he could not be deported, despite the grave threat he posed, because he would not receive a fair trial in Jordan. This was because of the prospect that evidence that might have been obtained by torture would be admitted against him. The Supreme Court allowed the government's appeal and restored the decision of SIAC. The case is now being appealed by Othman to the European Court of Human Rights.

D. LIBYA

There have been two cases involving the deportation of Libyans who posed a risk to national security. We allowed their appeals and that conclusion was upheld on appeal to the Court of Appeal.

Again there was a Memorandum of Understanding, and a monitoring arrangement. On paper, there was nothing to prevent return. The two would probably face serious terrorist charges on return and could face capital charges. We concluded that the monitoring body, the Qadhafi Development Foundation headed by one of Colonel Qadhafi's sons, would not be independent and at the times when needed most, would ally itself most strongly with the Libyan government. Indeed, the UK case put very little weight on its role.

We accepted that the Libyan assurances had been given in good faith, and that there had been a very significant change in outlook in the Libyan regime including Colonel Qadhafi and the senior regime officials or inner circle, towards the West, that it had renounced terrorism, that it had cooperated in the removal of weapons of mass destruction, and that it had proved itself now to be trustworthy. There was clearly a much better diplomatic relationship between the UK and Libya, and there were burgeoning commercial and other ties that reflected that change. The UK government contended that the regime was pragmatic and had changed its stance toward the West because pragmatically it needed investment to survive, which could only come from the West and it would not jeopardize that by breaching the Memorandum of Understanding. The Libyan government saw itself as threatened by the same Islamist activities as did the West and thus as a partner in counter-terror and intelligence. There had, however, been no domestic changes that altered the views of the regime about Islamist extremists and the threat that they posed to its survival.

The issue in the end came down to whether the word of Colonel Qadhafi and his inner circle by itself, given in good faith, would be effective enough in the range of circumstances that could present themselves to prevent a real risk of torture or ill-treatment arising. The UK government's evidence included that of a former ambassador to Libya who said that it was "well-nigh unthinkable" that the Libyan government would breach its assurances. We felt unable to accept that view; although we recognized his expertise, we were not obliged to defer to it.

We concluded that although it was probable that there would be no ill-treatment, there remained a real risk of ill-treatment for someone in detention for so long, awaiting trial, being tried, and in prison after conviction. Although there were incentives to comply, the absence of an effective monitoring system meant that breaches would not be deterred or detected. There were no other institutions of Parliament, freedoms of expression or assembly, political parties, trade unions, media, even population groups with distinct voices whose support or quiescence Colonel Qadhafi would be keen to obtain by obviously avoiding ill-treatment.

We undertook the same process as with Algeria and Jordan, of considering the political background in the country, the terms of the agreement, means of monitoring adherence to it, the diplomatic and other ties that underpinned the arrangements and encouraged compliance, but here we were not satisfied that the real risk of severe ill-treatment had been eliminated. We also thought that any trial would be a flagrant denial of fair trial rights.

E. GENERAL THEMES

I propose now to draw some general themes together, conscious that I have referred only to the UK experience, although there are other circumstances in which deportation with assurances has been tried.

One conclusion the Special Immigration Appeals Commission came to strongly in considering other instances cited to it where there had been breaches of assurances given only to individuals rather than to governments, or given only at a middle-ranking governmental or official level, or given where there had been no particular previous diplomatic contact, is that the judicial role in deciding whether the degree of risk would breach international obligations was vital.

This role enabled issues to be raised, and tested. This itself had an effect on the scope of assurances given and their verification. It prevented the assessment of the political or diplomatic background being simply the government's view, rather than a judicial assessment. It tested the experience of other removals. It is right that the assessment, in a system governed by the rule of law, of whether an act would breach the *ECHR* is made by judges.

1) Parties to the Assurances

I start with the parties to any assurance. Those that we have considered involve assurances to the UK government, rather than to the individual. This is important because it gives the UK government a role and standing to concern itself in the way in which the country of return treats its own national. It would not otherwise have that ability and there are examples of even friendly nations being rebuffed when they have tried to intervene in cases of concern about dual nationals. There are also examples of assurances, in instances cited to SIAC, said to have been given to individuals that were deniable or that lacked any teeth for enforcement.

The assurances in the cases decided by SIAC had been given or plainly endorsed at the highest level by the governments in question, giving the assurance in a political and diplomatic process that they have been persuaded to engage in, knowing in each case that it would be the subject of judicial scrutiny and comment. In each case, the arrangements were also accepted by the security services of the country. Assurances by a diplomat, a high-ranking security officer, or a medium-ranking minster may cause concern about whether they reflect the will of the true powers in the land. Those are important considerations when dealing with countries of variable stability or where the power lines may be unclear or deniable. I would add consideration of the manner of negotiation is useful as well in judging what matters to the country of return.

2) Scope of Assurances

Assurances about torture cannot be wholly separated from consideration of the lawfulness of detention before, during, and after trial (*ECHR*, Article 5) or from issues of fairness of trial (*ECHR*, Article 6). This came across to us very strongly in all cases we heard. There is a strong interrelationship.

Detention pre-trial—where, duration, access to lawyers, family and judge—impacts on the prospects of ill-treatment, as well as on Article 5. The location itself of some detention may make torture more or less likely and has been the subject of assurances (whether that it would not be security detention or would not involve a particular prison). The physical conditions of detention, post-conviction imprisonment, and the death-row phenomenon can create breaches of *ECHR*, Article 3. The way in which allegations that a confession was obtained by torture are considered by a trial court goes to the fairness of a trial, but it also affects the risk of the use of torture to obtain it.

So the apparently more straightforward issue of assurances that an individual will not be tortured links to problems concerning the way in which a trial will be conducted. That is a more difficult topic for assurances because the usual national court of trial, applying its usual rules and governed by its usual outlook is less readily changed, if it can be affected at all, by assurances. Assurances over where someone is to be detained are quite different in effect or visibility from assurances over judicial independence or how the admissibility of evidence allegedly obtained by torture will be judged.

3) Text

It is clear that the political background and diplomatic relationship and other ties with the receiving country and the assessment of each country's interests are very necessary parts of the evaluation of the effectiveness of assurances. It is very far from a simple examination of the textual adequacy of the agreement.

The text of the assurances can be of importance, however, because on occasions there may be a precise adherence to the terms and no more; and there are other areas where the text may be less explicit for certain reasons, about the real intent of the assurance.

1. Death penalty assurances may be given essentially informally but at a high political level: explicit formal assurances may be seen as infringing the constitutional functions of the judiciary or trespassing on Presidential, Royal, or other institutional prerogatives. Political or diplomatic assessment and judicial decision is then called for, but in all the SIAC cases the outcome was clear. Algeria in fact did not execute terrorists; in Jordan

the death penalty for Othman would have occasioned a major outcry and there was no prospect of a capital charge; in Libya, execution was unlikely but it was less clear how long any commutation would take and the death row phenomenon was one aspect of our ill-treatment concerns.

2. Assurances that run counter to the applicable law of the country of return have not been accepted or relied on. This is particularly significant in relation to fair trial assurances.
3. Assurances about how a trial would be conducted, usually couched in reassuring, bland generalities have been unpersuasive where they conflict with what is in evidence about the actual trial procedures.
4. There have been debates about how valuable language such as "respecting human dignity" or "in conformity with internationally recognised standards" is as a prohibition on torture. States have been unwilling to accept a specific reference to torture because that could be seen as an acknowledgment of a practice of torture that they deny. But the political context has been clear: states have known what the purpose of the assurances was in relation to *ECHR*, Article 3, and that that would be scrutinized by SIAC. They have known what it was about.
5. More problematic could be the debate over what acts were permissible within "internationally recognized standards"—stress and duress, or sensory deprivation could be debatable areas. We took the view in Othman, in which this issue was most pressed, that it would have been extremely undesirable to have had any explicit delineation of precisely what or for how long was prohibited, which would have been taken as permitting anything not excluded. Rather we took the view that in that particular political context but it would be true of Algeria and Libya too, the clear obligation of the receiving country was seen by it as "hands off, no quibbles."
6. But we do not rely on any assurances unless they were contained the open material. This avoids issues of deniability.

4) Verification and Monitoring

Monitoring or other means of verification of compliance with the assurances has three principal purposes: first, to deter breaches and to encourage compliance particularly among lower-ranking officials possibly acting against instructions; second, to enable diplomatic measures to be taken swiftly to prevent a situation developing in which a breach may take place but has not yet occurred; and, third, to enable sanctions to be brought to bear if necessary. But that would represent a failure of the assurances.

In the absence of some effective system of verification as to whether someone is in detention, and if so where, and in what conditions, the sending state would be wholly dependent on the word of the receiving state. We have accepted that compliance with assurances for visits to those in detention, by lawyers and family members who can report to an identified person in the British Embassy, UK, and NGOs on what they see and are told, can be sufficient verification of those matters. This was the position in Algeria where no specific monitoring was agreed.

We declined to accept as adequate monitoring by a body, the Qadhafi Development Foundation, which was closely allied to and would share, at difficult times, the same interest as the Libyan regime.

On the whole, countries of return have been reluctant to accept foreign diplomatic monitoring as too intrusive on sovereign sensitivities, and that sort of monitoring failed Agiza because of diplomatic sensitivities by Sweden toward Egypt. Some countries are reluctant to accept international NGO access, or access by such bodies to specific security police prisons, which is where the greater risks arise, for similar reasons.

But major NGOs have also refused, as a matter of principle, to be involved in this process, because they dislike deportation with assurances as a matter of principle. So monitoring and verification systems have proved to be difficult, perhaps unexpectedly difficult.

However such verification systems, though with flexibility over form and varying with the risks being run, have reinforced our conclusions about the genuineness of the receiving state's intentions, its political commitment and the direction of any political changes.

We recognize that a verification process can be subverted for example by last-minute changes in place of detention, or by saying that the person in question does not wish to see the monitor—but those acts would obviously be reported to the sending state and should trigger rapid diplomatic intervention. A deported person may refuse to discuss treatment, perhaps for fear of further ill-treatment or reprisal, and we recognize that some torture can be difficult to detect. The monitors, therefore, need to be aware of the risk and trained to detect its signs, in order to report to the UK, or both governments.

However, it is because there are problems that can arise and create risks in that way, that assurances and an agreement for monitoring by itself may not be enough for lawful deportation. Monitoring or verification needs to be judged in the context of the receiving state's political intentions developed over time, its institutional capability to adhere to the assurances, and its desire to avoid a breach or accusation of a breach of diplomatic promises specifically given to a friendly power. All of these issues therefore interlock in satisfying a court about the degree of risk which a deportee would run.

5) Principle

A number of objections in principle are commonly made to the use of assurances in deportations to countries where there would otherwise be a real risk of torture or cruel, inhuman or degrading treatment:

1. International law prohibits torture absolutely; that means that it is never justified, and never excused. But that is very different from saying that absolutely no risk must be taken that a person on return might be tortured. The European Court of Human Rights requires only that there be no real risk of torture; removal is forbidden only if serious or substantial grounds are demonstrated for believing that a person would be tortured on return. That legal test is very important. A mere possibility that someone would be tortured is not sufficient to prevent his removal. International law does not prohibit removal in those circumstances. As SIAC and the European Court of Human Rights have held, the proper application of international law requires a court to reach a fact-sensitive conclusion about the real degree of risk that would be run and about the effectiveness of assurances in reducing that degree of risk to a level low enough to permit return. The fact that, in the absence of such an assurance, a real risk might exist cannot dictate a conclusion that the assurance is inevitably irrelevant in law or ineffective in fact. An objection in principle to deportation in such circumstances such as is voiced by some NGOs and United Nations representatives is an invitation to disregard the law.
2. A second objection in principle is that a system of seeking assurances for individuals from states which will continue to torture those without such assurances leads to double standards and undermines endeavours to enforce international conventions to which those states are already parties. But this objection too would be an invitation to disregard the law, if an assurance would be sufficiently effective. And if it leads to double standards, that implicitly concedes a degree of effectiveness for such assurances. For my part in any event, I cannot see why assurances, monitored and adhered to, would not play their part instead in raising human rights standards and reducing abuses.

   Rather more directly effective would be assistance in the development of police investigatory techniques that enabled such states to advance more rapidly from overreliance on confessions, which is a significant cause of the incidence of torture, or recording interrogations.
3. It is often asked why a state that is acknowledged routinely to breach international conventions on torture to which it is a party should be

thought likely to adhere to what is often seen, slightingly, as a mere bilateral legally unenforceable agreement. It is, of course, true that these Memorandums of Understanding or Exchanges of Letters are not enforceable domestically or in any international court, although I remain largely skeptical of any advantage claimed for the legal enforceability of international conventions. But diplomatic agreements do carry their own legal status; they have significance in the eyes of the two states and in the views of other states with which the assuring state may have diplomatic, commercial, and other ties.

It is in the bilateral nature of the specifically negotiated assurances that their strength lies. Of course, much depends on the domestic political background in the country of return, its security and legal structures, and its motivation for entering into the assurances. But what the bilateral assurances add is this:

a. the specific interest of the deporting state in the well-being of the individual, and a specific role, directly or indirectly, sometimes only implicitly, to interest itself in what happens to him; and
b. the risk of some sanction—diplomatic, military, intelligence, commercial, aid, or other aspect of the relationship—being placed on the relationship as a result of a breach.

That can add considerably to the potential effectiveness of a bilateral assurance over a multilateral international convention. The degree to which it adds depends on a number of factors coming together—the degree of political commitment on both sides, the diplomatic background, a willingness, with incentives, to adhere to assurances without sanctions and to enforce adherence down the line, the willingness of the removing state to impose sanctions perhaps to its own detriment, and on its ability, of course, to discover or deter breaches.

4. We considered whether the UK had any real interest in pursuing the well-being of those it had deported as a threat to its own national security. We concluded that it did. An aspect to which we gave some weight was that the UK government did give evidence of pursuing human rights concerns contrary to its more immediate interests. More importantly, deportation of foreigners who threatened national security to North Africa and Middle East states is an important part of the UK government strategy for dealing with the Islamist terrorist threat; it is a high-profile policy. Any significant breach of an assurance by a receiving state would be a real problem for the UK government in dealing with appeals to SIAC. Indeed, any Western state with an interest in de-

porting Islamists would have an interest in keeping the receiving state to its bilateral assurances to the UK; for example, the breach of assurance by Egypt to Sweden in the case of Agiza would create significant difficulties for any deportation to Egypt, and had to be considered in UK deportations anyway.

F. CONCLUSION

Deportation of foreign nationals who threaten it is a legitimate part of a State's right to protect itself and its citizens. If the exercise of that right is inhibited in order to protect the deportees' human rights, taking further measures that then enable the lawful deportation of such individuals is likewise legitimate. It is for the courts to judge whether the measures proposed are effective enough to that end.

PART FIVE

NATIONAL SECURITY OVERSIGHT AND REVIEW

CHAPTER 13

Tests of Maturity: An Australian Perspective

IAN CARNELL
INSPECTOR-GENERAL OF INTELLIGENCE AND SECURITY, AUSTRALIA

A. INTRODUCTION

The attacks of 11 September 2001 in New York and Washington, DC, thrust counter-terrorism onto the centre stage of public and parliamentary debate and government activity in Australia. Further incidents, such as the attacks in Bali in October 2002, Madrid in March 2004, London in July 2005, and Bali in October 2005 ensured continuing prominence of the issue.

By 2006 the Australian government had responded by committing over $8.3 billion in additional funding to security agencies and functions; new and revamped security arrangements ranging across prevention, preparedness, response and recovery; as well as over thirty pieces of legislation.[1] Yet there were, and remain, a number of sharp controversies.

Among the controversial issues are: the introduction of new criminal offences, including "preventative" offences; the balance between the powers of security agencies and individual liberties, including the adequacy of protections and safeguards around those powers; the willingness or otherwise of government to revisit and if necessary rebalance these matters; the ability of courts to deal with counter-terrorism cases, including the protection of classified information and the admissibility of certain material; the separation of

1 Australian Government, *Protecting Australia Against Terrorism 2006: Australia's National Counter-terrorism Policy and Arrangements* (Canberra: Department of Prime Minister and Cabinet, 2006).

power between the executive and the judiciary; and, both the use of, and behaviour by, parts of the media.

In this paper my intention is to give a satellite view of this Australian experience (up to 31 March 2008), with particular reference to legislative reviews and other activities in which I have had some involvement.[2]

B. ENVIRONMENT

To understand the concerted attention paid to counter-terrorism in Australia after 11 September 2001 it needs to be appreciated that up until that point (to the extent that it was in public consciousness), the general sense was that terrorism or politically motivated violence was not directed toward Australia itself.

Although there had previously been isolated instances of politically motivated violence in Australia, these were toward the interests of foreign governments or entities within Australia. For example, in February 1978 a bomb exploded in a garbage bin outside a hotel in Sydney where delegates to a Commonwealth Heads of Government Regional Meeting were staying, with three people being killed and six injured. On 6 April 1992 several Mujahideen e-Khalq supporters vandalized the Iranian Embassy in Canberra and assaulted embassy officials. In February 1999 sixty-five pro–Kurdistan Workers Party protesters occupied the Greek Consulate-General in Sydney, protesting the arrest of Kurdish leader Abdullah Ocalan.

Following the events in the United States of America and Bali, there was a sharp public realization that Australia, Australians, and Australian interests were themselves targets. Since 2001, public statements by al-Qa'ida's leaders and other terrorists have singled out Australia for criticism and encouraged attacks on it. Australia is identified as part of the West and as such, an enemy. There have also been references to Australia's alliance with the United States, its regional and global counter-terrorism efforts, and its military commitments in East Timor, Afghanistan, and Iraq.

These events were also for many Australians a jolt about the methods that could be employed by those willing to resort to politically motivated violence. The terrorist threat was now seen as primarily one of a deliberately indiscriminate, catastrophic incident occurring without warning. This is to be contrasted

2 I have been the Inspector-General of Intelligence and Security since March 2004, an independent statutory position that reviews the legality and propriety of the activities of the six intelligence and security agencies. Formal inquiries (with coercive powers and associated protections) are conducted, including of the Inspector-General's own motion, as well as numerous inspections of agency records (i.e., compliance audits).

with there being a negotiation to achieve certain political objectives (for example, by people hijacking a plane or occupying an embassy), making demands in return for the release of hostages, and often largely happy to have drawn attention to their cause.

C. NEW CRIMINAL OFFENCES

One of the key government responses was the enactment into the Commonwealth *Criminal Code* of new offences that would prohibit certain organizations and conduct of particular kinds.

Committing a terrorist act was one of these new offences. Notably, there were also new offences introduced in relation to what were called "preliminary acts," that is, planning or preparation; providing or receiving training; collecting or making documents likely to facilitate terrorism; providing or collecting funds; and, possessing things connected with a terrorist act.[3] These all carried high potential penalties.

The policy view behind these changes was that there must be a strong emphasis on the prevention of a terrorist incident. The argument was that it was no longer enough to be focused on responding to an incident when or as it occurred—the consequences could be too great.

In the same vein a number of "organizational" offences were also enacted. These covered the conduct of directing the activities of a terrorist organization; membership of an organization; recruiting to join a terrorist organization; providing or receiving training to or from a terrorist organization; receiving from or making funds available to a terrorist organization; supporting or resourcing a terrorist organization; and, associating with a terrorist organization.[4]

While this emphasis on prevention is understandable, it does not sit entirely comfortably with established Australian legal traditions. There are now a significant number of cases before the Australian courts that may indicate how comfortable that fit is.[5]

---

3 *Criminal Code Act 1995* (Cth.) [*Criminal Code*], Schedule — the *Criminal Code*, chapter 5, Part 5.3, Division 101.

4 *Ibid.*, Division 102.

5 In addition to the cases in this article, Mr. Belal Khazaal has pleaded not guilty in the New South Wales Supreme Court to charges of making a document *(ibid.*, s. 101.5) and incitement (*ibid.*, ss. 11.4 and 101.1). Nine other people in New South Wales have been committed on charges of conspiring in preparation (*ibid.*, ss. 11.5 and 101.6). Thirteen people in Victoria have been committed on charges of being members of a terrorist organization and various others of the new offences. Two others in Victoria have been

Notably, there are two potential overlays as to how some of these cases may unfold. The first is a belief by some in the Australian Federal Police (AFP) that "we were directed, we were informed to lay as many charges under the new terrorist legislation against as many suspects as possible because we wanted to use the new legislation."[6] The second is a phenomenon suggested by the current Attorney General of "a degree of judicial blowback" sparked by suspicions about such a politicized area.[7]

D. SECURITY LEGISLATION REVIEW COMMITTEE

One condition for passage of some of the key legislation was that there be a review after three years by an independent committee. Such a committee was formed in the second half of 2005. After taking submissions and holding public hearings, it produced a report in June 2006.[8]

This Security Legislation Review Committee (SLRC) was chaired by a retired New South Wales Supreme Court judge, the Honourable Simon Sheller QC, AO, and had seven other members. Two were nominees of the Law Council of Australia, one was a nominee of the Attorney General, and four people were *ex-officio* members. I was one of the *ex-officio* members. The SLRC's report was unanimous, with the exception of one aspect on which the two points of view were set out in the report (I might note that the disagreement was over how the process for proscribing a terrorist organization should be reformed, not the need for reform).

One of the fundamental debates the SLRC had to consider was whether these new offences were indeed necessary, or whether existing criminal law (much of which is set in State and Territory, rather than Commonwealth, legislation), could have dealt adequately with conduct or potential conduct of concern.

After careful consideration the SLRC was satisfied that in general such a set of new offences was necessary. This was particularly because of the need to address prevention and because differences between the criminal law in each State and Territory could render dealing with cross-border events potentially

---

charged with three offences, including making funds available to the Liberation Tigers of Tamil Eelam (LTTE).

6 Evidence of Federal Agent Lam Pakstun, *R. v. Ul Haque*, voir dire open transcript, 24 October 2007. Sally Neighbour, "Charge Suspects To Test Terror Laws" *The Australian* (13 November 2007).

7 *The Weekend Australian* (26–27 January 2008) 3.

8 Security Legislation Review Committee, *Report of the Security Legislation Review Committee* (Canberra: Attorney General's Department, 2006) [SLRC].

difficult. There was also an argument that terrorism is a serious crime that warranted higher penalties.

As a committee we noted that there had been no apparent abuse of the new provisions to date, although it was very early days (at the time of our deliberations little had come before the courts in a substantive way). We therefore recommended that a further review be scheduled and that consideration be given to creating a position of independent reviewer (along the lines of the role Lord Carlile of Berriew QC plays in the United Kingdom). The SLRC had only been authorized to conduct one review.

However, we still gave close scrutiny to the existing provisions. This was particularly with tests of proportionality, clarity, and fairness in mind. The SLRC was conscious that there was no sunset clause on the provisions under review and that Australia does not have a charter of human rights.[9]

We recommended that there be a number of legislative changes, of which the most significant were that:

- The offence of associating with a terrorist organization transgressed the fundamental human right of freedom of association and interfered with ordinary family, religious, and legal communication. We concluded that the interference with human rights was disproportionate to anything that could be achieved by way of protection of the community if the section were enforced. We recommended that the relevant provisions be repealed (and if considered necessary, a further support offence be created).
- Advocating the doing of a terrorist act was one of the grounds for proscribing an organization as a terrorist organization, but the definition of "advocates" was on its face broad and potentially far-reaching. We recommended removal of that part of the definition that was particularly broad.
- Some of the subsections applied strict liability to elements of a criminal offence. We took the position that where criminal offences involved heavy penalties of imprisonment, neither the offences, nor elements of them, should be of strict liability.
- The process whereby an organization was proscribed as a terrorist organization required significant reform to make it a fairer and more transparent process.

---

9 The Attorney General in the new government elected in November 2007 has said publicly that there will be a consultative process about a Commonwealth charter of rights, having regard to the charters already in place in the State of Victoria and the Australian Capital Territory.

The SLRC was also troubled by the damaging effect on community relations of aspects of the new laws and the limited dissemination of accurate information about them. The SLRC emphasized that legislative refinements should be seen as an essential part of effective security strategies, not a soft approach to security. The report commented:

> Events in recent years have had a profound impact on Muslim and Arab Australians. The biggest impacts are a considerable increase in fear, a growing sense of alienation from the wider community and an increase in distrust of authority. The SLRC has serious concerns about the way in which the legislation is perceived by some members of Muslim and Arab communities.
>
> The SLRC recommends that greater efforts be made by representatives of all Australian governments to explain the security legislation and communicate with the public, in particular the Muslim and Arab communities, to understand and address the concerns and fears of members of those communities so that practical and immediate programs can be developed to allay them.
>
> The SLRC also believes that the amendments it has recommended to the proscription, advocacy, association, and strict liability elements of Part 5.3 of the *Criminal Code* would contribute to a reduction in fear and sense of alienation by at least some Muslim and Arab Australians. By doing so, there will be an enhancement, not a diminution, of anti-terrorism efforts. The dynamics for the development of so called homegrown terrorism must be reduced rather than provoked.[10]

E. RESPONSE AND FURTHER REVIEW

The then Commonwealth Attorney General, the Honourable Philip Ruddock MP, responded with a statement that the government's preliminary view was to oppose the SLRC recommendations concerning reform of the proscription process and removal of the association offence, but that detailed consideration would be given to all the recommendations. He said that the government agreed with the need to engage with the community on security issues and that the government had already taken some steps in this regard.[11]

As provided for in the legislation, the SLRC's report was subsequently reviewed in two parts by a Committee of the Commonwealth Parliament, the Parliamentary Joint Committee on Intelligence and Security (PJCIS). The

10 SLRC, above note 8 at 5–6.

11 Philip Ruddock, Media Release, 111/2006 (15 June 2006).

first PJCIS review covered all recommendations except those relating to the proscription process, and a report on this first review was produced in December 2006.[12] The second PJCIS review covered the proscription process and a report was issued in September 2007.[13]

It soon became clear from submissions to the PJCIS that the government did not support many of the SLRC proposals for change,[14] including any further formal review.

When the PJCIS produced its first report (on aspects other than proscription) in December 2006, it was evident that it agreed with most of the SLRC recommendations. Notably, the PJCIS report, prepared by a committee comprising five government members and four from the Opposition, was unanimous. Most of the PJCIS members had had extensive experience and none held, while on the PJCIS, a ministerial or like position (although a number had previously).

The PJCIS did strongly support the notions of an independent reviewer being appointed, the need to improve community relations, and amendment of the strict liability elements. The committee also supported review of the association offence, but did not specifically endorse its removal, and was not prepared to go as far as the SLRC in repealing "advocacy" as a basis for proscribing an organization. The PJCIS also made some additional recommendations, including that the offence of membership of a terrorist organization be replaced with one of participation in such an organization, and that there should be clarification that the offences do not include conduct regulated by the law of armed conflict.

The government did not issue a formal response to this PJCIS report during the remainder of its term (the Howard government was defeated in elections held on 24 November 2007).

The PJCIS report on proscription, tabled in September 2007, rejected the SLRC proposals for some fundamental reforms to the process, but took the opportunity to reiterate support for an independent reviewer and the removal

12 Austl., Parliamentary Joint Committee on Intelligence and Security, *Review of Security and Counter Terrorism Legislation*, Parl. Paper No. 423/06 (4 December 2006).

13 Austl., Parliamentary Joint Committee on Intelligence and Security, *Inquiry Into the Terrorist Organisation Listing Provisions of the Criminal Code Act 1995*, Parl. Paper No. 201/07 (20 September 2007) [PJCIS Report 2007].

14 Australian Government, *Government comments on Recommendations of the Security Legislation Review Committee (the Sheller Review)*, Submission No. 14, online: Parliamentary Joint Committee on Intelligence and Security: Committee activities (inquiries and reports): Review of Security and Counter Terrorism Legislation www.aph.gov.au/house/committee/pjcis/securityleg/subs/sub14.pdf.

of strict liability from the terrorist offence provisions. Several minor changes were also recommended.[15]

F. SEDITION

Another key review was conducted by the Australian Law Reform Commission (ALRC) in early 2006 into amendments made to the sedition provisions in the Commonwealth *Criminal Code* by the *Anti-Terrorism Act 2005* (Cth). The changes were described as "modernization" of long-standing sedition offences, replacing them with a suite of five offences built around the concept of prohibiting a person from "urging" others to use "force or violence" in a number of prescribed contexts, and with a specific defence of "good faith."[16]

The Attorney General had issued terms of reference for a review to the ALRC as a result of a commitment he gave to the government backbench committee when the Bill was about to be introduced into the Parliament.[17]

The ALRC report was finalized in July 2006 and tabled in Parliament in September 2006. The ALRC supported the general direction of the 2005 changes, but made several recommendations to enhance the shift. One of these was to remove the term "sedition," on the basis that it did not actually describe the new offence, and "it was closely associated in the public mind with its origins and history as a crime rooted in criticising—or 'exciting disaffection' against—the established authority."[18]

A key recommendation was that the offences should be subject to a requirement of intention, that is, that that person must intend that the urged force or violence will occur. The ALRC explained that such an amendment "would help remove from the ambit of the offences any rhetorical statements, parody, artistic expression, reportage and other communications that the person does not intend anyone will act upon," and hence reflect the high value placed on freedom of expression.[19] The ALRC rejected the idea that an offence of "encouragement" or "glorification" of terrorism should be introduced into federal law.[20]

---

15 PCJIS 2007, above note 13.

16 Australian Law Reform Commission, *Review of Sedition Laws: Discussion Paper* (Canberra: Australia Law Reform Commission, 2006) at 9.

17 Austl., Cth., Senate, *Parliamentary Debates* (18 October 2006) at 56.

18 Australian Law Reform Commission, *Fighting Words: Report on the Review of Sedition and Related Laws* (ALRC Report 104) (Canberra: Australian Law Reform Commission, 2006) at 10, online: www.alrc.gov.au/report-104.

19 *Ibid.* at 14.

20 *Ibid.* at 12–13.

The then Attorney General issued a media statement simply noting that the ALRC supported the shift made in the provisions, and that the government would give careful consideration to the commission's report.[21] No further response was made by the government during the rest of its term.

G. EARLY PROSECUTIONS

Australian experience has been developing with terrorism-related prosecutions. One early case that received substantial publicity—that of Mr. Jack Roche—was conducted under earlier legislation, not the new offences. He pleaded guilty in May 2004 to conspiracy to destroy by means of explosives official premises of internationally protected persons with intent to endanger the lives of internationally protected persons (section 8(3C)(a) of the *Crimes (Internationally Protected Persons) Act 1976*). Mr. Roche was sentenced to nine years' imprisonment with a non-parole period of four years, six months. The West Australian Court of Criminal Appeal upheld the sentence.[22]

In New South Wales in early 2005, Mr. Zaky Mallah pleaded guilty to recklessly making to another person a threat to cause serious harm to a Commonwealth public official, but he was not convicted by a jury on charges brought under section 101.6(1) of the *Criminal Code* (preparation for planning a terrorist act). He was sentenced to imprisonment for two years and six months, and served one year and eight months before release on a good behaviour order.[23]

The sentencing decision by Chief Justice Wood included sharp criticism of the behaviour of certain media personnel. Mr. Mallah came to public attention as a result of a passport refusal and firearms offences and came "to enjoy, if not to crave, the media attention." The police used an undercover operative and it was to this operative that Mr. Mallah conveyed the threat about causing harm to certain government agencies. Despite some criticism of this approach, the undercover operative's information was admitted as evidence. Chief Justice Wood commented:

> It does seem to me to have been regrettable that some sections of the media took up the Prisoner as a person of interest, and gave him an entirely underserved and unnecessary exposure, particularly if it be the fact, as he has claimed, that he was paid for his cooperation.

---

21 Philip Ruddock, News Release, 177/2006 (13 September 2006).

22 *R. v. Roche*, [2005] WASCA 4.

23 *R. v. Mallah*, [2005] NSWSC 317 [*Mallah*].

> Had real fears been entertained as to his potential dangerousness, then the preferable course surely would have been to pass any relevant information concerning him, to the appropriate policing and security agencies. Had he been dismissed as an attention seeker, of no moment, then there surely would have been no occasion to give him the extensive public exposure which he obviously enjoyed and indeed craved. . . .
>
> To continue discussions with a suspect in the position of the Prisoner, or to give him publicity, risks trampling all over any covert operation that may have been mounted under strict controls by professional policing and intelligence agencies, thereby potentially frustrating the collection of valuable intelligence that may have prevented a genuine terrorist event. Any investigation of such a person is far better left to professional agencies with the necessary training and access to intelligence, and should, in my view, be absolutely avoided by the media.
>
> Furthermore, placing a person such as the Prisoner into the public spotlight is not only likely to encourage him to embark on even more outrageous and extravagant behaviour but, perhaps more importantly, it risks unnecessarily heightening the existing public concerns about terrorist activity as well as encouraging or fanning divisive and discriminatory views among some members of the community.[24]

These comments were ignored by the media reporting on the case.[25]

1) *Thomas* Case

Mr. Jack Thomas was convicted by a jury for receiving funds from a terrorist organization and for possessing a false passport. [26] These convictions were overturned on appeal by the Victorian Supreme Court of Appeal in August 2006.[27]

The central issue in the appeal was the admissibility of records of interview taken by the Australian Federal Police in Pakistan, where Mr. Thomas had been detained by the authorities. At first instance Cummins J. had ruled the records were admissible, saying:

---

24 *Ibid.* at paras. 33–34 and 36–37.

25 On media impact see also Human Rights and Equal Opportunity Commission, *Isma*ع*—Listen: National consultations on eliminating prejudice against Arab and Muslim Australians*, online: Australian Human Rights Commission: Race Discrimination Publications: 2004 www.hreoc.gov.au/racial_discrimination/isma/report/index.html.

26 *DPP v. Thomas*, [2006] VSC 120. Mr. Thomas was also found not guilty on a charge of providing support or resources to a terrorist organization.

27 *R. v. Thomas*, [2006] VSCA 165 [*R. v. Thomas (1)*].

> I consider the provisions of Part IC of the Crimes Act (Commonwealth) applied to the interview on 8 March 2003.... Thus, ordinarily, the accused should, pursuant to section 23G(1)(b) of the Act, have been informed by the investigating officers that he may communicate with or attempt to communicate with a legal practitioner of his choice and arrange or attempt to arrange for a legal practitioner to be present during the questioning, and the questioning should have been deferred for a reasonable time to allow that communication or presence to occur. The officers, rather than inform the accused of that dual right, informed him that "this right will not be available to you today" (question 29). Normally, failure to avail an interviewee of that right would be fatal to the admission of a subsequent interview. That is, because the right is an important right in the system of justice. However, that requirement is not absolute. Here, the officers had ascertained that the provision would not be permitted in Pakistan. They were faced with the choice of conducting an interview or postponing it for an indefinite period to an indefinite place. Had the officers sought to utilise that situation for a collateral purpose, or as a pretext, or opportunistically to defeat or deflect the requirements of Part IC of the Act I would have had no hesitation in ruling the interview inadmissible. Further, I would unhesitatingly excuse the interview if I considered it unfair to admit it. However, I consider the officers acted reasonably, honestly and fairly in all the circumstances.[28]

The Court of Appeal took a different view, ruling that the admissions by Thomas were not made voluntarily. While "nothing occurred in the interview itself that could be seen to overbear the will of the applicant and thereby restrict, in a practical sense, his available choices and the manner of their exercise," nonetheless:

> there can be little doubt that it was apparent to the applicant, at the time of the AFP interview, as it would have been to any reasonable person so circumstanced, that, if he was to change his current situation of detention in Pakistan and reduce the risk of indeterminate detention there or in some unidentified location, co-operation was far more important than reliance on his rights under the law. Indeed, it is apparent that he believed—and, we would add, on objectively reasonable grounds—that insistence upon his rights might well antagonise those in control of his fate.[29]

While quashing the convictions on this point, the Court went on to comment on the other grounds of appeal, saying that it would have been prepared, had

---

28 *DPP v. Thomas*, [2005] VSC 523 at paras. 5–6.

29 *R. v. Thomas (1)*, above note 27 at para. 85.

it been necessary to do so, to uphold a submission that Justice Cummins' exercise of discretion to admit the evidence miscarried.[30]

However, this was not the end of the matter, because Mr. Thomas will be retried on the basis of statements made by or attributed to him that were screened on television or published in newspapers.[31]

Mr. Thomas was also subjected to a control order—a subject that I will discuss later in this article.

2) *Lodhi* Case

Mr. Faheem Khalid Lodhi was found guilty by a jury in New South Wales on three of four charges in June 2006. The three charges concerned doing an act in preparation for a terrorist act (making inquiries concerning the availability of chemicals); possessing a document connected with preparation for a terrorist act (instructions as to how to manufacture poisons, explosives, detonators, and incendiary devices); and, collecting documents connected with preparation for a terrorist act (maps of the electricity supply system). He was sentenced to concurrent terms of imprisonment totalling twenty years, with a non-parole period of fifteen years.[32]

One interesting aspect of the trial process was that consideration was given to the appointment of special counsel. In the UK, special counsel are appointed by the Law Officers of the Crown to represent the interests of an organization or other appellant in proceedings involving national security material. The special counsel see all material, whether classified or not, and participate in the proceedings. However, they are not permitted to disclose any part of the classified material to those whom they represent.

In the *Lodhi* matter, the presiding judge, Whealy J., was satisfied that the *National Security Information (Criminal and Civil Proceedings) Act 2004* (Cth) (*NSI Act*) did not prohibit the appointment of special counsel. In a subsequent article he observed:

> The appointment of special counsel in Australia is a novel concept. So far as I am aware, special counsel has not been appointed in Australia, either within or outside the confines of the National Security Information Act. Although the utility of the appointment of special counsel has been doubted, I consider that it could be a useful weapon in the armoury of a trial judge in a situation where there is a clash between a national security claim and a suggestion that

30 *Ibid.* at paras. 96–115.

31 *R. v. Thomas (No 3)*, [2006] VSCA 300.

32 *R. v. Lodhi*, [2006] NSWSC 691.

> the defence will be substantially prejudiced or interfered with in the conduct of the case.[33]

In the same article Justice Whealy also wrote about what a challenging experience being a trial judge in a terrorist trial was—reflecting on what is required to ensure a fair trial in the face of "the frequent barrage of articles and commentary in the media, certainly on a weekly if not a daily basis, involving terrorism and terrorists." He was sharply critical of the considerable complexities of the *NSI Act*.[34]

Mr. Lodhi appealed his conviction and also sought leave to appeal against his sentence, but both were dismissed by the NSW Court of Criminal Appeal.[35]

The court rejected an objection to the constitutional validity of the *NSI Act*, particularly provisions in it as to the weight to be given to the risk to national security in considering disclosure of information or the calling of a witness. The court did not accept that this breached the Australian Constitution by the executive usurping judicial power.

Another ground rejected was that the Crown could not prove that when he acted in the way specified in the charges, he had determined when, how, where, or by whom the relevant terrorist act might be carried out. The court accepted that proof of these matters was not necessary for conviction—the offences were aimed at preparatory acts.

H. AGENCY POWERS

The Australian law enforcement and intelligence agencies have been provided with significantly increased powers and capabilities in recent years. (These were outside the terms of reference for the SLRC mentioned earlier.)

The most controversial of these in Parliament and general public debate (at least at the federal level) have been the following three:

- The enactment of a capacity for the domestic security agency (Australian Security Intelligence Organisation (ASIO)) to obtain warrants for compulsory questioning and, in defined circumstances, detention.[36] This category of warrant was added to the ASIO legislation in 2003 following lengthy and heated debate in the Parliament.

33 Justice A.G. Whealy, "Difficulty in Obtaining a Fair Trial in Terrorism Cases" (2007) 81 Austl. L.J. 743 at 750.

34 *Ibid.*

35 *Lodhi v. R.*, [2007] NSWCCA 360.

36 *Australian Security Intelligence Organisation Act 1979* (Cth.), Part III, Division 3.

- The enactment of legislation in 2005 allowing for "control orders," whereby upon application by the Australian Federal Police, a court may place certain requirements on an individual, including the prohibition or restriction of specified activities, for example, communicating or associating with specified people, a curfew, or wearing a tracking device.[37]
- The enactment, also in 2005, of legislation at the Commonwealth level of preventative detention orders whereby a person can be detained by police for a limited period without being charged.[38] Similar legislation was subsequently enacted in each of the States and Territories.

I have had a close interest in these ASIO warrants for compulsory questioning in that I have an important role as a safeguard from the abuse of power. I view the requests for such warrants in order to satisfy myself that the legislative requirements are met, and I attend on at least the first day of questioning. If I have a concern, the questioning must if necessary be suspended while my concern is addressed.

None of the warrants to date (fifteen as at 30 June 2007) have involved detention. If this were to occur, I have the power to enter any place of detention to satisfy myself that the published protocols for conditions of detention are being applied.[39]

My experience has been that ASIO has acted professionally and appropriately in carrying out these questioning warrants. The predecessor of the PJCIS also reviewed the use and operation of this category of warrant in 2005.[40] The committee was able to view video recordings and described the questioning as "very formal and certainly polite and dispassionate, if persistent."[41] The committee was essentially satisfied that ASIO's conduct in respect of the warrants had been proper.

Nonetheless the committee agreed with a number of submissions, including mine, that there was scope to refine the legislative provisions, and that a sunset clause should remain. Sunset clauses inserted in legislation have the effect of bringing to an end the nominated provisions at a specified date, unless further legislation sets a new date for expiration. The provisions inserted into

---

37 *Criminal Code*, above note 3, Part 5.3, Division 104.

38 *Ibid.*, Division 105.

39 *Inspector-General of Intelligence and Security Act 1986* (Cth.), s. 19A.

40 Austl., Parliamentary Joint Committee on ASIO, ASIS and DSD, *Review of Division 3 Part III of the ASIO Act 1979 - Questioning and Detention Powers*, Parl. Paper No. 454/2005 (30 November 2005) [*Review*, 454/2005].

41 *Ibid.* at para. 1.44.

the *ASIO Act* allowing for questioning warrants had originally had a three-year sunset clause (that is, 23 July 2006).

Six recommendations by the PJCIS were accepted in full, six in part only, and seven were rejected by the government.[42] Two points of disagreement I would highlight are:

- The committee believed that the latest date that should be set for the new sunset clause should be November 2011.[43] However, the government used the majority it had gained in the Senate (the upper house) after the 2004 election to have the amending legislation set a date of July 2016.
- The committee recommended that the "prescribed authority," a retired judge who oversees the questioning, should be provided with a copy of the statement of facts and grounds on which the warrant was issued (so that they can better gauge the relevance of questions being asked). This was rejected by the government and not included in the amending legislation.

I. CONTROL ORDERS

As I noted earlier, legislation allowing for control orders was enacted in 2005. These can be issued by a court upon an application by the Australian Federal Police, the making of which has been approved by the Attorney General.[44]

1) *Thomas* Case

Two control orders have been issued to date. The first was issued in August 2006 and concerned Mr. Jack Thomas. It was an interim order, and required him, among other things, to remain at his residence between midnight and 5 a.m., not contact a list of people involved with terrorism, and to use only specified means of electronic communication.

Mr. Thomas challenged the constitutionality of control orders. A decision by the High Court was published in August 2007 in which a majority upheld the validity of the provisions.[45]

---

42 Related materials available online: Parliamentary Joint Committee on ASIO, ASIS and DSD: Committee activities (inquiries and reports) www.aph.gov.au/house/committee/pjcaad/reports.htm.

43 Austl., Cth., Senate, *Parliamentary Debates* (13 June 2006) at 82–106 (particularly 88).

44 *Criminal Code*, above note 3, Part 5.3, Division 104.

45 *Thomas v. Mowbray*, [2007] HCA 33.

In Australia, the Commonwealth Parliament has limited and specific powers in the written Constitution. One key area of argument in this appeal by Mr. Thomas concerned the scope of the defence and external affairs heads of power in the Commonwealth Constitution, but I do not propose to canvass that in this paper. Rather, I wish to highlight the divergent views on the issue of whether the control order provisions were invalid because they confer on a federal court what was argued to be non-judicial power, contrary to Chapter III of the Commonwealth Constitution.

Chief Justice Gleeson rejected the argument that there was a conferral of non-judicial power, stating:

> The power to restrict or interfere with a person's liberty on the basis of what that person might do in the future, rather than on the basis of a judicial determination of what the person has done, which involves interfering with legal rights, and creating new legal obligations, rather than resolving a dispute about existing rights and obligations, is in truth a power that has been, and is, exercised by courts in a variety of circumstances.[46]

The Chief Justice's view was that if the argument was that such a power could only be exercised by the executive branch of government, then:

> The advantages, in terms of protecting human rights, of such a conclusion are not self-evident. In *Fardon*, I indicated that the exercise of powers, independently, impartially and judicially, especially when such powers affect the liberty of the individual, would ordinarily be regarded as a good thing, not something to be avoided.... To decide that such powers are exclusively within the province of the executive branch of government would be contrary to our legal history, and would not constitute an advance in the protection of human rights.[47]

Clearly for the Chief Justice, pragmatism about who is best trusted by the community to approve use of a sensitive power was a compelling factor.

While a majority of the other justices agreed with the Chief Justice that the control order provisions were not incompatible with judicial power, there was a notable dissent on this issue by Justice Hayne. In his view, what set these provisions apart from other cases argued to provide supporting authority was "the indeterminacy of the criterion that the courts are required to apply—'for the purpose of protecting the public from a terrorist act.'"[48]

---

46 *Ibid.* at para. 15.

47 *Ibid.* at para. 17.

48 *Ibid.* at para. 475.

His view was:

> It is a criterion that seeks to require federal courts to decide whether and how a particular order against a named person will achieve or tend to achieve a future consequence: by contributing to whatever may be the steps taken by the Executive, through police, security and other agencies, to protect the public from a terrorist act. It is a criterion that would require a federal court to consider future consequences the occurrence of which depends upon work done by police and intelligence services that is not known . . .[49]

Justice Hayne considered this was "a judgement ill-fitted to judicial determination," and noted the contrast of the Australian provisions with those of section 83.3 of the Canadian *Criminal Code*—where a "peace officer" lays information before a judge and the issue for judicial determination is whether the judge is "satisfied by the evidence adduced that the peace officer has reasonable grounds for the suspicion." Justice Hayne noted that the Canadian scheme "does not require, as provisions now in issue do, the court to decide for itself what is necessary or desirable for protection of the public."[50]

Mr. Thomas has not been subject to a further control order, but has entered into undertakings in the Federal Magistrates Court that are similar to the conditions contained in the interim control order.

2) *Hicks* Case

The second control order—also an interim one—was imposed by a federal magistrate on Mr. David Hicks upon his release from jail in December 2007.

Mr. Hicks had been captured by Northern Alliance forces in Afghanistan in December 2001 and transferred by US forces to Guantanamo Bay in early 2002. He was charged, but these charges lapsed when the US Supreme Court ruled the original military commission system unconstitutional. Mr. Hicks was re-charged, and pleaded guilty in March 2007 to a charge of providing material support for terrorism. He was sentenced to seven years' imprisonment, with all but nine months suspended in line with a pre-trial agreement. In May 2007 Mr. Hicks was returned to Australia to serve the remainder of his sentence.

The interim control order contained eight conditions, including a curfew and a proviso that Mr. Hicks must report to the police in person three times a week.

49 *Ibid.* at para. 476.

50 *Ibid.* at paras. 502 and 514.

In a recent book, the Australian journalist Ms. Leigh Sales has observed:

> Hicks was a tool for those seeking to portray the left as "soft on terror" but was also used by those who argued that Howard was the Bush administration's puppet. Hicks didn't really matter as a person, except to those personally close to him, such as his family and Major Mori. For many others, he was merely a useful political device.
>
> Ultimately the outcome of the Hicks case does not serve the causes of either the left or the right. Those who believe Hicks is a terrorist will be infuriated that the legal process was so mishandled that he will always be able to claim he pleaded guilty only to escape the harsh conditions at Guantanamo Bay. Those who believe his trial was rigged will chafe at the injustice and Hicks's inability to ever clear his name.[51]

The book outlines the very successful "public relations offensive" that was undertaken by Hicks' father and his defence lawyer, Major Mori:

> When Hicks was first detained in 2001, the newspaper headlines almost universally condemned him as a traitor or terrorist. Just before his guilty plea, they were almost entirely sympathetic. Hicks was no longer the bad guy; the Howard government and the Bush administration were. With help from Terry Hicks, Mori successfully changed the media focus from Hicks's own conduct to the flawed legal process. Of course the shift was not all the result of their efforts—the Bush administration's failure to deal with the case in a timely fashion and its tarnished credibility relating to Iraq and Guantanamo Bay were also major factors.[52]

J. PREVENTATIVE DETENTION ORDERS

As noted earlier, legislation allowing for preventative detention orders (PDOs) against a person was enacted by the Commonwealth Parliament, and also subsequently by State and Territory Parliaments.

The preconditions for issue of a PDO include that there is threat of an imminent terrorist attack (that is, within fourteen days), or that a terrorist attack has occurred.

---

51 Leigh Sales, *Detainee 002: The Case of David Hicks* (Melbourne: Melbourne University Press, 2007).

52 *Ibid.* at 222–23.

In the Commonwealth scheme, a PDO can only be for a maximum of twenty-four hours. Because of constitutional differences, the State and Territory schemes allow a maximum of fourteen days.

No PDOs have yet been issued (as of 31 March 2008).

K. *HANEEF* CASE

Interestingly, the most controversial of the changes to law enforcement powers has not been control orders or preventive detention orders, but rather the questioning provisions in the *Crimes Act 1914* (which had been amended without exciting much attention in 2004 to lengthen the time a person could be held for questioning prior to being charged).

This is because these powers were used in the case of Dr. Mohamed Haneef. Two second cousins of Dr. Haneef, with whom he had contact when himself in the UK, were arrested there following attempted terrorist bombings in London and Glasgow on 29 and 30 June 2007, respectively. Dr. Haneef, at that time an employee in a Queensland hospital, was arrested by the AFP on 2 July 2007. The detention period for someone arrested for a terrorism offence is four hours, but this can be extended by a magistrate in certain circumstances. There is in the legislation provision for questioning to be suspended or delayed for reasons such as inquiries being needed across different time zones or translations being required (so called "dead time").[53]

On 14 July 2007, Dr. Haneef was charged with intentionally providing resources (in the form of a SIM card he had left behind in the UK) to a terrorist organization. He was granted bail on 16 July 2007 but the Minister for Immigration and Citizenship then cancelled his business (long stay) visa.

The basis of the visa cancellation was that the minister reasonably suspected that Dr. Haneef did not pass the character test, because of his "association" with his cousins.

The prosecution collapsed on 27 July 2007 when the Director of Public Prosecutions announced that he would offer no evidence. There had been an embarrassing error by the prosecutor over where the SIM card had been found in the UK. The DPP conducted an inquiry and the prosecutor in his office was subsequently demoted.[54]

---

53 *Crimes Act 1914*, (Cth.), s. 23CB.

54 Director of Public Prosecutions, News Release (12 October 2007); *The Australian* (24 October 2007).

Dr. Haneef left Australia voluntarily but his legal representatives successfully pursued an appeal against the cancellation of his visa. The appeal was upheld in August 2007 by the Federal Court,[55] and the Full Bench of the Federal Court dismissed an appeal by the minister against that decision in December 2007.[56] A key precedent relied on by the minister was rejected by the Full Bench in ruling that in the context of the *Migration Act 1958* and the character test, "association" must involve "some sympathy with, or support for, or involvement in, the criminal conduct of the person, group or organisation with whom the visa holder is said to have associated with."[57]

Another dimension to this matter were claims of official "leaks" and release into the public domain by defence lawyers of the police record of interview. This sparked a debate about the propriety of defence lawyers commenting to the media, or releasing material to the media, while the matter concerned was before the court.[58]

The new government elected in November 2007 had committed itself during the election campaign to a judicial inquiry into the *Haneef* case. On 13 March 2008, the Attorney General announced that a former NSW Supreme Court judge, the Honourable John Clarke QC, would conduct the inquiry.

L. *UL-HAQUE* CASE

Another public embarrassment to both police and ASIO in late 2007 was the dismissal of charges against a medical student, Mr. Izhar Ul-Haque, of having trained with a terrorist organization (Lashkar-e-Taiba). A NSW Supreme Court judge ruled three police interviews were inadmissible because of the conduct of the ASIO and police officers prior to the interviews.

Justice Adams considered the behaviour of the ASIO officers had involved unlawful detention and attempts to overbear Mr. Ul-Haque in the hope that he would cooperate. Justice Adams concluded that there had been "oppressive conduct," that the circumstances adversely affected the truth of admissions made, and that the evidence had been obtained improperly. The effect of provi-

55 *Haneef v. Minister for Immigration and Citizenship*, [2007] FCA 1273.

56 *Minister for Immigration and Citizenship v. Haneef*, [2007] FCAFC 203.

57 *Ibid.* at para. 130.

58 John H. Phillips, "Practical Advocacy" (2007) 81 Austl. L.J. 918. There has also been debate about leaks apparently from official sources—see, for example, *Review*, 454/2005, above note 40 at paras. 5.32–5.38.

sions in the *Evidence Act 1995* was therefore that the formal police interviews were not admissible.[59]

In November 2007 I announced that I would conduct an inquiry under the *Inspector-General of Intelligence and Security Act 1986* into the conduct of the ASIO officers (and should avoid public comment at this stage lest possible bias be read into anything I might state).

M. *HABIB* CASE

No discussion of terrorism issues in recent years would be complete without reference to the subject of extraordinary rendition. The previous government's official position had been that "persons should only be transferred to another country through recognised legal means or where legal authority exists, such as extradition."[60]

An action against the Australian government has been commenced by Mr. Mamdouh Habib, an Australian citizen born in Egypt, who alleges that he was rendered from Pakistan, with the complicity of Australian officials, to Egypt where he was tortured. Ultimately he was moved to Guantanamo Bay, but was not charged and was returned to Australia in 2005. This action is still underway.

Mr. Habib has been unsuccessful in defamation action against a media company,[61] and also in an appeal against the cancellation of his passport and the refusal of a new one.[62]

I should note that apart from Mr. Habib's claims, official reports such as those produced by Mr. Dick Marty (for the Committee on Legal Affairs and Human Rights of the Council of Europe),[63] and a report prepared by the Intelligence and Security Committee in the United Kingdom[64] have not pointed to

59 *R. v. Ul-Haque*, [2007] NSWSC 1251.

60 Austl., Cth., Senate, *Parliamentary Debates* (4 October 2005) at 85.

61 *Habib v. Nationwide News Pty Limited*, [2008] NSWSC 181.

62 *Re Habib and the Minister for Foreign Affairs, Habib and the Director-General of Security*, [2007] AATA 1908.

63 Council of Europe, P.A., Committee on Legal Affairs and Human Rights, *Alleged secret detentions and unlawful inter-state transfers of detainees involving Council of Europe member states*, Doc. 10957 (12 June 2006), online: Council of Europe: Parliamentary Assembly http://assembly.coe.int/main.asp?Link=/documents/workingdocs/doc06/edoc10957.htm.

64 UK, Intelligence and Security Committee, *Rendition*, Cmnd. 7171 (July 2007), online: National Archives: Cabinet Office: http://webarchive.nationalarchives.gov.uk/+/http://www.cabinetoffice.gov.uk/intelligence/special_reports.aspx .

Australian involvement in rendition flights or identified any other Australian who may have been the subject of rendition.

N. ACCOUNTABILITY OF AGENCIES

Naturally the changes in agency powers that I have canvassed have raised debate about monitoring and accountability.

In Australia some commentators have tunnel vision about how to construct an accountability framework—they seem unable to look beyond the possibilities of courts.

Professor John McMillan, an eminent lawyer in the field of administrative law and the current Commonwealth Ombudsman, has noted that discussion about the rule of law in Australian legal and academic circles often has more to say about the role of courts than about the true broad focus of the doctrine, which is limiting and controlling the behaviour of governments.[65]

Of course, the judiciary plays an absolutely vital role in ensuring that executive government is subject to the law and not above it. Our courts have a very proud history in this regard and it would be alarming to try to contemplate our system having a less effective judicial arm.

However, there are some limitations in what the judiciary can do in protecting rights. The range of issues that receive judicial scrutiny is in fact adventitious and episodic.[66] Additional, non-judicial mechanisms are also important in safeguarding the rule of law.

In the case of my role, I have already touched on the close scrutiny given to ASIO warrants, but this is only one example of how the additional powers and capabilities are monitored.

Through an inspection program my office aims at comprehensive, regular, and ongoing review of the exercise of all significant agency powers and capabilities. This can have the benefit of identifying issues at an early stage and thus stop them becoming magnified. The normative effect on behaviour within the agencies is considerable.

I also spend time speaking with new recruits and existing staff in the Australian agencies to emphasize the necessity of them acting legally and properly. I believe that only if they have the trust and confidence of the community will

---

65 John McMillan, "The Ombudsman and the Rule of Law" (2005) 44 AIAL Forum 1 at 3.

66 John McMillan, "The Role of the Ombudsman in Protecting Human Rights" (Address delivered at University of Melbourne Faculty of Law, 21 July 2006), online: Commonwealth Ombudsman: Speeches and Presentations: 2006 http://ombudsman.gov.au/docs/speeches/omb-role_protect_human_rights-july06.pdf.

they continue to be entrusted with the range of special powers and capabilities they currently have.

Another dimension to my role since the controversy over Iraq and weapons of mass destruction has been inquiring into the legality and propriety of our key assessment agency, the Office of National Assessments. The central concern is whether there is improper political or policy influence on the key judgments made in assessments.

O. CONCLUSIONS

The need for government to be seen as responding and in charge can create, in the words of Stephen Flynn (who wrote on America's counter-terrorism efforts), a situation where the mantra becomes "act now" rather than necessarily "act effectively."[67]

From a pragmatic point of view that may be unavoidable, but a key test for liberal democracies in the area of counter-terrorism is willingness to revisit what was done, and if necessary modify the measures introduced, to ensure balance and proportionality. This is particularly so if some elements may be counterproductive—such as adding to the sense of alienation and discrimination which members of Muslim communities can suffer. Arguably a willingness to do so by government has not been strongly demonstrated in Australia on experience to date.

Another key feature in the Australian experience so far has been acceptance of the concept of targeting prevention through criminal offences, but a significant number of cases are "still in the pipeline," and it is too early for a conclusive view. That experience with the pending prosecutions, and the scale of those proceedings, will also reveal whether the procedural framework in the *NSI Act* for the handling of security matters is sufficiently workable.

Some media behaviour will presumably continue to pose challenges about proper conduct by the media and about ensuring proceedings are fair. There seems to be much less enthusiasm for discussion about media responsibilities compared to what are asserted to be media rights and freedoms.

The admissibility of evidence, as influenced by the circumstances prior to and surrounding formal police interviews, has produced some sharp lessons for police and government officials.

At the same time the actual exercise of the special powers most controversial when introduced (ASIO questioning and detention warrants, control orders

67 Stephen Flynn, *America the Vulnerable* (New York: Harper Perennial, 2005) at 162–63.

and preventive detention orders) has been modest and not provided the dire consequences that some commentators warned would eventuate. Arguably, the close attention these measures received in development, and the inclusion of non-judicial forms of monitoring and review in the schemes implemented, have contributed to this. Yet it must be said that the interplay of the mechanisms (including police questioning powers) has not apparently had much attention, and would seem ripe for review.

CHAPTER 14

Intelligence Services Commissioner for the United Kingdom

THE RIGHT HONOURABLE SIR PETER GIBSON
INTELLIGENCE SERVICES COMMISSIONER, UNITED KINGDOM

It was the Roman satirical poet Juvenal who wrote "*Quis custodiet ipsos custodes?*" ("Who will keep watch on those who keep watch?"). Those words were written in a totally different context nearly two thousand years ago. But they have a resonance today. Governments, anxious to provide security for their citizens, rely on their national intelligence services to combat terrorism and other threats and to that end they give those services more and more extensive and intrusive powers to keep watch on those thought to threaten mischief. But they also recognize the need to reassure the public that those services are properly accountable and subject to the rule of law. A popular television series in England called *Spooks* had the Chief of MI6 with manic abandon sloshing petrol over the Director General of MI5 with a view to setting him alight. No doubt many who watched that program firmly believe that that is just the sort of skulduggery that the security services get up to and would be sadly disappointed by the more humdrum actuality.

To return to Juvenal's question, different countries have provided different answers to fit their own particular circumstances. The United Kingdom was somewhat slow to acknowledge publicly even the existence of its intelligence services and even slower to accept the need for their accountability, the tension between secrecy and accountability yielding to the former until quite recently. Now there are Acts of Parliament that spell it out: "There shall continue to be a Security Service," thereby acknowledging that MI5 did exist prior to the *Security Service Act 1989*. Similarly, in 1994 the *Intelligence Services Act* provided that there should continue to be a Secret Intelligence Service, MI6, and a Government Communications Headquarters, GCHQ.

With those Acts came the formal statement of the functions of each of those agencies. The functions of MI5 are the protection of national security and in particular its protection against threats from espionage, terrorism, and sabotage, from the activities of agents of foreign powers and from actions intended to overthrow or undermine parliamentary democracy by political, industrial, or violent means, to safeguard the economic well-being of the UK against threats posed by the actions or intentions of persons outside the British Islands, and to act in support of the activities of the police forces and other law enforcement agencies in the prevention and detection of serious crime. The functions of MI6 are to obtain and provide information and to perform other tasks relating to the actions or intentions of persons outside the British Islands, but it can only do so in the interests of national security or the economic well-being of the UK or in support of the prevention or detection of serious crime. GCHQ's functions are to monitor or interfere with electromagnetic, acoustic, and other emissions and any equipment producing such emissions and to obtain and provide information derived from or related to such emissions or equipment and from encrypted material to the armed forces, the government, and certain other organizations, but only in the interests of national security or in the interests of the UK's economic well-being in relation to the actions or intentions of persons outside the British Islands and to provide advice and assistance about languages (including terminology used for technical matters) and cryptography and other matters relating to the protection of information and other material to the armed forces, the government, and other organizations.

The Acts formally established the oversight mechanisms that Parliament intended for those agencies.

First, there is political oversight in that each of the agencies is expressed to be under the authority of the Secretary of State, and his personal approval and in general his signature to a warrant are required for intrusive surveillance and interception of communications activities carried out by those agencies. Ministers set budgets for each agency, deciding how much is to be spent on security and intelligence, and are accountable to Parliament for what the agencies do or fail to do operationally.

Second, there is parliamentary oversight of MI5, MI6, and GCHQ in the form of the Intelligence and Security Committee, comprising nine parliamentarians with cross-party membership drawn from both Houses of Parliament. The committee's statutory remit is to examine the expenditure, administration, and policy of the three agencies and to report to the Prime Minister annually, the reports being laid before Parliament together with the government's responses to them.

Third, there is independent judicial oversight in that there are two commissioners, the Interception of Communications Commissioner and the Intelligence Services Commissioner, who keep under review separate categories of activity of the three agencies and of certain other governmental bodies with intrusive powers. Each commissioner is required to be the holder or past holder of high judicial office. The thinking behind that requirement is no doubt first that the holder of high judicial office is independent of government and likely to form his own disinterested judgment, second that he is likely to have experience of eliciting facts, and third that by virtue of his judicial position he may be seen to carry authority. There is also a tribunal, the Investigatory Powers Tribunal, whose statutory function it is to investigate, among other things, complaints by individuals about the conduct of the agencies toward them or about the interception of their communications, and, if it upholds the complaint, the tribunal has the power to order such remedial action as it sees fit. This includes the award of damages, and in one case damages were awarded. A Court of Appeal judge is the current president of the tribunal.

The Interception of Communications Commissioner reviews the issue and operation of warrants permitting the interception of mail and telecommunications and the acquisition of communications data by the three agencies, the Ministry of Defence, and law enforcement agencies, and the arrangements for handling that material. He is required to report annually to the Prime Minister who lays the report before Parliament. The current Interception of Communications Commissioner is a retired Court of Appeal judge.

I can say a little more about the job of the Intelligence Services Commissioner because that is, and has been since April 2006, my own role. The more important of the commissioner's statutory functions are:

1. to keep under review the exercise by the Secretary of State of his powers to issue, renew, and cancel warrants for entry on or interference with property or with wireless telegraphy, such warrants being in practice issued by the Home Secretary or the Secretary of State for Northern Ireland;
2. to keep under review the exercise by the Secretary of State of his powers to give, renew, and cancel authorizations for acts done outside the UK, authorizations in practice issued by the Foreign Secretary;
3. to keep under review the exercise and performance by the Secretary of State of his powers and duties in relation to the activities of the agencies and (save for Northern Ireland) of Ministry of Defence officials and

members of the armed forces with regard to the grant of authorizations for intrusive surveillance, that is to say, covert surveillance in residential premises or a private vehicle in a manner likely to reveal private information about a person;

4. to keep under review the exercise and performance by members of the intelligence services of their powers and duties with regard to two matters:
   a. the grant of authorizations for directed surveillance, that is to say, covert surveillance that is not intrusive surveillance but is undertaken for the purposes of a specific investigation or operation in such a manner as is likely to result in the obtaining of private information about a person; and
   b. the conduct and use of covert human intelligence sources (undercover officers, agents, informants, and the like); and
5. to keep under review the exercise and performance in places other than Northern Ireland by Ministry of Defence officials and members of the armed forces with regard to the grant of authorizations for directed surveillance and the conduct and use of covert human intelligence sources.

There are detailed criteria laid down in the governing Acts that must be fulfilled if a warrant or other authorization is to be issued lawfully. Thus the Secretary of State can only authorize the placing of a surveillance device in someone's house or car if he believes such action is necessary in the interests of national security or for preventing or detecting serious crime or in the interests of the UK's economic well-being. He must also believe that the authorized surveillance is proportionate to what is sought to be achieved and he must have regard to whether the information sought to be obtained could reasonably be obtained by other means. Since the *Human Rights Act* came into force in 2000, account must be taken by the decision-maker of any adverse effect on human rights. Such rights can be interfered with but only if the statutory safeguards of necessity and proportionality are satisfied. Account must be taken of any collateral intrusion into the lives of those not directly connected with the operation. Time limits are set for the currency of any warrant or authorization, normally twelve months, but there are provisions for renewal and also in the event of an emergency. In such urgent cases an official is able to sign the warrant in place of the Secretary of State but can only do so if the Secretary of State has expressly authorized the issue of the warrant and if it is to continue, it must then be renewed under the hand of the Secretary of State within a few days. The commissioner in conducting his review looks out for any failure to observe what is required by law.

The commissioner is required to report annually to the Prime Minister, and the report is laid before Parliament and published. The practice has been to put sensitive material in an annex that, if the Prime Minister so decides after consultation with the commissioner, is excluded from the report laid before Parliament and from publication. That means that few statistics are or can be revealed.

In the area of the Intelligence Services Commissioner's functions the UK has opted for a system where in general Parliament has not required any judicial involvement prior to the warrant or other authorization or decision but has given the Secretary of State the function of taking the relevant decision. Instead the commissioner is given the function of review. A duty of cooperation is imposed on every member of an agency, every departmental official, and every member of the armed forces to disclose or provide to the commissioner all such documents and information as he may require. He can review retrospectively what has been done by calling for the papers leading up to the warrant or other authorization or other relevant decision and if appropriate seeing the case officers and talking to them about what has happened. The commissioner generally meets all the relevant Secretaries of State every year. The practice has been for the commissioner to visit each of the agencies and other relevant government offices twice a year, and to make inspections overseas. He is provided with a list of all current warrants and authorizations and a list of all those which have been cancelled since his last visit. From those lists he chooses those cases the papers for which he wishes to see and those for which he would like to meet the officers concerned.

It cannot be pretended that the commissioner sees all the documentation relating to all the warrants, authorizations, and other decisions taken in his area of oversight, but past experience has shown that in general he sees enough to be reasonably confident that the Secretary of State and the agencies and other departments have complied and are complying with their statutory obligations. These days they make full use of the growing numbers of legal advisers available to them, including at times the Law Officers, to ensure that they act within their powers. Independent specialist barristers are occasionally consulted on points of particular difficulty. When things do go wrong, as inevitably they do because of human error, the error is promptly acknowledged to the commissioner and explanations are sought by the commissioner and given for any such failure, together with assurances as to the measures taken to avoid use of material incorrectly obtained and to prevent a recurrence. The errors are noted and commented on by the commissioner in the annual report. Happily, the errors are comparatively rare and, as a proportion of the increasing number of cases, becoming rarer because of the care taken and the well-practised procedures adopted to ensure compliance.

Finally, how does one answer Juvenal's question in relation to the commissioner himself? Who keeps watch on him in the performance of his functions? To whom is he accountable? The honest answer is that really no one has been given that function. The commissioner does in practice meet the Intelligence and Security Committee once a year for a fairly informal discussion on matters of mutual interest, but that committee has no power to summon the commissioner or otherwise to require him to give evidence nor has any other parliamentary committee. The Prime Minister, being the person who appoints the commissioner, retains powers to dismiss him, but only on certain dire events such as bankruptcy or conviction imposing a sentence of imprisonment or misbehaviour or incapacity. No doubt it is expected that the past or present holder of high judicial office will be, like Caesar's wife, above suspicion, though that perhaps is a simile bringing little reassurance. Juvenal posed his question in the context of a flirtatious wife, the husband of whom was advised to keep her under strict watch, and it was that advice that prompted Juvenal to ask the question, "Who will keep watch on those who keep watch?"

CHAPTER 15

The Role of Canada's Security Intelligence Review Committee in Safeguarding Human Rights While Protecting National Security

THE HONOURABLE GARY FILMON
CHAIR, SECURITY INTELLIGENCE REVIEW COMMITTEE, CANADA

A. INTRODUCTION

The Security Intelligence Review Committee (SIRC), which I chair, enjoys a unique perspective on different forms of review and oversight and the ways in which democratic governments can safeguard human rights while protecting national security. Although I do not pretend to know all of the answers to these complex and difficult questions, I believe that Canada has developed a thoughtful and balanced approach which by and large, has stood the test of time.[1]

In order to discuss the Canadian model of security intelligence review, it is necessary to go back more than thirty years. At that time, Canada was grappling with a violent separatist movement in Quebec characterized by a number of bombings, kidnappings, and murders. The responsibility for countering this threat largely rested with Canada's Security Service—then part of the Royal

1 Sources relied on for this chapter are: Security Intelligence Review Committee, *SIRC Annual Report 2006–7: An Operational Review of the Canadian Security Intelligence Service* (Ottawa: Public Works and Government Services Canada, 2007); Commission of Inquiry into the Actions of Canadian Officials in Relation to Maher Arar, *A New Review Mechanism for the RCMP's National Security Activities* (Ottawa: Public Works and Government Services Canada, 2006); Security Intelligence Review Committee, *Reflections: Twenty Years of Independent External Review of Security Intelligence in Canada* (Ottawa: Security Intelligence Review Committee, 2005); and Ward Elcock, Address (John Tait Memorial Lecture, delivered at the Annual Meeting of the Canadian Association for Security and Intelligence Studies, Vancouver, 16–18 October 2003).

Canadian Mounted Police. The Security Service engaged in several illegal activities, including break-ins, arson, and theft targeted at left-leaning media and political parties (including one that was poised to form a provincial government). Once exposed by the media, the government of the day came under enormous pressure to ensure that such abuses would never happen again.

B. THE McDONALD COMMISSION

The government decided to establish the McDonald Commission, an independent inquiry that recommended that Canada create a new civilian security intelligence service, separate and distinct from its national police force. The Canadian Security Intelligence Service (CSIS) would collect intelligence to advise the government on threats to national security, while law enforcement agencies would continue to collect evidence used to prosecute national security and other criminal offences.

With the passage of the *CSIS Act* in 1984, Canada became one of the first democratic countries anywhere in the world to establish a legal framework for its security service. Canada had legislation that clearly defined the mandate and limits of state power to collect national security intelligence. And equally significant, the *CSIS Act* created a framework to keep those powers in check. Specifically, the *CSIS Act* described in detail how the Service's work was to be monitored through a rigorous system of political and judicial controls, including two bodies—each with a distinct mandate—to watch over CSIS.

The first body is the Inspector General of CSIS. The Inspector General is an *internal* review body that provides the Minister of Public Safety with a knowledgeable set of "eyes and ears" on CSIS operations. In effect, the Inspector General acts as an early warning system, to ensure that anything illegal or worrisome is quickly brought to the minister's attention. Although independent of CSIS itself, the Inspector General is part of the minister's bureaucratic apparatus.

C. SECURITY INTELLIGENCE REVIEW COMMITTEE

The second body is the Security Intelligence Review Committee. SIRC is an *external* review mechanism that does not report to any minister, but directly to Parliament and therefore ultimately to all Canadians. SIRC is fully independent in what it chooses to examine and how it goes about its work.

SIRC's mandate is limited to reviewing CSIS, which can sometimes be problematic when other federal departments or agencies are also involved in a particular investigation. This was highlighted by a recent commission of inquiry headed by Mr. Justice Dennis O'Connor, which examined the actions of Canadian officials in relation to Maher Arar, a Canadian citizen who was sent to Syria against his will by American authorities, where he was detained and tortured, before being allowed to return to Canada. O'Connor recommended that statutory gateways be established to allow Canada's review bodies to exchange information and conduct joint investigations, when more than one federal department or agency may be involved.

SIRC's role is relatively easy to describe, if rather complex to execute. The committee has two basic functions: (1) to conduct retrospective reviews into CSIS operations; and, (2) to investigate complaints against CSIS. SIRC has, in law, the absolute authority to examine all of the Service's activities and has full access to its files, no matter how highly classified that information may be. The sole exception is Cabinet confidences, meaning deliberations among ministers.

SIRC's reviews are done by assessing the Service's activities and operations against four instruments that together form the legislative and policy framework of the Service. These are: (1) the *CSIS Act* and other applicable legislation; (2) ministerial direction; (3) national requirements for security intelligence; and, (4) CSIS operational policies.

In each of its reviews, the committee examines several essential questions, such as:

- Did CSIS have reasonable grounds to suspect a threat to the security of Canada?
- Was the level of investigation proportionate to the seriousness of the threat?
- Did exchanges of information between CSIS and domestic and foreign partners comply with the agreements and caveats governing information-sharing?
- And last but not least, did the Service's investigation respect the rights and freedoms of individuals who were either the focus of, or who may have been implicated in, the investigation?

Normally, SIRC reviews take several months to complete and involve examining thousands of pages of documents. Once a review is completed, copies are sent to the Director of CSIS and the Inspector General; in some special cases, they are sent directly to the Minister of Public Safety. Declassified summaries, with any national security and privacy concerns removed, are also included in

SIRC's annual report to Parliament. Since its creation, SIRC has completed 177 reviews, containing 391 recommendations.

SIRC also investigates complaints brought against CSIS by individuals or groups. These complaints can be about "any act or thing done by the Service"; denials of security clearances to federal government employees and contractors; referrals from the Canadian Human Rights Commission in cases where the complaint relates to the security of Canada; and, very infrequently, minister's reports in respect of the *Citizenship Act*. Recently, SIRC became an alternative redress mechanism to hear complaints from individuals denied permission to board an aircraft under Canada's Passenger Protect Program or "no-fly" list. In these cases, SIRC is not the primary avenue of redress; it only becomes involved when the complainant believes that information or advice provided to Transport Canada by CSIS was behind the transport minister's decision to place the individual on the list.

When SIRC accepts jurisdiction in a complaints case, it functions as a quasi-judicial, administrative tribunal. The complainant has a right to an oral hearing presided over by one or more committee members whose role is similar to a judge. At the conclusion of the investigation, SIRC issues a report containing findings and recommendations to the Minister of Public Safety, the Director of CSIS, and in some cases, the deputy minister of the government department involved. A declassified report on the investigation is also provided to the complainant. To date, SIRC has issued 130 written complaints reports.

In SIRC's view, having review and complaints under one body has proven advantageous. Reviews give us the expertise to evaluate and investigate complaints more fully; at the same time, complaints give us another "window" on CSIS operations, particularly their impact on the lives of ordinary Canadians. In some jurisdictions, these functions are kept separate; but Canada's experience suggests that there are real benefits in having them under one roof.

SIRC's recommendations are non-binding, whether they stem from reviews or complaints. The scheme that Parliament created was not meant to have SIRC substitute for either the Director of CSIS, who is accountable to the Minister of Public Safety; or for the minister, who is accountable to Parliament in the Canadian system. Nevertheless, CSIS has implemented the majority of SIRC's recommendations and has publicly acknowledged that SIRC has made it a better organization. In 2003, then CSIS Director Ward Elcock said publicly at the annual meeting of the Canadian Association for Security and Intelligence Studies:

> Twenty years of constant review activity have resulted in many recommendations on how we could run things differently, and many of these recom-

mendations have mirrored adjustments that have been made to the Service's management procedures. SIRC's comments have extended into the heart of how the organization is run, including matters of source-handling, investigative methods, targeting decisions and other core functions.

...

Do we always share SIRC's views? No in some cases, yes in some ... but that is not the point. The point is that the review process remains an ongoing debate on ways to ensure that the principles of the legislation are sustained as we evolve and adapt to new threats. That is what the legislators intended.

D. *CANADIAN CHARTER OF RIGHTS AND FREEDOMS*

A key objective for SIRC is to ensure that CSIS acts lawfully and therefore does not undermine Canadians' fundamental rights and freedoms. In Canada, the concept of human rights is anchored in our Constitution by the *Canadian Charter of Rights and Freedoms*, which celebrated its twenty-fifth anniversary in 2007.

Most of the rights and freedoms enshrined in the *Charter* are not new; indeed, Canadians had enjoyed many of them as a matter of practice over the years. They derived from federal legislation, international treaties to which Canada is a signatory as well as common law jurisprudence. However, with the adoption of the *Charter*, these rights and freedoms became guaranteed in Canada, meaning that all federal and provincial laws must respect them. Canadians also gained the power to apply to the courts if they felt that the state had infringed upon or denied their *Charter* rights.

The *Charter* offers protection for everyone in Canada of certain basic rights and freedoms essential to maintaining our free and democratic society. Section 2 guarantees four fundamental freedoms:

1. Freedom of conscience and religion;
2. Freedom of thought, belief, opinion and expression, including freedom of the press;
3. Freedom of peaceful assembly; and
4. Freedom of association.

Canada's *Charter* also provides everyone with basic legal rights, such as the right to life, liberty, and security; the right not to be arbitrarily detained or imprisoned; the right not to be subjected to cruel and unusual treatment or punishment; and the right to be protected from unreasonable search and seizure.

Section 1 of the *Charter* makes these rights subject to such "reasonable limits" as "can be demonstrably justified in a free and democratic society." In other words, the government may legally limit an individual's *Charter* rights; this limitation clause has been used to prevent a variety of objectionable conduct such as hate speech and obscenity. It is important to note, however, that the Supreme Court of Canada has established criteria that must be satisfied to override a constitutionally protected right or freedom, in order to protect Canadians from unreasonable interference by government. This limitation clause is not unique to Canada's *Charter*; the *European Convention on Human Rights*, for example, sets out several similar limitations.

In performing its duties, SIRC at times must consider *Charter* issues. For example, our 2006–7 annual report discussed a review into the case of Mohammed Mansour Jabarah, an admitted al-Qa'ida member and Canadian citizen, who planned to bomb American and Israeli embassies in Southeast Asia. Despite his admissions, he could not be charged under the *Criminal Code*, since his terrorist activities took place on foreign soil and pre-dated Canada's *Anti-terrorism Act*. SIRC's review raised questions regarding CSIS's contention that Jabarah's self-incrimination and decision to surrender himself to American authorities were made freely and voluntarily. The committee concluded that Jabarah was "arbitrarily detained" by CSIS in violation of section 9 of the *Charter* and that his right to silence as protected by sections 7 and 11 (c), as well as his right to counsel under section 10, was breached. Furthermore, his right to remain in Canada as protected by section 6 of the *Charter* (mobility rights) was violated. In this particular case, SIRC concluded that CSIS strayed from its security intelligence mandate into the area of law enforcement.

Regardless of whether SIRC is investigating complaints or conducting reviews, the committee always attempts to balance individual rights with the state's interest in ensuring national security. For example, are the means employed by CSIS proportionate to the threat; are they fair and not arbitrary; and are Canadians' rights impacted as little as possible during CSIS's investigation, recognizing the State's duty to ensure the safety of its citizens?

In a landmark 2007 ruling, the Supreme Court of Canada found that a procedural aspect of our security certificate system was unfair and therefore incompatible with the *Charter*. (Security certificates allow the Government of Canada to detain without charge or trial, foreign nationals or permanent residents who are suspected of being a threat to national security, prior to their removal from Canada.) In its decision, the Supreme Court drew attention to the merits of a little-known feature of SIRC's complaints investigations.

When SIRC hears a complaint, it employs an independent, security-cleared counsel to represent the interests of complainants when they must be excluded from a hearing room for security reasons. SIRC's counsel is expected to vigorously cross-examine CSIS witnesses in the absence of the complainant's counsel. Once the *ex parte* portion of the hearing is concluded, the complainant is given a summary of the hearing, which provides as much information as possible without disclosing national security information. This ensures procedural fairness while balancing national security concerns.

In response to the Supreme Court's decision, the Government of Canada introduced legislation that received royal assent in February 2008. The Act provides for the use of special advocates to represent and protect the interests of individuals, in a reformed security certificate regime. However, several experts have noted that these special advocates do not exercise the same powers enjoyed by SIRC counsel, which in their view could impair the effectiveness of the special advocates.

E. CONCLUSION

For twenty-four years, SIRC has strived to perform its work in an objective, fair, and balanced way. The committee recognizes that in a free society, individual rights are meaningless without real and lasting human security. We believe that democracies must use every resource at their disposal to counter threats to national security, but in doing so must uphold the principles of accountability, respect for individual rights, and absolute adherence to the rule of law.

Human rights and national security objectives may at times appear to clash. But in a healthy democracy where rights and freedoms have constitutional protection, they can—indeed, they must—co-exist. It is SIRC's view that the demands of public safety and democratic values are not in conflict with each other; rather, they are complementary.

LIST OF CONTRIBUTORS

- The Honourable Yorick Aler, *Judge, Court of Appeal, The Hague, The Netherlands*
- The Honourable Aharon Barak, *President Emeritus, Supreme Court of Israel*
- Ian Carnell, *Inspector-General of Intelligence and Security, Australia (2004–2010)*
- Stanley A. Cohen, *Department of Justice, Canada*
- The Honourable Sir Andrew Collins, *Judge, Administrative Division, High Court of Justice, England and Wales, United Kingdom*
- The Honourable Gary Filmon, *Chair, Security Intelligence Review Committee, Canada (2005–2010)*
- Angela Gendron, *Canadian Centre of Intelligence and Security Studies, Carleton University*
- The Right Honourable Sir Peter Gibson, *Intelligence Services Commissioner, United Kingdom*
- The Right Honourable Lord Brian Hutton, *Chair, Investigation into the Circumstances Surrounding the Death of Dr. David Kelly, United Kingdom (2003–2004)*
- The Honourable Ian Bruce Josephson, *Judge, Supreme Court of British Columbia, Canada*
- Jean-Claude Marin, *Procureur de la République, Tribunal de Grande Instance de Paris, France*
- The Honourable Sir Duncan Ouseley, *Chair, Special Immigration Appeals Commission, United Kingdom*
- Christopher K. Penny, *Norman Paterson School of International Affairs, Carleton University, Canada*
- The Honourable Richard A. Posner, *Judge, United States Seventh Circuit Court of Appeals*
- Lorenzo Vidino, *Belfer Center, Kennedy School of Government, Harvard University, United States of America*

Printed and bound by CPI Group (UK) Ltd, Croydon, CR0 4YY

15/09/2026

14962400-0002